WEALTH AND POVERTY IN THE INSTRUCTION OF AMENEMOPE AND THE HEBREW PROVERBS

SOCIETY
OF BIBLICAL
LITERATURE

DISSERTATION SERIES

David L. Petersen, Old Testament Editor
Pheme Perkins, New Testament Editor

Number 142

WEALTH AND POVERTY IN THE INSTRUCTION OF AMENEMOPE
AND THE HEBREW PROVERBS

by
Harold C. Washington

Harold C. Washington

Wealth and Poverty in the Instruction of Amenemope and the Hebrew Proverbs

PJ
1559
.A7W28
1994
seab

Scholars Press
Atlanta, Georgia

WEALTH AND POVERTY IN THE INSTRUCTION OF AMENEMOPE AND THE HEBREW PROVERBS

Harold C. Washington

© 1994
The Society of Biblical Literature

Library of Congress Cataloging in Publication Data
Washington, Harold C., 1956–
    Wealth and poverty in the Instruction of Amenemope and the Hebrew
Proverbs / Harold C. Washington.
        p.   cm. — (Dissertation series ; no. 142)
    Includes bibliographical references.
    ISBN 0-7885-0072-4 (cloth). — ISBN 0-7885-0073-2 (paper)
    1. Instruction of Amenemope. 2. Poverty in literature. 3. Wealth
in literature. 4. Bible. O.T. Proverbs—Criticism,
interpretation, etc. 5. Wisdom literature—Relation to Egyptian
literature. 6. Egyptian literature—Relation to the Old Testament.
7. Poverty—Biblical teaching. 8. Wealth—Biblical teaching.
I. Title. II. Series: Dissertation series (Society of Biblical
Literature) ; no. 142.
PJ1559.A7W37   1995
223'.7067—dc20   94-40162
                                                  CIP

Printed in the United States of America
on acid-free paper

To my parents,
William Harold and Violet Woodle Washington

CONTENTS

PREFACE

As the SBL Dissertation Series precludes the updating of bibliography, it might be worthwhile to mention here two recent developments. First, significant contributions to the study of the New Kingdom Egyptian necropolis workers' settlement at Deir el-Medinah have been made since this project was completed. Details are available in recent volumes of the *Annual Egyptological Bibliography*. Secondly, the studies of J. P. Weinberg devoted to the *Bürger-Tempel-Gemeinde* model for post-exilic Judean society have been translated by D. Smith-Christopher and issued in a volume of collected essays: *The Citizen-Temple Community* (JSOTSup 151; Sheffield: JSOT Press, 1992).

For support and advice I would like to thank my dissertation adviser, Professor C. Leong Seow, as well as the other faculty who served at various stages of the project on my dissertation committee: Professors Patrick D. Miller, Jr., J. J. M. Roberts, and Katharine D. Sakenfeld. I am grateful to Professor Tryggve Mettinger, University of Lund, for giving me an inspiring introduction to the Hebrew wisdom literature and to Professor Schafik Allam, University of Tübingen, who instructed me in the Egyptian language and also gave helpful advice on Egyptological questions. I am indebted to the Fulbright-Hays and Charlotte W. Newcombe foundations for fellowship support of my work on the dissertation, and to my colleagues at Saint Paul School of Theology, as well as my student assistant, Kathy Simmons, for support and assistance during the final stages of this project.

Finally I want to thank Pam Gordon for her critical acumen, personal support, and irreplaceable companionship. She gives new meaning to the words אשת חיל (Prov 31:26).

ABBREVIATIONS

The abbreviations found in this work are those of the "Instructions for Contributors" to the *Journal of Biblical Literature*, with the addition of the following:

AEL	*Ancient Egyptian Literature*, M. Lichtheim
ÄHG	*Ägyptische Hymnen und Gebete*, J. Assmann
DEM	Deir el-Medinah
EG	*Egyptian Grammar*, A. Gardiner
GM	*Göttinger Miszellen. Beiträge zur ägyptologische Diskussion*
HÄB	Hildesheimer Ägyptologische Beiträge
JSSEA	*Journal of the Society for the Study of Egyptian Antiquities*
O.	Ostracon
OTWSA	*Ou-Testamentiese Werkgemeenskap in Suid Afrika*
PNWS	Proto-Northwest Semitic
P. Anast.	Papyrus Anastasi
P. BM	Papyrus British Musuem
RP	*Racial Proverbs*, S. Champion
SAK	*Studien zur altägyptischen Kultur*
SAIW	*Studies in Ancient Israelite Wisdom*, J. Crenshaw
SPOA	*Les sagesses du Proche-Orient ancien*
VESO	*The Vocalization of the Egyptian Syllabic Orthography*, W. F. Albright
Wb	*Wörterbuch der ägyptischen Sprache*, A. Erman and H. Grapow
ZÄS	*Zeitschrift für ägyptische Sprache und Altertumskunde*

TABLES

INTRODUCTION

Wealth and poverty are mentioned more frequently in the book of Proverbs than in any other section of the Hebrew Bible.[1] The book of Proverbs, however, gives no coherent view of the rich and the poor; rather it presents a complicated world of moral discourse. Some passages assert baldly that riches belong properly to the wise:

> The crown of the wise is their wealth,[2]
> but the garland of fools is folly (14:24; cf. 8:18; 3:16).

Wealth is described as the reward for a life of modest piety:

> The reward for humility and fear of Yhwh
> is riches and honor and life (22:4; cf. 10:22).

The Proverbs often suggest that poverty is self-inflicted:

---

[1] See the tabulation of relative frequency of vocabulary items for rich and poor in T. Donald, "The Semantic Field of Rich and Poor in the Wisdom Literature of Hebrew and Accadian," *Oriens Antiquus* 3 (1964) 27–41.

[2] Commentators often find this verse problematic because of its ethical implications. Many emend עָשְׁרָם, "their wealth," to עָרְמָתָם, "their prudence," following LXX's use of the adjective πανοῦργος, "versatile, shrewd" (used to translate עָרוּם in 14:8; so Ehrlich, Toy, Oesterley, Gemser, Ringgren, BHK, BHS.) But the LXX Proverbs typically convert concrete Hebrew terms for wealth and poverty into moralistic abstractions. The glorification of wealth in the Hebrew Proverbs is regularly replaced with pietistic language (cf. LXX Prov 21:20; 14:23). The reading πλοῦτος αὐτῶν=MT עָשְׁרָם, is attested in the Greek tradition (see A. J. Baumgartner, *Etude critique sur l'état du Livre des Proverbes d'apres les principales traductions anciennes* [Leipzig: W. Drugulin, 1890] 140). The MT reading עָשְׁרָם should be retained.

Whoever loves pleasure will suffer want;
whoever loves wine and oil will not be rich (21:17).
A slack hand causes poverty,
but the hand of the diligent makes rich (10:4).

It is not surprising therefore that some interpreters have depreciated the social ethic of the wisdom literature, and of Proverbs in particular. The sages' indifference to the poor is contrasted to the outcries of the Hebrew prophets against social injustice.[3] Theologian J. L. Segundo dismisses the sapiential literature as the product of an era during which "the historical vocation of Israel was ... lost from view."[4] G. von Rad, one of the most sensitive interpreters of Hebrew wisdom, asserts that the sages experienced the poor and poverty in Israelite society as merely a "sting in the conscience." Von Rad observes:

> The sentences often judge poverty very coolly and unemotionally, for often enough it is the person's own fault. In a word, it is simply there.[5]

This apparently supercilious attitude of the sages toward the poor is often attributed to the upper-class origins of Hebrew wisdom.[6] The Proverbs, it is maintained, were assembled for the instruction of scribes, diplomats, and officials of the Judean monarchy. We can detect in them an aristocratic bias, the class-ethic of a "wisdom school."[7] The sayings which blame the poor for their suffering thus reflect class conceit; those which associate wealth with right conduct function ideologically to legitimate the position of the superior social classes.

The sayings mentioned so far, however, express only one point of view found in the book of Proverbs. Other passages indicate clearly that the sages took a grave view of the suffering of the oppressed:

---

[3] For example, C. van Leeuwen, *Le Développement du Sens Social en Israël avant l'ère Chrétienne* (Studia Semitica Neerlandica 1; Assen: Van Gorcum, 1955) 153-172; and J. D. Pleins, "Biblical Ethics and the Poor: The Language and Structures of Poverty in the Writings of the Hebrew Prophets" (Ph.D. diss., University of Michigan, 1986) 258-290; cf. J. D. Pleins, "Poverty in the Social World of the Wise," *JSOT* 37 (1987) 61-78.

[4] *Liberation of Theology* (Maryknoll: Orbis, 1976) 112.

[5] *Wisdom in Israel* (Nashville: Abingdon, 1972) 76.

[6] See especially R. Gordis, "The Social Background of Wisdom Literature," *HUCA* 18 (1944) 77-118.

[7] B. Kovacs, "Is There a Class-Ethic in Proverbs?" in *Essays in Old Testament Ethics. J. P. Hyatt, In Memoriam*, ed. J. L. Crenshaw and J. T. Willis (New York: Ktav, 1974) 171-89. Kovacs concludes: "Court and king sayings, instruction and discipline, an ethic of restraint, observance of proprieties, and a

There are those whose teeth are swords,
whose teeth are knives,
to devour the poor from off the earth,
the needy from among mortals (Prov 30:14; cf. Mic 3:2-3).

In fact, of all the passages in Proverbs which take an evaluative stance
on wealth and poverty, less than a third imply that the rich and the poor
deserve their fates.[8] More frequent is the recognition that much existing
wealth and poverty is the result of murder, extortion, and deceit (1:10-
19; 13:23; 11:1). Although some proverbs express a definite social
conservatism (e.g., 30:21-23),[9] others would be quite unsettling to the
self-satisfied rich:

A slave who deals wisely will rule
over a child who acts shamefully,
and will share the inheritance
as one of the family (17:2; cf. 27:18).

A critical stance toward wealth *eo ipso* is not uncommon in the
Proverbs (e.g., 11:4, 28). There are numerous injunctions against
greed and exploitation (e.g. 15:27; 30:14), and much explicit concern
for the poor (17:5; 22:22; etc.).

Some interpreters assume that these proverbs—and not the
former group, where the rich are praised and the poor are blamed—
reflect the genuine social outlook of the sages. Affirmative concern for
the poor is so essential to wisdom, it is argued, that Isaiah's advocacy
of the oppressed in Jerusalem can be attributed to "wisdom
influence".[10] The special regard for the lowly in Deuteronomy has
likewise been ascribed to sapiential provenance.[11]

The ambiguity of the book of Proverbs' teaching on the ethical
problem of wealth and poverty demonstrates the need for greater clarity

---

system of authority suggest a professional ethic of administrators or officials"
(186).

[8] N. Gottwald, *The Hebrew Bible: A Socio-Literary Introduction* (Philadelphia:
Fortress, 1985) 573.

[9] See R. C. Van Leeuwen, "Prov 30:21-23 and the Biblical World Upside
Down," *JBL* 105 (1986) 599-610.

[10] J. W. Whedbee, *Isaiah and Wisdom* (Nashville: Abingdon, 1971) 94-110.

[11] M. Weinfeld, *Deuteronomy and the Deuteronomic School* (Oxford: Oxford
University Press, 1972) 265-73, 282-297. Cf. F. C. Fensham, "Widow, Orphan,
and the Poor in Ancient Near Eastern Legal and Wisdom Literature," *SAIW* 161-
171. All suggestions of wisdom influence should be considered in light of J.
Crenshaw's criticism: "Method in Determining Wisdom Influence upon
'Historical' Literature," *SAIW* 481-94.

concerning the social context of the book of Proverbs: For whom was this literature written and what social function did it serve? The present study will pursue this question, taking the theme of wealth and poverty in Proverbs as a test case in the social location and function of the Hebrew wisdom literature. My procedure will be to reconstruct so far as possible the social-historical settings in which the diverse traditions found in Proverbs emerged and to interpret the influence of these settings on the development of the material. By social-historical settings I mean both the broader social and economic circumstances of the society in which the materials were formed as well as the particular social setting of the individuals who preserved these traditions (e.g., scribal class, wisdom school?). The argument that an elite social setting has shaped proverbial expressions on wealth and poverty will be tested, as well as the possibility that some traditions originated in a folk setting.

Since the pioneering studies of Gressmann, Baumgartner, and Fichtner,[12] it has been recognized that Hebrew wisdom belongs to the broader international wisdom tradition of the ancient Near East, and that an adequate historical understanding of the Proverbs is impossible apart from this context. For this reason I have chosen to compare the social location and function of the Hebrew Proverbs with that of a prime example of the ancient Near Eastern wisdom tradition, the Egyptian Instruction of Amenemope. Amenemope has been selected as the main object of comparison, first, because Amenemope's demonstrable influence upon the book of Proverbs is greater than that of any other wisdom text from the ancient Near East. Amenemope is the structural model for the collection of thirty sayings known as the "Words of the Wise" (Prov 22:17–24:22), and is the material source for nine of the first ten of these sayings. There are also significant points of contact between Amenemope and the other sub-collections of Proverbs.[13] It happens that a large amount of the material common to Amenemope and Proverbs deals with the theme of wealth and poverty.

---

[12] H. Gressmann, *Israels Spruchweisheit im Zusammenhang der Weltliteratur* (Berlin: C. Curtius, 1925); W. Baumgartner, *Israelitische und altorientalische Weisheit* (Tübingen: Mohr, 1933); J. Fichtner, *Die altorientalische Weisheit in ihrer israelitisch-jüdischen Ausprägung: Eine Studie zur Nationalisierung der Weisheit in Israel* (BZAW 42; Giessen: A. Toepelmann, 1933).

[13] Especially important for the theme of wealth and poverty are the antecedents in Amenemope (9:5–8; 16:11–12) to the "better" sayings of Prov 15:16–17; 16:8; 17:1. The affinities between Amenemope and sections of Proverbs other than 22:17–24:22 are discussed fully in J. M. McGlinchey, "*The Teaching of Amen-em-*

Amenemope has been chosen for comparison with Proverbs, secondly, because we are better equipped in the case of Amenemope than with any other example of Egyptian Instruction to reconstruct the social-historical circumstances which shaped the attitudes toward wealth and poverty in the text. We have more material pertinent to the social and economic history of late New Kingdom Egypt, when Amenemope was written, and we are better informed about the scribal class of this time than of any other period. Indeed, we have more detailed information about the context of Amenemope than we do about the circumstances of post-exilic Judah in which the redaction of the Hebrew Proverbs was completed. Earlier study of Amenemope by Egyptologists and biblical scholars has concentrated on its literary history. The text has not been interpreted extensively against the social-historical background in which it emerged. The results of such an inquiry will provide a comparative basis for interpreting the Hebrew Proverbs, as well as shedding light on an important stage in the development of ancient Near Eastern wisdom.

This study is divided into two parts: Part One treats the Instruction of Amenemope, Part Two examines the Hebrew Proverbs. The two parts follow a parallel procedure, beginning with the attempt to date the composition of each text. Next I describe the social-historical setting of the composition, identifying the class of people for whom the text was composed and sketching the social and economic history of the period. Against this background the views of wealth and poverty in each text are interpreted. We may now proceed to the Instruction of Amenemope.[14]

___

ope and The Book of Proverbs" (D.S.T. diss., Catholic University of America, 1938; 46-104).

[14] For review of earlier secondary literature on the theme of wealth and poverty in Amenemope and Proverbs, see H. Brunner, "Die religiöse Wertung der Armut im alten Ägypten," Saeculum 12 (1961) 319-44; and R. N. Whybray, Wealth and Poverty in the Book of Proverbs (JSOTSup 99; Sheffield: JSOT, 1990). The principally literary treatments of Brunner and Whybray set the point of departure for the social-historical investigation pursued here.

PART ONE
THE INSTRUCTION OF AMENEMOPE

I
INTRODUCTION TO AMENEMOPE

"The Instruction of Amenemope" is the name conventionally given to the Egyptian literary text contained in Papyrus 10,474 of the British Museum. Amenemope is familiar to biblical scholars chiefly because of its affinities to the Hebrew Proverbs. In Egyptian literature, however, Amenemope is arguably the finest example of the Instruction genre, both for its literary qualities and its state of textual preservation. The papyrus is twelve feet one and one-half inches long, an average of ten inches wide, frayed at the ends. It contains twenty-seven columns of text written in a cursive hieratic script, for the most part in black ink, with red ink employed in a few special cases.[1] Each column contains from nineteen to twenty-three lines, the total number of lines amounting to five hundred fifty-one (including the scribal colophon).

---

[1] Red ink is used for the title line ("Beginning of the teaching for life," 1.1), the author's name ("Amenemope, the son of Kanakht," 2.11), two of the author's titles ("The overseer of grains who controls the measure," 1.15; and "The overseer of grains, [provider] of foods, 2.5), chapter headings (e.g., 3.8; 4.3; 5.9), and two lines where the scribe apparently wished to note a difficulty in the text (8.6; 12.11). Line citations for Amenemope refer to the column number followed by the line number in that column, a decimal point separating the two numbers. On the variety of reasons for using alternating black and red ink in Egyptian papyri, see J.

The papyrus was discovered in a Theban tomb and presented to
the British Museum by E. A. W. Budge in 1888. For over thirty years
the text was virtually unknown to the scholarly world.[2] In 1922 Budge
published an account of the papyrus together with hieroglyphic
transcription and translation of large portions of the text.[3] In the
following year Budge issued a proper *editio princeps*, with an
introductory account of the text accompanied by photographic plates of
the whole papyrus, hieroglyphic transcription and translation.[4] It was
soon recognized that a wooden writing tablet at the Turin Museum
contained thirty lines of the same text (24.1–25.9).[5] H. O. Lange
utilized the additional evidence of the Turin tablet and made a fresh
study of the entire text, issuing a much improved transcription and
German translation with notes.[6] The best account of the text of
Amenemope is now to be found in I. Grumach's Basel dissertation,
Untersuchungen zur Lebenslehre des Amenope.[7] Translations of

---

Černý, *Paper and Books in Ancient Egypt* (London: H. K. Lewis, 1952) 24–25.

[2] L. Le Page Renouf read the text soon after Budge brought it back to London,
and discussed one line (8.13) in an 1888 publication: "Is אֲבְרֵךְ (Gen. xli,43)
Egyptian? The Thematic Vowel in Egyptian," *Proceedings of the Society of
Biblical Archaeology* 11 (1888–89) 6–8; and Budge included a photograph of one
column of the papyrus in his *By Nile and Tigris: A Narrative of Journeys in Egypt
and Mesopotamia on Behalf of the British Museum between the Years 1886 and
1913* (London: J. Murray, 1920) 1.337.

[3] "The Precepts of Life, by Amen-em-Apt, the Son of Ka-nekht," *Recueil
d'études égyptologiques dédiées à la mémoire de Jean-François Champollion*
(Paris: E. Champion, 1922) 431–46.

[4] *Facsimiles of Egyptian Hieratic Papyri in the British Museum with
Descriptions, Summaries of Contents, Etc.* (Second Series; London: Harrison and
Sons, 1923) 9–18, 41–51; pls. 1–14. Essentially the same transcription and
translation appeared in Budge's publication of the following year: *The Teaching of
Amen-em-Apt, Son of Kanekht* (London: Martin Hopkinson, 1924) 93–234.

[5] W. Spiegelberg, Review of Budge, *Facsimiles of Egyptian Hieratic Papyri*,
Second Series, *OLZ* 27 (1924) col 185.

[6] *Das Weisheitsbuch des Amenemope aus dem Papyrus 10,474 des British
Museum herausgegeben und erklärt* (Det Kgl. Danske videnskabernes Selskab,
Historisk-filologiske Meddelelser 11,2; Copenhagen: Andr. Fred. Høst, 1925).

[7] (Münchner ägyptologische Studien 23; Munich: Deutscher Kunstverlag, 1970)
see the appendix, following p. 198. Except when noted otherwise, transliterated
Egyptian citations from Amenemope in the following agree with Grumach's text. I
have normalized the transliteration of the text according to the rules given by W.
Schenkel, *Materialien zur Vorlesung: "Einführung in die klassisch-ägyptische
Sprache und Schrift"* (Tübingen: W. Schenkel, 1985) 2.5; with the exception of
substituting y for German j.

Amenemope have also been published by A. Erman, F. Ll. Griffith, Fr. W. von Bissing, J. A. Wilson, W. K. Simpson, M. Lichtheim, and H. Brunner.[8]

---

[8] A. Erman, "Das Weisheitsbuch des Amen-em-ope," *OLZ* 27 (1924) cols. 241-52 (a German revision of Lange's translation, which was originally prepared in Danish: "En ny Visdomsbog fra det Gamle Aegypten," *Nordisk Tidskrift*, 1924, 94-107); F. Ll. Griffith, "The Teaching of Amenophis the Son of Kanakht. Papyrus B.M. 10474," *JEA* 12 (1926) 191-231; Fr. W. von Bissing, *Altägyptische Lebensweisheit* (Bibliothek der Alten Welt, Reihe der Alte Orient; Zurich: Artemis, 1955) 80-90; J. A. Wilson, *ANET* 421-424 (excerpts); W. K. Simpson, *The Literature of Ancient Egypt: An Anthology of Stories, Instructions, and Poetry*, 2nd edition (New Haven: Yale University, 1973) 241-65; M. Lichtheim, *Ancient Egyptian Literature*, Vol. II, *The New Kingdom* (Berkeley: University of California Press, 1976) 146-63; and M. Lichtheim, "Some Corrections to My *Ancient Egyptian Literature*, I-III," *GM* 41 (1980) 67-74 (on Amenemope, pp. 68-69); H. Brunner, *Altägyptische Weisheit: Lehren für das Leben* (Zurich and Munich: Artemis, 1988). Except when otherwise noted, translated quotations from Amenemope are by Lichtheim.

II
THE DATE OF AMENEMOPE

The dating of the Instruction of Amenemope has been intensively discussed since the text was first published. Earlier proposals ranged from the sixteenth to fourth century BCE.[1] Today it is clear that Amenemope originated no later than the period of the Egyptian New Kingdom (a chronology of the period is given in Table 1 below).[2]

---

[1] Proposals for the date of composition include the following: Budge: eighteenth dynasty, probably in the reign of Amenhotep I (c. 1510 BCE, *The Teaching of Amen-em-apt*, 96); A. Erman: c. 1000 BCE, "Eine ägyptische Quelle der 'Sprüche Salomos'," *Sitzungsberichte der Preussischen Akademie der Wissenschaften zu Berlin: Phil.-hist, Klasse*, 15 (1924) 86; W. Spiegelberg: twenty-second dynasty (c. 950–750 BCE, Review of Budge, *Facsimiles of Egyptian Hieratic Papyri*, OLZ 27 [1924] col. 185); H. Gressmann: c. 900 BCE ("Ägypten im Alten Testament," *Vossiche Zeitung* June 22, 1924, 2); Lange: 1100–300 BCE, most likely Persian or Hellenistic period (*Das Weisheitsbuch des Amenemope*, 13–14); W. O. E. Oesterley: later than the eighth century, perhaps as late as the beginning of the sixth century BCE ("The 'Teaching of Amen-em-ope' and the Old Testament," *ZAW* 45 [1927] 18–19; *The Wisdom of Egypt and the Old Testament in the Light of the Newly Discovered 'Teaching of Amen-em-ope'* [London: SPCK, 1927] 8–10); E. Drioton: just before or during the Persian period (a translation made into Egyptian from a Hebrew original, "Une colonie israélite en Moyenne Egypte à la fin du VIIe siecle av. J.-C.," In *A la Rencontre de Dieu: Memorial Albert Gelin* [Bibliothèque de la faculté catholique de théologie de Lyon 8; Le Puy: Xavier Mappus, 1961] 181–191).

[2] The relative chronology of the New Kingdom is for the most part secure, but competing systems for the absolute chronology of dynasties Eighteen to Twenty exist. Much discussion has been motivated by uncertainty whether astronomical

TABLE 1. CHRONOLOGY OF THE EGYPTIAN NEW KINGDOM PERIOD

Eighteenth Dynasty			
Ahmose	1552–1527	Amenhotep III	1402–1364
Amenhotep I	1527–1506	Amenhotep IV/	
Tuthmosis I	1506–1494	Akhenaten	1364–1347
Tuthmosis II	1494–1490	Smenkhare	1351–1348
Hatshepsut	1490–1468	Tutankhamen	1347–1337
Tuthmosis III	1490–1436	Ay	1337–1333
Amenhotep II	1438–1412	Horemheb	1333–1305
Tuthmosis IV	1412–1402		
		Twentieth Dynasty	
Nineteenth Dynasty		Sethnakht	1186–1184
Ramesses I	1305–1303	Ramesses III	1184–1153
Seti I	1303–1289	Ramesses IV	1153–1146
Ramesses II	1289–1224	Ramesses V	1146–1142
Merenptah	1224–1204	Ramesses VI	1142–1135
Amenmesses	1204–1200	Ramesses VII	1135–1129
Seti II	1200–1194	Ramesses VIII	1129–1127
Siptah	1194–1188	Ramesses IX	1127–1109
Twosret	1194–1186	Ramesses X	1109–1099
		Ramesses XI	1099–1069

observations dated by dynasty in the ancient sources (in particular, the sighting of the star Sirius recorded in the calender of the Ebers medical papyrus) were made at Memphis, rendering the so-called "high" chronology, or at Thebes, requiring the "low" chronology. There is a difference of some twenty years for most dates in the two respective systems (e.g. 1515 or 1490 BCE for the accession of Thutmose III). For details, see W. Helck, *Geschichte des alten Ägypten* (Handbuch der Orientalistik, I,1.3; Leiden: Brill, 1968) 141–42; E. Hornung, *Untersuchungen zur Chronologie und Geschichte des Neuen Reiches* (Ägyptologische Abhandlungen 11; Wiesbaden: Harrassowitz, 1964) esp. pp. 15–23; E. F. Wente and C. C. van Siclen, "A Chronology of the New Kingdom," in J. H. Johnson and E. F. Wente, eds., *Studies in Honor of George R. Hughes* (Chicago: Oriental Institute Press, 1977) 217–61; P. Aström, ed., *High, Middle or Low? Acts of an International Colloquium on Absolute Chronology Held at the University of Gothenburg 20th–22nd August 1987* (Gothenburg: Paul Aström); D. O'Connor, "New Kingdom and Third Intermediate Period, 1552–644 BC, Prolegomena: Chronology," in B. G. Trigger et al., eds. *Ancient Egypt: A Social History* (Cambridge: Cambridge University Press, 1983) 183–85. The low chronology has gained ground in recent discussion (cf. K. A. Kitchen, *The Third Intermediate Period in Egypt* [Warminster: Aris and Phillips, 1973], and M. L. Bierbrier, *The Late New Kingdom in Egypt (c. 1300–664 B.C): A Genealogical and Chronological Investigation* [Warminster: Aris and Phillips, 1975]; L. W. Casperson, "The Lunar Date of Ramesses II," *JNES* 47 [1988] 181–84) and is followed here. The dynastic dates in Table 1 follow those of the chronological table in D. O'Connor, "New Kingdom and Third Intermediate Period," 184.

The text can be dated securely to the late Ramesside period on the basis of four types of evidence: (1) paleographical data, (2) personal names, (3) loan words, and (4) chapter headings.[3]

PALEOGRAPHICAL DATA

Papyrus BM 10,474, the only complete witness to Amenemope, is a relatively late copy. It is assigned on paleographical grounds to the twenty-sixth to twenty-seventh dynasties, or sixth century BCE.[4] Two wooden writing tablets with fragments of the text are slightly earlier. The Turin tablet (no. 6237 = Amenemope 24.1–25.9), probably dates to the twenty-sixth dynasty. A second, in the Pushkin Museum of Moscow (I1d324 = Amenemope 6.10–7.1), is from the twenty-sixth or twenty-fifth dynasties. A third tablet (Louvre, E.17173 = Amenemope 2.15–18) is much earlier, probably twenty-second to twenty-first dynasties.[5] To these are to be added an ostracon (Cairo, no. 1840 = Amenemope 3.9–4.10) of the twenty-second to twenty-first dynasties, and a papyrus fragment (Stockholm, no. 18416 = Amenemope 10.18–14.5) of the twenty-first dynasty.[6]

---

[3] Thematic considerations also place Amenemope in the Ramesside era. See G. Bryce, *A Legacy of Wisdom: The Egyptian Contribution to the Wisdom of Israel* (Lewisburg: Bucknell University Press, 1979) 219 n. 35; H. Brunner, "Der freie Wille Gottes in der ägyptischen Weisheit," *SPOA* 103–120. Most recently D. Römheld, in his study of Amenemope and Prov 22:17–24:22, has concurred with the view taken here, that a twentieth-dynasty date for the text is most likely (*Wege der Weisheit: Die Lehren Amenemopes und Proverbien 22,17–24,22* [BZAW 184; Berlin: de Gruyter, 1989] 7).

[4] R. J. Williams, "A People Come Out of Egypt: An Egyptologist Looks at the Old Testament," *Congress Volume: Edinburgh*, 242 (VTSup 28; Leiden: E. J. Brill, 1975); cf. Williams, "The Sages of Ancient Egypt in the Light of Recent Scholarship," *JAOS* 101 (1981) 10.

[5] All three are published and discussed by G. Posener, "Quatre tablettes scolaires de basse époque (Aménémopé et Hardjedef)," *RdE* 18 (1966) 45–65.

[6] Cairo ostracon: B. Peterson, "A Note of the Wisdom of Amenemope 3.9–4.10," *Studia Aegyptiaca* 1 (1974) 323–27; Stockholm fragment: B. Peterson, "A New Fragment of *The Wisdom of Amenemope*," *JEA* 52 (1966) 120–128; Pls. 31–31a. There are two additional text fragments which may contain the title of Amenemope (1.1). A wooden tablet (Turin Suppl. 4661) of the twenty-sixth to twenty-fifth dynasties bears the words ḥ3t-ᶜ m sb3yt m ᶜnḫ, "beginning of the teaching for life" (see Posener, "Une nouvelle tablette d'Aménémopé," *RdE* 25 [1973] 251–2); and a hieratic graffito at Medinet Habu consists of the same text (see W. F. Edgerton, *Medinet Habu Graffiti Facsimiles* [Oriental Institute Publications 36; Chicago: University of Chicago Press, 1937] pl 10, no. 30). It is uncertain, however, whether these fragments should be taken as witnesses to

Amenemope is thus attested to have been in circulation as early as the twenty-first dynasty, 1069–945 BCE. Creative literary activity in Egypt, however, otherwise came to a halt with the end of Ramesside rule in the previous twentieth dynasty, when unified government of Egypt disintegrated. As W. F. Albright argues, it is unlikely that a text such as Amenemope could have been created and promulgated after this time:

> In view of the otherwise complete drying up of Egyptian literary inspiration with the fossilizing of the classical tongue after the end of the Ramesside Age, it is very risky to date the composition of the Maxims of Amenemope after the end of the second millenium.[7]

Moreover, since the fragments from the twenty-first dynasty are student exercises, we must allow some decades to have elapsed before Amenemope became a standard exercise text.[8] This would mean that Amenemope was written not during the twenty-first dynasty, from which our earliest fragments have survived, but sometime during the earlier twentieth dynasty, 1186–1069 BCE.

PERSONAL NAMES

The name Amenemope (*Imn-m-ipt* 2.11), is a common New Kingdom name, especially well attested for the twentieth dynasty.[9] The name

---

Amenemope, because the superscription could also apply to other texts (see Posener, *RdE* 9 [1951] 119, no. 58, and his reference to *Wb* 1.199,6; J. Ruffle, "The Teaching of Amenemope and its Connexion with the Book of Proverbs" [M.A. thesis, University of Liverpool, 1964] 19. Both fragments exhibit the shift of genitive *n* to *m* which is found in Amenemope 1.1, but this is not decisive because the exchange is increasingly common in late Egyptian.

[7] W. F. Albright, "Some Canaanite-Phoenician Sources of Hebrew Wisdom," *Wisdom in Israel and The Ancient Near East*, fs. Rowley, 6 (VTSup 3; Leiden: E. J. Brill, 1955) 6. See also A. Gardiner, *Ancient Egyptian Onomastica* (London: Oxford University Press, 1947) 1.24.

[8] R. J. Williams, "The Sages of Ancient Egypt in the Light of Recent Scholarship," 10; cf. Williams, "A People Come Out of Egypt," 242. J. Ruffle ("The Teaching of Amenemope," 24) argues likewise that the appearance of Amenemope on an ostracon indicates its use as a standard text for scribal instruction, suggesting in turn that it had been in existence for some time, "since a brand new work would hardly achieve this distinction overnight."

[9] Final -t is silent by the New Kingdom period; thus the conventional transcription: Amenemope. Gardiner (*Ancient Egyptian Onomastica*, 1.24) reads the name as Amenope, maintaining that *m* was regularly assimilated to a preceding *n* (likewise Grumach, *Untersuchungen zur Lebenslehre des Amenope*, 1 n. 1). The

occurs with very high frequency among the twentieth-dynasty textual remains from the Theban necropolis at Deir el-Medinah.[10] The name Amenemope is also prominent among the priestly and noble families of the nineteenth and twentieth dynasties.[11]

Amenemope is quite common as a scribal name during this period. At least two of the scribes who supervised work at Deir el-Medinah were named Amenemope.[12] A scribe of the same name is the attributed author of the "Onomasticon of Amen[em]ope," which Gar-

---

name occurs as *Amanappa* in six Amarna letters (see J. A. Knudtzon, *Die El-Amarna Tafeln mit Einleitung und Erläuterungen* [Leipzig: J. C. Hinrichs, 1908–1915] nos. 73, 77, 82, 86, 87, 93; Griffith, "The Teaching of Amenophis," 197). This Akkadian form reflects the assimilation of *m* to the following consonant, but this is inconclusive evidence for the appropriate reading of the Egyptian. Generally the fuller spelling has been retained by Egyptologists (e.g., Lichtheim, *AEL* 2.149; cf. D. Römheld, *Wege der Weisheit: Die Lehren Amenemopes und Proverbien 22,17-24,22* (BZAW 184; Berlin: de Gruyter, 1989] 9 n. 16). For attestation of the name, see H. Ranke, *Die ägyptischen Personennamen* (Glueckstadt: J. J. Augustin, 1935-52) 1.27, no. 18. On the name in general, see also J. Ruffle, "The Teaching of Amenemope," 23.

10 Besides the scribes named below, note the following: Amenemope, father of the foreman Nebnufer; Amenemope, "guardian of the tomb;" a policeman named Amenemope, who dates to the reign of Ramesses XI; two fishermen named Amenemope during the reigns of Ramesses III–VI and Ramesses IX–XI; and four necropolis craftsmen named Amenemope whose attested dates span the reigns of Ramesses III–IX (J. Černý, *A Community of Workmen at Thebes in the Ramesside Period* [Cairo: Institut français d'archéologie orientale, 1973] 123, 150, 264; M. Gutgesell, *Die Datierung der Ostraka und Papyri aus Deir el-Medineh und ihre ökonomische Interpretation. Teil I: Die 20. Dynastie* [HÄB 19; Hildesheim: Gerstenberg, 1983] 216, 218; cf. Index, 597).

11 See the genealogical reconstructions of M. L. Bierbrier, *The Late New Kingdom in Egypt*: Amenemope, son of Amenhotep I (pp. 7–8, Chart II); Amenemope, Third Prophet of Amun, son of Tjanefer I (pp. xiv, 5–11, 16–17, 115–16, 120 nn. 63 & 80, charts I–III); Amenemope, son of Imiseba (p. 15, Chart IV).

12 (1) Amenemope, scribe active at Deir el-Medinah in years 35 and 37, which must be of Ramesses II. He is evidently identical with the "king's scribe in the Place of Truth, Amenemope," owner of tomb no. 215 at Deir el-Medinah. This scribe also named one of his two sons Amenemope. (2) Amenemope, "scribe of the Tomb," in office from year 1 of Ramesses IV to year 2 of Ramesses V. He is most likely identical with the scribe Amenemope, son of the scribe Minmose, occuring in tomb no. 334 (J. Černý, *A Community of Workmen at Thebes*, 194–96, nos. 3–4; M. Gutgesell, *Die Datierung der Ostraka und Papyri aus Deir el-Medineh*, 1.212, 298).

diner dates to the twentieth dynasty.[13] The name occurs very frequently in the scribal miscellanies of this period, usually as the name of a scribe.[14] It is also the name of the inept scribe to whom the Satirical Letter of Papyrus Anastasi I is addressed.[15] Papyrus BM 10,474 contains on the side opposite to our Instruction text, a group of proverbs gathered under the name Amenemope (with different titles from Amenemope son of Kanakht).[16]

The name of Amenemope's father, Kanakht (2.11), became fashionable during the latter part of the twentieth dynasty, and is otherwise attested no later than the twentieth dynasty.[17] The name of Amenemope's wife, Tawosre (3.7) is common in the New Kingdom from the eighteenth dynasty on.[18] The name of Amenemope's son, Hor-em-maakher (3.4) is otherwise unknown before the late period.[19] Griffith claims to have found an example of this name from the twelfth dynasty, but J. Ruffle shows that this is actually another name.[20] The fact that the name Hor-em-maakher is otherwise unknown until the

---

[13] *Ancient Egyptian Onomastica*, 24–25.

[14] See R. Caminos, *Late Egyptian Miscellanies* (Brown Egyptological Studies 1; London: Oxford University Press, 1954) 73, 75, 83, 86, 88, 91–92, 95–96, 100, 103–04, 326, 446.

[15] Newly edited by H.-W. Fischer-Elfert, *Die Satirische Streitschrift des Papyrus Anastasi I* (Kleine Ägyptische Texte; Wiesbaden: O. Harrassowitz, 1983); see the English translation of J. A. Wilson, *ANET*, 475–79. The composition dates probably to the nineteenth dynasty.

[16] Budge, *Facsimiles of Hieratic Papyri*, Second Series, 18. Griffith, "The Teaching of Amenophis," 227, J. M. McGlinchey, "*The Teaching of Amen-em-ope* and *The Book of Proverbs*," 18.

[17] A scribe of the Tomb at Deir el-Medinah by the name of Kanakht is known from an ostracon of the late twentieth dynasty. Virtually all examples of the name date from the same period: O. Cairo '244,2; '642,II,2; Kanakhte, son of Sety, P. Turin Cat. 2057–2058, (year 16 of Ramesses IX); 1932, vo. III,2 (Ramesses X) and 2018, *passim* (year 8 of Ramesses XI) (J. Černý, *A Community of Workmen at Thebes*, 220 no. 60; cf. Albright, "Some Canaanite-Phoenician Sources of Hebrew Wisdom," 6; Ranke, *Die ägyptischen Personennamen*, 1.338 no. 7; Ruffle, "The Teaching of Amenemope," 23.) For two possibly earlier attestations of the name, see Černý, ibid.

[18] Ranke, *Die ägyptischen Personennamen*, 1.355, no. 22.

[19] Ranke, *Die ägyptischen Personennamen*, 1.247, no. 22.

[20] Ruffle observes that the name cited by Griffith, $M3^c$-$ḫrw$-$ḥr$ is a $sḏm.f$ form, but $Ḥr$-m-$m3^c$-$ḥrw$ (Amen 3.4) is a non-verbal sentence (Griffith, "The Teaching of Amenophis," 226; Ruffle, "The Teaching of Amenemope," 23; Ranke, *Die ägyptischen Personennamen*, 1.144, no. 22.

Saite and Persian periods thus militates against pushing the date of composition back too early in the New Kingdom period. The best interpretation of the evidence from personal names suggests a date in agreement with the paleographical evidence, during the twentieth dynasty.

LOAN WORDS

In New Kingdom sources, foreign loan words are recognizable by their appearance in the so-called syllabic orthography (group-writing). The practice of syllabic orthography, although it was not consistently applied, was intended to imitate the cuneiform syllabaries for the purpose of indicating the vocalization of unfamiliar words.[21] For

---

[21] The existence of a syllabic orthography in Egyptian was first systematically proposed by W. M. Mueller, *Asien und Europa nach altägyptischen Denkmälern* (Leipzig: W. Engelman, 1893) 58-91. Mueller's theory was rejected by virtually all the members of the Berlin School (Sethe, Erman, and their students). Erman's student Max Burchardt published a valuable collection of all the evidence available at the time for Semitic loan words in Egyptian (*Die altkanaanäischen Fremdworte und Eigennamen im Ägyptischen* [Leipzig: J. C. Hinrichs, 1909-1910]), but he accepted the view of Sethe and denied the vocalic nature of the syllabic writing. In 1934 Albright took up Mueller's case and established the existence of a vocalized syllabic orthography in New Kingdom Egyptian: *The Vocalization of the Egyptian Syllabic Orthography* (American Oriental Series 5; New Haven: American Oriental Society, 1934). Albright's system was challenged (W. F. Edgerton, "Egyptian Phonetic Writing, from its Invention to the Close of the Nineteenth Dynasty," *JAOS* 60 [1940] 473-506), but a continuing accumulation of evidence has supported the Mueller-Albright theory (W. Albright, "Northwest-Semitic Names in a List of Egyptian Slaves from the Eighteenth Century BC," *JAOS* 74 [1954] 222-33; E. Edel, "Neue Keilschriftlichen Umschreibungen Ägyptischer Namen aus den Bogazköytexten," *JNES* 7 [1948] 11-24; and "Neues Material zur Beurteilung der syllabischen Orthographie des Ägyptischen," *JNES* 8 [1949] 44-47; W. Albright and T. Lambdin, "New Material for the Egyptian Syllabic Orthography," *JSS* 2 [1957] 113-27; W. A. Ward, "Notes on Egyptian Group-Writing," *JNES* 16 [1957] 198-203.) For a more recent survey of the material, with new syllabic tables, see W. Helck, *Die Beziehungen Ägyptens zu Vorderasien im 3. und 2. Jahrtausend v. Chr.* (Ägyptologische Abhandlungen 5; Wiesbaden: Harrassowitz, 1962) sect. 36: "Asiatische Fremdworte im Ägyptischen," 551-606. See also, however, a more cautious summary of the evidence in J. Černý and S. I. Groll, *A Late Egyptian Grammar* (Rome: Biblical Institute Press, 1975) par. 1.2. Černý-Groll point out that while the syllabic writings occur mostly in foreign words, they are also found in purely Egyptian words. Note also the criticism of Helck's work by J. Janssen, "Semitic Loan-Words in Egyptian Ostraca," *JEOL* 19 (1966) 443-48.

example, the PNWS term *ʾallānu (> BH אַלּוֹן; cf.

Ugaritic ʾaln; Akkadian al(i)ānu), "oak tree," is transcribed in late Egyptian (with the help of weak consonants to indicate vowels): ʾal-l(2)-lú-na (P. Anast. I.19,3).

Albright maintains that the syllabic orthography reached its height of development midway through the eighteenth dynasty, around the reign of Amenhotep III (1402–1364 BCE). Through the nineteenth dynasty a fair degree of regularity in the syllabic transcription of foreign terms was maintained. In the twentieth dynasty, however, after the reign of Ramesses III (1184–1153) along with the political disintegration and general decline of scribal standards during the period, there was a marked corruption of the syllabic orthography system.[22] This deterioration continued into the twenty-first dynasty, and by the tenth century the syllabic orthography is for all practical purposes defunct.

The Instruction of Amenemope contains a number of apparent Semitic loan words. Syllabic orthography is used in the transcription of these terms with varying degrees of regularity. Albright judged that the spelling of Semitic loan words in Amenemope precludes a date of composition before the 1100's BCE, but he never set out the evidence for this determination.[23] The only detailed discussion of Semitic loan material in Amenemope is by R. O. Kevin.[24] Kevin, however, argues that Amenemope was translated into Egyptian from a Hebrew original. He thus assembles *ex hypothesi* an unlikely list of thirty-five "Semiticisms" in Amenemope, of which only eight at most have any value.[25] Kevin does not consider the issue of syllabic orthography in this material, and he confuses cognate terms in Egyptian and Semitic with true loans. For example, no. 6 in Kevin's list is the Egyptian verb of being *iw*, which is cognate to BH היה.[26] The verb *iw* in its many uses is as frequent in Egyptian as היה in Hebrew. If its appearance were a mark of Semitic influence, practically every sentence in Egyptian could be considered under this category.

---

[22] For further details and examples see Albright, *Vocalization of the Egyptian Syllabic Orthography*, 12–15.

[23] Albright mentions only in passing his summary judgment of the loan words in Amenemope: "Some Canaanite-Phoenician Sources of Hebrew Wisedom," 6.

[24] "The Wisdom of Amen-em-apt and its Possible Dependence upon the Hebrew Book of Proverbs," *JAOS* 14 (1930) 115–157.

[25] Cf. Ruffle, "The Teaching of Amenemope," 432–33.

[26] "The Wisdom of Amen-em-apt and its Possible Dependence upon the Hebrew Book of Proverbs," 133.

It seems appropriate therefore to reconsider the matter of Semitic loan vocabulary in the Instruction of Amenemope. The Semitic loan words in Amenemope which are pertinent to dating the composition of the text are as follows:[27] (a) Amen 15.3; 18.2: *i(4)-śi* (Albr. *VESO,* III.C.2: *ʾi-ṭi*), "who? which? where?" =BH אִ־יֹ (< PNWS *ʾyy-ðī*), "which?".[28] This term occurs widely in New Kingdom sources, both inscriptions[29] and papyri.[30] The two writings in Amenemope are almost identical. In 15.3 the second element *śi* is written with a full syllabic complement (the *ʾaleph* sign) which is absent in 18.2.

(b) Amen 6.14; 7.17; 18.12, 15: *ꜥ-š-ga*, "to misappropriate," =BH עָשַׁק, "to oppress, extort".[31] The identical verbal root occurs once in a Ramesside letter (Pap. British Museum 10100),[32] and the form *ꜥšq* occurs three times, twice as a verb (P. Harris 1,3,9; Medinet Habu 108,4), and once as a substantive (in a papyrus fragment identified by Gardiner as belonging to P. Turin 1882).[33] The

---

[27] Syllabic values follow Helck, *Die Beziehungen Ägyptens zu Vorderasien,* 601–02, with additional references to Albright, *The Vocalization of the Egyptian Syllabic Orthography,* 31–32.

[28] Burchardt, *Die altkanaanäischen Fremdworte,* 2.11, no. 189; Kevin, "The Wisdom of Amen-em-apt," 132, no. 5; Griffith, "The Teaching of Amenophis," 211; Ruffle, "The Teaching of Amenemope," 193; R. J. Williams, "The Alleged Semitic Original of the *Wisdom of Amenemope, JEA* 47 (1961) 106; Helck, *Die Beziehungen Ägyptens zu Vorderasien,* 554, no. 18; Černý-Groll, *Late Egyptian Grammar,* par. 61.8; L. H Lesko and B. S. Lesko, *A Dictionary of Late Egyptian* (Berkeley, California: Scribe Publications, 1982) 1.61.

[29] Inscr. dédic. 57 (H. Gauthier, *La grande inscription dédicatoire d'Abydos* [Cairo: Imprimerie de l'Institut français d'archéologie orientale, 1912]); Kuban 15 (P. Tresson, *La stèle de Koubân* [Cairo: Imprimerie de l'Institut français d'archéologie orientale, 1922]) Mariette, Abydos II, 54 (A. Mariette, *Abydos, description des fouilles executées sur l'emplacement de cette ville* [Paris: A. Franck, 1869–80]).

[30] P. Anast. I, 10.9; 19.8; 21.5; P. Anast. 5, 20.4; P. BM 10052, 13.7.

[31] Burchardt, *Die altkanaanäischen Fremdworte* 2.16, no. 287; Ruffle, "The Teaching of Amenemope," 164; Williams, "The Alleged Semitic Original of the *Wisdom of Amenemope,*" 105–06.

[32] J. Černý, *Late Ramesside Letters* (Bibliotheca Aegyptiaca 9; Brussels: 1939), 30R12; E. Wente, *Late Ramesside Letters* (Studies in Ancient Oriental Civilization 33; Chicago: University of Chicago Press, 1967) no. 30, p.66, 67 n. e.

[33] Lesko, *Dictionary of Late Egyptian,* 1.91. For the P. Turin 1882 fragment, A. Gardiner, "A Pharaonic Encomium," *JEA* 41 (1955) 30 and pls. 7–11; "A Pharaonic Encomium, II," *JEA* 42 (1956) 8–20. This text can be dated quite closely, according to Gardiner, by a reference (5,9) to Ramesses IV (1153–46 BCE;

interchange of g and q is common in late texts,[34] and is well attested in Amenemope,[35] so the two forms ⁽šg and ⁽šq can be taken as evidence of the same root in Egyptian.

(c) Amen 15.2: p-ha, "snare, fetters,"=BH פַּח (< PNWS *paḥḥu), "bird-trap".[36] This is related to the feminine noun pḥȝt, "stocks," mentioned in the scribal training literature as punishment for idle students.[37] Both the masculine and feminine forms are found in the love poetry of P. Harris 500.[38] The syllabic transcription of this term in Amenemope is incomplete.

(d) Amen 7.6 ma-k-ma-rú-ta, "fishing net,"=*makmarot, as feminine plural equivalent to BH מִכְמָר, "fishing net".[39] In Egyptian the term is attested only in Amenemope.

(e) Amen 26.11: ma-da-qa-ta, "jug, jar,"=PNWS *maṣṣiqatu (a maqtilatu-form noun from disused root *nṣq, parallel to BH יצק < *wṣq); Akkadian maziqda (CAD 10:1.438; apparently a loan word in Akkadian, it occurs only in EA, in a list of cargo from Egypt; compare BH מוּצֶקֶת, from יצק).[40] The existence of *nṣq in PNWS is established

---

"A Pharaonic Encomium II," 8).

[34] Černý-Groll, Late Egyptian Grammar, par. 1.11.

[35] See Lange, Das Weisheitsbuch des Amenemope, 14.

[36] Kevin, "The Teaching of Amen-em-apt," 133, no. 8; Ruffle, "The Teaching of Amenemope," 433; Lesko, Dictionary of Late Egyptian, 1.180.

[37] P. Anast. 4, 11.12; P. Anast. 5, 18,2; P. Turin A, vs. 1.6. See Caminos, Late Egyptian Miscellanies, 184.

[38] 2.12; cf. 8.3,6. Text: W. M. Mueller, Die Liebespoesie der alten Ägypter (Leipzig: J. C. Hinrichs, 1899).

[39] W. Spiegelberg, Review of Budge, Facsimiles of Egyptian Hieratic Papyri, col. 185; Lange, Das Weisheitsbuch des Amenemope, 47; P. Humbert, "En marge du dictionnaire hébraïque," ZAW 62 (1949) 201; Ruffle, "The Teaching of Amenemope," 168; Helck, Die Beziehungen Ägyptens zu Vorderasien, 562, no. 127; Lesko, Dictionary of Late Egyptian, 1.249.

[40] Burchardt, Die altkanaanäischen Fremdworte, 2.29, no. 552; Kevin, "The Teaching of Amen-em-apt," 133, no. 13; Lange, Das Weisheitsbuch des Amenemope, 130; Albright, The Vocalization of the Egyptian Syllabic Orthography, 44 (VIII.9); T. Lambdin, "Egyptian Words in Tell El Amarna Letter No. 14," Or ns 22 (1953) 367; Ruffle, "The Teaching of Amenemope," 225; Williams, "The Alleged Semitic Original of the Wisdom of Amenemope," 106; J. Janssen, Two Ancient Egyptian Ship's Logs: Papyrus Leiden I 350 verso and Papyrus Turin 2008+2016 (Leiden: Brill, 1961) 59, 71–72; J. Janssen, Commodity Prices from the Ramessid Period: An Economic Study of the Village of Necropolis Workmen at Thebes (Leiden: Brill, 1975) 330 n. 7; Grumach, Untersuchungen zur Lebenslehre des Amenope, 170; Lesko, Dictionary of Late Egyptian, 1.260.

by a frequent variant transcription in Egyptian, preserving the *n*: *ma-an-ḏa-qa-ta*.[41] In both spellings, the word is found exclusively in New Kingdom sources, predominantly later ones.[42] The word has a full syllabic spelling in Amenemope, although the *i*-class vowel of the second syllable is not preserved in the Egyptian orthography.

(f) Amen 6.3: *ši-ra-di-má*.[43] A Semitic origin for this term has been supposed. It is written in full syllabic orthography and seems to be presented as a foreign term.[44] The determinative (for "tree," "foliage") and the context suggest some translation such as "branch," "leaves." The derivation, however, remains unclear.[45] The word is known only from Amenemope.

(g) Amen 15.1: *ša-ba-di*, "stick," =BH שֵׁבֶט (< PNWS **šabṭu/šibṭu*), "rod, staff."[46] This loan word is especially frequent in the scribal training literature.[47] Again the syllabic orthography is complete, but should perhaps be considered corrupt since the *i*-class vowel is not represented.

(h) Amen 18.12: *kú-t(a)-m-t*, "gold," =BH כֶּתֶם.[48] The term is apparently derived from Akkadian *kutimmu*, which itself is a Sumerian

---

[41] P. Anast. 4, 12.11=5, 4.1; Gardiner, *Ramesside Administrative Documents* 34, 13; P. BM 5637 *vso.* 4; P. BM 5639a *vso.* 6.9/10; Albright, *The Vocalization of the Egyptian Syllabic Orthography*, 44 (citations in Helck, *Die Beziehungen Ägyptens zu Vorderasien*, 563, no. 135). Compare the parallel roots in BH: נצר/יצר and נצב/יצב.

[42] For the spelling found in Amenemope, cf. Wente, *Late Ramesside Letters* 9R11; 31V1; Gardiner, *Ramesside Administrative Documents* 22,2R10; Pap. Turin 2008+2016 2R10.

[43] Helck, *Die Beziehungen Ägyptens zu Vorderasien*, 569, no. 201.

[44] Cf. Lange, *Das Weisheitsbuch des Amenemope*, 43: "appears to be a Semitic word."

[45] For a review of the proposals, see Grumach, *Untersuchungen zur Lebenslehre des Amenope*, 43.

[46] Burchardt, *Die altkanaanäischen Fremdworte*, 2.43, no. 842; Ruffle, "The Teaching of Amenemope," 193; Helck, *Die Beziehungen Ägyptens zu Vorderasien*, 570, no. 220; Caminos, *Late Egyptian Miscellanies*, 249.

[47] Any 8.8; P. Sallier 1, 6.6; P. Anast. 5, 16.6; P. Turin 39.7; Turin Love Poems 1.8; P. Chester Beatty 5, rt. 7.2.

[48] Burchardt, *Die altkanaanäischen Fremdworte*, 2.52, no. 1036; Kevin, "The Teaching of Amen-em-apt," 132, no. 3; Albright, *The Vocalization of the Egyptian Syllabic Orthography*, 61, XVII, C.9; Ruffle, "The Teaching of Amenemope," 203; Williams, "The Alleged Semitic Original of the *Wisdom of Amenemope*," 106; Helck, *Die Beziehungen Ägyptens zu Vorderasien*, 574, no. 264.

loan word.[49] Thus the word is ultimately foreign to both Egyptian and Semitic. Alternation between feminine and masculine forms of a substantive, as we find here, is not uncommon. Compare Akk. *kutinnu* and BH כְּתֹנֶת; Akk. *tiāmat* and BH תְּהוֹם (and cf. BH כֶּתֶר/כֹּתֶרֶת, כְּתָב/כְּתֹבֶת). The term also occurs in Egyptian (P. BM 10569 12.2) as *ku-t(a)-m*, where the spelling without final -*t* approximates BH כֶּתֶם. This term is attested in Egyptian only from the twentieth dynasty,[50] and not until the Hellenistic period does the word become very frequent in Egyptian.

Mention must also be made of two Egyptian verbs in Amenemope which have been falsely identified as Semitic loan words. For the word *mš3p*, (Amen 9.14; 16.17; 19.19; 20.12; 27.3), a Semitic origin has been proposed.[51] Kevin connects this with Hebrew מַשְׁאָב, "water-course, channel" (a *hapax* in BH, Judg 5.11).[52] The Hebrew term apparently did enter Egyptian as a loan word. The form *mš3b*, followed by the sign for water and the determinative for a canal or body of water (*EG*, N36) is attested in the late Egyptian Onomasticon of Amenope.[53] This is not the word which appears in Amenemope, however. The latter is a verb denoting physical action, not a noun, from the root *mšp*, not *š³b*. In four out of five passages in Amenemope the verb occurs in a compound construction: negative imperative *m-ir mšp* (9.14) or *mtwk mšp* (16.17; 19.19; 27.3) plus infinitive *r-wḫ3*, "to seek". Context suggests a meaning for *mšp* such as "endeavor" or "trouble oneself,"[54] a conjecture which is supported also by Amen 20.12 and the single other occurrence of *mšp* as a verb in P. Anastasi 7.2,7.[55] There is no known Semitic root to compare with this Egyptian verb.

The term *mšᶜf* (Amen 7.4) has been compared to Hebrew שֹׁאַף,

---

[49] Albright, *The Vocalization of the Egyptian Syllabic Orthography*, 61; T. Lambdin, "Egyptian Loan Words in the Old Testament," *JAOS* 73 (1953) 152.

[50] Pap. Harris 1.5,12;6,3; Medinet Habu 107,15.

[51] Kevin, "The Wisdom of Amen-em-apt," 133; Ruffle, "The Teaching of Amenemope," 178.

[52] cf. *Wb* 2.155; Burchardt, *Die altkanaanäischen Fremdworte*, 2.27, no. 506.

[53] A. Gardiner, *Ancient Egyptian Onomastica*, 1.9*, 42; Lesko, *Dictionary of Late Egyptian*, 1.245; cf. Helck, *Die Beziehungen Ägyptens zu Vorderasien*, 562, 117.

[54] Lichtheim, *AEL* 2.152: "Do not strain to seek;" Grumach, *Untersuchungen zur Lebenslehre des Amenope*, 64: "*Strebe nicht nach*".

[55] Lange, *Das Weisheitsbuch des Amenemope*, 57.

"to pant, gasp,"[56] and translated as a D participle: "the fishes are gasping."[57] The equivalence of Egyptian ꜥ and Northwest Semitic ꜣ is not impossible.[58] There is no D-stem of שׁאף in Hebrew, however; it occurs only in G. Moreover, a D-stem verbal form would be unlikely to survive in Egyptian even if it did exist in Northwest Semitic.[59] P. Anastasi 4.15,9 contains a compound form, *s*, "pool, lake," with an old perfective (pseudo-participle) of *šꜥf*, "to surround, capture," thus: "a confined pool, reservoir."[60] Grumach reads a participle of the same root, following the preposition *m*, in Amen 7.4, translating *"die Fische sind zusammengedrängt."*[61] This gives an acceptable meaning, and eliminates the need to explain the term as a Semitic loan word.

To summarize: Amenemope contains at least seven Semitic loan words which are otherwise in use in Egyptian only during the New Kingdom period, for the most part the late New Kingdom. One of these (*kú-t(a)-m-t*, "gold") is attested only from the twentieth dynasty on. The spelling of these terms is for the most part syllabic, but imperfect in the representation of vocalization. The presence of these terms in Amenemope clearly places the text in the late New Kingdom literary milieu. Some uncertainty regarding the existence and development of the practice of syllabic orthography among New Kingdom scribes must be acknowledged. If Albright's reconstruction of the development of syllabic orthography is basically correct, however, then the spelling of these terms accords with the composition of the text during the twentieth dynasty.

---

[56] Lange, *Das Weisheitsbuch des Amenemope*, 47; E. Drioton, "Le Livre des Proverbes et la Sagesses d'Aménémopé," *Sacra Pagina: Miscellanea biblica congressus internationalis Catholici de re biblica* (ed. J. Coppens, A. Descamps, and E. Massaux; Bibliotheca ephemeridum theologicarum Lovaniensium 12–13; Gembloux: J. Duculot, 1959) 231; Ruffle, "The Teaching of Amenemope," 168. Lesko, *Dictionary of Late Egyptian*, defines Egyptian *mšꜥf* as "to snap," cf. Helck, *Die Beziehungen Ägyptens zu Vorderasien*, 562, 120.

[57] Griffith, "The Teaching of Amenophis," 203; cf. Lange: *"die Fische schnappen nach Luft."*

[58] See W. Albright, "Northwest-Semitic Names in a List of Egyptian Slaves," 228, no. 17; cf. Ruffle, "The Teaching of Amenemope," 168.

[59] Note, however, the substantive *mú-ḫa-bí-ša-ya* (P. Petersb. 1116 B, 70), apparently a D participle related to PNWS *ḫbš*, "to bind" (Helck, *Die Beziehungen Ägyptens zu Vorderasien*, 561, no. 105).

[60] Caminos, *Late Egyptian Miscellanies*, 212.

[61] *Untersuchungen zur Lebenslehre des Amenope*, 50. Cf. Lichtheim, *AEL* 2.151, "the fish are crowded together."

CHAPTER HEADINGS

Amenemope is divided into thirty numbered sections, each denoted in Egyptian as a *ḥt*, "house".[62] Although this usage may have its roots as far back as the sixth dynasty in Egypt, it occurs in Egyptian literary texts only during the late New Kingdom.[63] Amenemope is the only text of the Instruction genre to contain chapter divisions with the numbered superscription *ḥt*. Since this usage accords with other compositions from the Ramesside period, we may accept it as additional evidence in support of a twentieth-dynasty date.[64]

In sum, the paleographical evidence for a twentieth-dynasty date is corroborated by several other features of the text: proper names, loan words, and chapter headings. We conclude then that Amenemope was composed during the reigns of the later Ramesside twentieth dynasty, 1186–1069 BCE, and turn to examine the social-historical background of the period.

---

[62] Arabic *bayt*, Syriac *baytā*, and Sumerian *š* are used in the same way. See A. M. Blackman, "The Use of the Egyptian Word *ḥt* 'House' in the Sense of 'Stanza'," *Or* 7 (1938) 64–67.

[63] These include P. Chester Beatty I; P. British Museum 10188; and P. Chester Beatty 9 (Blackman, "Use of the Egyptian Word *ḥt*," 64).

[64] Cf. Grumach, *Untersuchungen zur Lebenslehre des Amenope*, 3 n. 9; Ruffle, "The Teaching of Amenemope," 56.

III

THE SOCIAL-HISTORICAL BACKGROUND TO AMENEMOPE

THE EVIDENCE FROM DEIR EL-MEDINAH

A wealth of archaeological data for New Kingdom Egypt has come from the site of Deir el-Medinah. This evidence is especially useful for our understanding of the context in which Amenemope was composed, because it comes from the same time, place, and social milieu as our Instruction text: The bulk of the material belongs to the period of the twentieth dynasty, it is from the vicinity of Thebes, and it reflects the social world of mid- to lower-level non-agricultural functionaries of the Ramesside state.

Deir el-Medinah is the Arabic name for the site of a small New Kingdom village containing approximately 70 houses, located in a desert valley on the west bank of the Nile just south of Thebes.[1] The inhabitants, designated "Workers of the Royal Tomb," *rmṯ-yst n pȝ ḥr*, or "Servants in the Place of Truth," *sḏm-ʿš m st mȝʿt*, were artisans charged with the construction and decoration of the royal tombs in the Valley of the Kings at Western Thebes.

The community of necropolis workers appears to have been founded in the late 16th century BCE by Amenhotep I.[2] Royal name-

---

[1] The Arabic name refers to a Coptic monastery which eventually occupied the site: "the monastery of the town." The ancient Egyptian residents seem to have called the place simply *dmi*, "the village."

stamps on the bricks of the enclosure wall indicate that the village itself
was constructed by Amenhotep I's successor, Thutmose I. Presumably
work ceased at the Theban necropolis during the Amarna years. A
similar workers' settlement has been uncovered at the Amarna capital,
suggesting that the craftsmen of the Theban necropolis may have been
transferred there to continue in service of the new regime. When the
pharaonic administration returned to Thebes (by c. 1345 BCE), activity
resumed at Deir el-Medinah, additional buildings were constructed, and
the village flourished until the later years of the twentieth dynasty. As
the Ramesside government deteriorated and turbulent social conditions
became increasingly dangerous, the site was finally abandoned under
Ramesses XI (1099–1069 BCE). The remaining workers were moved to
safer quarters inside the walled temple complex at Medinet Habu.[3]

Because Deir el-Medinah has been completely excavated, we
know this community better than we know any other group in ancient
Egyptian society.[4] Moreover, the necropolis workers are the only
members of the ancient Egyptian middle and lower classes about whom
we have detailed knowledge.[5] A large fund of non-literary ostraca and

---

[2] This is suggested by the fact that Amenhotep I and his mother, Ahmes-
Nefertari, were worshipped as patrons by the inhabitants of the village during later
periods. Disputes among workers were settled by oracular responses obtained from
a statue of Amenhotep I. (J. Černý, "Le culte d'Aménophis Ier chez les ouvriers
de la nécropole thébaine," *BIFAO* 27 [1927] 159–203).

[3] For overviews of the village and its history see J. Černý, "Egypt: From the
Death of Ramesses III to the End of the Twenty-First Dynasty." *Cambridge
Ancient History*, 3rd ed.; vol. 2, part 2; *History of the Middle East and the Aegean
Region c. 1380–1000 B.C.* (eds. I. E. S. Edwards, C. J. Gadd, N. G. L.
Hammond, and E. Sollberger; Cambridge: Cambridge University Press, 1975)
622; K. A. Kitchen, *Pharaoh Triumphant: The Life and Times of Ramesses II,
King of Egypt* (Warminster: Aris & Phillips, 1982) 185–205; M. Bierbrier, *The
Tomb-Builders of the Pharaohs* (London: British Museum Publications, 1982); C.
J. Eyre, "Work and the Organisation of Work in the New Kingdom," in *Labor in
the Ancient Near East* (ed. M. A. Powell; American Oriental Series 68; New
Haven, Connecticut: American Oriental Society, 1987) 168–80.

[4] A brief review of archaeological progress at Deir el-Medinah is given by
Bierbrier, *Tomb-Builders of the Pharaohs*, 125–44. Full excavation reports were
published by B. Bruyère, *Rapport sur les fouilles de Deir el Médinah*; 17 vols.
(Cairo: Institut francais d'archéologie orientale, 1924–53). Cf. also C. Bonnet and
D. Valbelle, "Le village de Deir el-Médineh. Reprise de l'étude archéologique,"
BIFAO 75 (1975) 429–446, and "Le village de Deir el-Médineh. Etude
archéologique (suite)," *BIFAO* 76 (1976) 317–42.

[5] See especially A. Eggebrecht, "Die frühen Hochkulturen: Das Alte
Ägypten," in A. Eggebrecht et al., *Geschichte der Arbeit: Vom Alten Ägypten bis
zur Gegenwart* (Cologne: Kiepenheuer & Witsch, 1980), 77–93. Our knowledge of
the community at Deir el-Medinah is supplemented by data from the worker's

papyri, along with abundant stelae and tomb inscriptions, have allowed detailed reconstruction of daily life in the village. The owners of several houses at Deir el-Medinah are known by name, and entire family histories at the village have been recovered.[6] Texts from the site have also yielded detailed information about a range of topics such as the organization of work at the necropolis, the wages and leave time granted, inheritance and other legal relations in the village, and religion among the workers.[7]

Much of the information from Deir el-Medinah illumines general conditions in Ramesside Egypt, such as the deteriorating pharaonic administration and consequent economic crises which presumably afflicted the entire country. It is hazardous, however, to rely exclusively on evidence from Deir el-Medinah for any aspect of the social history of the New Kingdom period because it was not a typical rural village.[8] The inhabitants of Deir el-Medinah, unlike those of an ordinary non-urban settlement, did not grow their own staple crops; they were dependent upon rations from the royal stores. The workers had the unique privilege of constructing for themselves decorated tombs

---

settlements at el-Lahun and el-Amarna. See. e.g., J. Janssen, "Prolegomena to the Study of Egypt's Economic History during the New Kingdom," in H. Altenmüller and D. Wildung, eds., *SAK* 3 (Hamburg: Helmut Buske, 1975) 134.

[6] K. Kitchen reproduces a ground plan of the village where eleven houses are identified with their owners (*Pharaoh Triumphant: The Life and Times of Ramesses II*, 189 fig. 59). M. Bierbrier's genealogical investigation of the New Kingdom devotes a chapter to the families of the workers at Deir el-Medinah (*The Late New Kingdom in Egypt*, 19-44).

[7] Besides the basic work of J. Černý, *A Community of Workmen at Thebes in the Ramesside Period*, see the following illustrative studies: J. Černý, "Prices and Wages in Egypt in the Ramesside Period," *Journal of World History* 1 (1954) 903–21; J. Janssen, "Absence from Work by the Necropolis Workmen of Thebes," *SAK* 8 (1980) 127-152; J. Černý, "Une famille de scribes de la nécropole royale de Thèbes," *Chron. d'Eg* 22 (1936) 247-50; P. W. Pestman and J. Janssen, "Burial and Inheritance in the Community of the Necropolis Workmen at Thebes," *JESHO* 11 (1968) 137-70; S. Allam, "Familie und Besitzverhältnisse in der altägyptischen Arbeitersiedlung von Deir el-Medineh," *Revue Internationale des Droit de l'Antiquité* 30 (1983) 17-39; S. Allam, *Das Verfahrensrecht in der Arbeitersiedlung von Deir el-Medineh* (Untersuchungen zum Rechtsleben im alten Ägypten 1; Tübingen: S. Allam, 1973); B. Gunn, "The Religion of the Poor in Ancient Egypt," *JEA* 3 (1916) 81-94; J. Clère, "Un monument de la réligion populaire de l'époque ramesside," *RdE* 27 (1975) 70-77.

[8] Cf. J. Janssen, *Commodity Prices from the Ramessid Period* (Leiden: Brill, 1975) 539-62.

in the hills overlooking the settlement—something otherwise enjoyed only by the elite of Egyptian society. Only with caution therefore can we extrapolate from evidence at Deir el-Medinah to general economic or social conditions in Egypt. The situation of the village's inhabitants cannot be equated with that of the peasants who occupied most of the country.

Yet it is precisely the peculiarities of Deir el-Medinah that make the site valuable as a backdrop to Amenemope. The number of individuals at Deir el-Medinah who bore the title *sš*, "scribe," was much higher than in an ordinary village.[9] The archaeological record of this exceptionally literate community thus reveals the very circles where texts like Amenemope were copied and studied by student scribes. The Instruction of Amenemope is not attested at Deir el-Medinah, but only because the village at Deir el-Medinah was abandoned before Amenemope had circulated widely enough in scribal circles to become a standard instructional text (under the twenty-first dynasty).[10] The earlier Instruction of Any, which addresses an audience similar to that of Amenemope and had considerable influence upon the author of Amenemope, is well attested at Deir el-Medinah.[11] The ostraca from Deir el-Medinah suggest that a favorite text in the village was the Instruction of Dua-Khety ("Satire of the Trades"), the standard *apologia* for the scribal profession.

The evidence from Deir el-Medinah thus supplies a richly detailed background against which to view the composition of Amenemope. When used with discretion, information from the village serves as a window into the broader economic and social history of the Ramesside period. It also illustrates the life of the professional class for whom the text of Amenemope was composed. We will therefore draw extensively on information from the village in reconstructing the social-historical background to the Instruction of Amenemope.

---

[9] The title *sš* was also often used at Deir el-Medinah as an abbreviation for *sš-qd*, "draftsman". Hence not every bearer of the title *sš* necessarily performed scribal duties. It is clear, however, that both the literacy rate and the number of professional scribes at Deir el-Medinah was unusually high. J. Baines estimates that 25–30% of the adult male personnel of the Tomb were fully literate, resulting in a literacy rate for the village of perhaps five times the rate for the country at large ("Four Notes on Literacy," *GM* 61 [1983] 90).

[10] In other words, if our judgment of the date of composition of Amenemope is correct, the settlement at Deir el-Medinah was at the height of its activity just as Amenemope was being written.

[11] At least eight ostraca from Deir el-Medinah are known to contain fragments of Any, and a papyrus from Deir el-Medinah contains about one-third of the text. See J. Černý, *Papyrus Hieratiques de Deir el-Medineh*, Vol I (Documents de

THE SETTING OF AMENEMOPE: SCRIBAL TRAINING
IN THE NEW KINGDOM PERIOD

The evidence concerning scribal education in ancient Egypt has been collected in several useful studies.[12] Here I wish to address two questions concerning this material from a social-historical perspective: (a) Did scribal training take place in an institutional setting that could properly be called a "school"? and (b) To what extent did the scribal students of the Egyptian New Kingdom comprise a social and economic elite?

Schools or Not?

Among biblical scholars the relationship of schools to wisdom literature has been the subject of lively debate. The Egyptian scribal school has often been posited as an institutional *Sitz-im-Leben* for the Instruction literature and thus it has been adduced as an antecedent to the hypothetical Hebrew "Wisdom School".[13] Amenemope, with its affinities to the book of Proverbs, has been taken as the prime example of a text from such a background.

M. V. Fox has observed that much confusion in this discussion has resulted from the failure to distinguish between two meanings of the word "school". The term can refer to (1) "an academy of learning," or to (2) "a group of thinkers characterized by certain attitudes and ideas, i.e. an intellectual 'circle' or 'movement'."[14] For the present I am concerned with the former sense of the word: "school" as an educational institution.[15] The question then is whether

---

Fouilles 8; Cairo: Institut français d'archéologie orientale, 1978) 2–3.

[12] See especially E. Otto, "Bildung und Ausbildung im alten Ägypten," *ZÄS* 8 (1956) 41–48; H. Brunner, *Altägyptische Erziehung* (Wiesbaden: Harrassowitz, 1957); R. J. Williams, "Scribal Training in Ancient Egypt,"*JAOS* 92 (1972) 214–221.

[13] E.g., H.-J. Hermisson, *Studien zur israelitischen Spruchweisheit* (WMANT 28; Neukirchen: Neukirchener, 1968); see the section titled "Die Ägyptische Schule," pp. 103–107; J. P. J. Olivier, "Schools and Wisdom Literature," *JNWSL* 4 (1975) 55–56; T. Mettinger, *Solomonic State Officials: A Study of the Civil Government Officials of the Israelite Monarchy* (CB OT Series 5. Lund: Gleerup, 1971) 140–57; A. Lemaire, *Les écoles et la formation de la Bible dans l'ancien Israël* (OBO 39; Göttingen: Vandenhoeck & Ruprecht, 1981) 34, 94 n. 73.

[14] "The Social Setting of the Wisdom Instruction: the Egyptian Example," paper delivered to the Hebrew Scriptures and Cognate Literature section of the Society of Biblical Literature Annual Meeting, November 19, 1989, Anaheim, California, 2.

[15] We can also use the word "school" in this sense to refer most concretely to

we can accurately refer to the setting of Amenemope as the New Kingdom Egyptian scribal school.

The scribal orientation of the Instruction of Amenemope is unmistakable. The author is identified as "the offspring of a scribe of Egypt" (1.14). The patron divinity of the scribal craft, Thoth, is often invoked (e.g., 4.19; 7.19; 17.7; 28.1). Most of the advice given is specific to the setting of the royal court or bureaucracy, where Egyptian scribes pursued their careers. Teachers' corrections are visible on the oldest fragments of Amenemope, making it clear that the text was used in scribal training.[16] But was Amenemope written for use in a "school"?

The Egyptian sources do not actually describe such a setting.[17] Nowhere in the ancient literature is there an explicit account of the organization of Egyptian scribal education. From indirect evidence, however, it is clear that literacy training took the form of task-oriented preparation of scribes for state service. Hence the educational arrangement resembled a network of guilds and apprenticeships rather than a school system.

There was in ancient Egypt no literacy training apart from the scribal profession—no "liberal arts education". This is true even if, as J. Baines and C. J. Eyre suggest, more young boys were given basic literacy training at Deir el-Medinah than ever went on to take a scribal post.[18] Surplus training was necessary in that setting because of high mortality rates. Students might never advance beyond the status of

---

the physical facilities which house such an institution. Thus the term "school" could designate any of the following: "(1) an institution for the instruction of children; (2) an institution for instruction in a skill, discipline, or business; or (3) the building or group of buildings in which instruction is given or in which students work and live" (adapting this definition from a standard dictionary: *The American Heritage Dictionary* [Boston: Houghton-Mifflin, 1985], 1098).

[16] The Stockholm papyrus fragment containing Amenemope 10.18–14.5 bears correction marks apparently made by a teacher (see B. J. Peterson, "A New Fragment of the Wisdom of Amenemope," and D. Römheld, *Wege der Weisheit: Die Lehren Amenemopes und Proverbien 22,17–24,22*, 7); the ostraca containing fragments of Amenemope appear to have been used for the same purpose.

[17] Cf. B. van de Walle, *La transmission des textes littéraires égyptiens* (Brussels: Fondation égyptologique Reine Elisabeth, 1948), 16–17, and note his caution regarding the existence of schools during the Old and Middle Kingdoms, "Problèmes relatifs aux méthodes d'enseignement dans l'Egypte ancienne," *SPOA* 193.

[18] "Four Notes on Literacy," 89.

draftsman (*sš-qd*), but their literacy training was motivated nonetheless by anticipation of an eventual scribal appointment. Formal education in reading and writing thus occurred only in preparation for scribal office and as a rule, the tutoring or apprenticeship which constituted professional training did not take place in a school. With the occasional exception of the centralized training of groups of students at the royal court, this pattern holds true through each of the historical periods of dynastic Egypt.

Old Kingdom

In the Old Kingdom period the typical practice is for officials personally to train suitable youths (theoretically their sons) in their own homes to be their successors.[19] This model of education is assumed in the oldest Instruction texts, Hardjedef, Kagemni, and Ptahhotep, and is reflected in the tomb paintings of the Old Kingdom as well.[20] There are some indications that during the Old Kingdom groups of youths were gathered at the royal court for organized training. Some officials, for example, describe themselves as having been "brought up among the royal children in the palace of the king."[21] The title "Chief Teacher of Royal Children" is attested for the Old Kingdom period, although its significance is not clear.[22] The basic pattern of education in the Old Kingdom, however, is the relationship of *magister-famulus*: the student, who is ostensibly the child of the teacher, serves as the official's amanuensis, apprentice, and eventual replacement in office.

---

[19] See H. Brunner, "Schreibunterricht und Schule als Fundament der Ägyptischen Hochkultur," in L. Kriss-Rettenbeck and M. Liedtke, eds., *Schulgeschichte im Zusammenhang der Kulturentwicklung* (Bad Heilbrunn: Julius Klinkhardt, 1983) 64; E. Otto, "Bildung und Ausbildung im alten Ägypten," 42; R. J. Williams, "Scribal Training in Ancient Egypt," 216.

[20] Cf. J. Baines: "The ideal of father and son in Old Kingdom tombs is of a father in the mature prime of life with a young son who is sometimes given a scribal title or scribal gear, and has thus started in a career, probably under his father as his amanuensis" ("Literacy and Ancient Egyptian Society," *Man* n.s. 18 [1983] 580).

[21] E.g., Ptahshepses of the fifth dynasty (K. Sethe, ed., *Urkunden des alten Reichs* (Urkunden des ägyptischen Altertums. Leipzig: J. C. Hinrichs, 1906-58) I, 51; see R. Williams, "Scribal Training in Ancient Egypt," 215; cf. *Urkunden des alten Reichs*. I, 98; 142; 254; 250).

[22] H. Brunner, *Altägyptische Erziehung*, 11-12.

First Intermediate

During the First Intermediate period the Egyptian phrase usually translated as "school" first appears in the tenth-dynasty tomb inscription of a nomarch at Siut.[23] This term, *ꜥt <n> sbꜣ*, remains in use from the Middle Kingdom to the Coptic period (*ansēbe*).[24] The literal meaning of the term, however, is simply "place of instruction." In none of the various contexts in which the phrase occurs from the tenth dynasty through post-Ramesside times does it necessarily denote a distinct educational institution.[25]

Other evidence from this period is sparse. A probable reference to group instruction at the royal court is found in the Herakleopolitan Instruction to Merikare. The young king is instructed:

> Do not kill a man whose virtues you know,
> with whom you once chanted the writings.[26]

The latter phrase must refer to the gathering of talented youths at the royal court for group instruction, which included the memorization and recitation or singing of the Instruction texts. The First Intermediate, however, was a period of increased local autonomy throughout the provinces. Most literate education, rather than occurring in centralized court schooling, must have continued in the pattern of local training by individuals.[27]

Middle Kingdom

The task of consolidating and expanding state control under the twelfth dynasty after the dissolute period of the First Intermediate

---

[23] *Siut* IV, 66; see Williams, "Scribal Training in Ancient Egypt," 215; and Brunner, *Altägyptische Erziehung*, 12.

[24] *Wb* 1.160, 12; W. E. Crum, ed., *A Coptic Dictionary* (Oxford: Clarendon, 1939), 12a.

[25] Cf. U. Kaplony-Heckel, "Schüler und Schulwesen in der Ägyptischen Spätzeit," *SAK* 2 (1974) 238.

[26] M. Lichtheim, *AEL* 1.101.

[27] J. Baines and C. J. Eyre detect a decline in the general competence of writing as well as a broadening of the social categories of people owning inscriptions in the First Intermediate period ("Four Notes on Literacy," 68). This is understandable since the breakdown of pharaonic rule in Memphis would have deprived literate culture of its center. Political decentralization resulted both in the diffusion of literacy training and a deterioration of the quality of writing.

required an enlarged bureaucracy. Thus with the emergence of the Middle Kingdom there is renewed evidence for the organized training of youth at the royal court.[28] For example, a high official Ikhernofret at Abydos under Sesostris III (twelfth dynasty) refers to his upbringing at the royal palace in terms similar to those of the Old Kingdom sources. Ikhernofret records the words of the king spoken to him:

> For you were brought up as a pupil of my majesty. You have grown up as foster child of my majesty, the sole pupil of my palace. My majesty made you a Companion [i.e., "courtier"] when you were a youth of twenty-six years.[29]

The superscript to the Instruction of Dua-Khety, also a twelfth-dynasty text, reflects a similar background:

> Beginning of the Instruction made by the man of Sile, whose name is Dua-Khety, for his son, called Pepi, as he journeyed south to the residence, to place him in the "school" [ʿt <n> sbȝ] for scribes among the sons of magistrates, with the elite of the resi-dence.[30]

This passage clearly attests to the sending of boys to the royal court for scribal training. It does not, however, indicate that literate education is entirely centralized at a palace school. The beginning student in this text can be described as "barely grown, still a child," but Dua-Khety's opening exhortations indicate that the boy is already literate:

> Set your heart on books! ...
> Read the end of the *Kemit*-book,
> You'll find this saying there ...

We can infer that the boy Pepi has already begun his studies under his father Dua-Khety, who himself is not merely literate but a sophisticated author.

Dua-Khety resides at Sile, a remote border fortress at the eastern Delta far from the capital city. The location of the author of a famous instructional text at such a remote site makes it clear that the practice of localized elementary training is quite widespread under the twelfth dynasty. Ostensibly the addressee of the text is Dua-Khety's son Pepi, who is sent to study with the "elite of the (royal) residence." Pepi,

---

[28] G. Posener, *Littérature et politique dans l'Egypte de la xiie dynastie* (Bibliothèque de l'Ecole des Hautes Etudes 307; Paris: Ecole des Hautes Etudes, 1956) 7–8.

[29] Stela of Ikhernofret (Berlin 1204) 5–7; translated by M. Lichtheim, *AEL* 1.124; Brunner gives additional examples (*Altägyptische Erziehung*, 16).

[30] Lichtheim, *AEL*, 1.185.

however, is an ideal figure for the broader audience of the text. We know from the attestation of the text during the New Kingdom period that Dua-Khety's instruction, with its satire of the occupations of villagers and rural folk, was read by scribal students in all locales. During the Middle Kingdom period when the text first became popular it must have been used in scribal families for the instruction of youth far beyond the confines of the royal palace.

New Kingdom

With the New Kingdom period our documentation for scribal training becomes abundant. At the same time, however, reference to the royal palace as a central training site for provincial youths ceases. Scribal education occurs in the widest range of settings, wherever scribal activity goes on.

It appears that scribal training in the New Kingdom is a two-stage process. The first stage, elementary training in reading and writing, is done locally and in groups. Numerous writing and drawing exercises found near the living quarters at Deir el-Medinah, for example, show that elementary education was pursued there. The volume of these ostraca is proof of group instruction. This is confirmed by texts from Deir el-Medinah which refer to groups of pupils. A letter, for example, from the scribe Thutmose urges that the "children" (*ꜥḏdw šryw*) not be allowed to desist from their lessons.[31] Similar deposits of ostraca elsewhere, though not as copious as those from Deir el-Medinah, indicate that elementary education occurred locally throughout New Kingdom Egypt.[32]

From the eighteenth-dynasty Instruction of Any we learn that a young scribal student can be expected to receive instruction locally but outside the family. Any tells the student to remember the debt he owes to his mother:

> She put you to "school" [*ꜥt <n> sbꜣ*] when you were ready to be instructed in letters, while daily she waited for you with bread and beer in her house (Any 7.20–8.1).[33]

---

[31] E. Wente, *Late Ramesside Letters*, 28; J. Baines, "Four Notes on Literacy," 88.

[32] H. Brunner, *Altägyptische Erziehung*, 19; B. van de Walle, *La transmission des textes littéraires égyptiens*, 16.

[33] See Williams, "Scribal Training in Ancient Egypt," 216. The translation here is by T. G. H. James, *Pharaoh's People: Scenes from Life in Imperial Egypt*

It is clear from this passage that the student continues to eat (and presumably sleep) at home while taking instruction outside the house.

This elementary training begins at an early age, perhaps around five years. Any mentions a period of only three years of infancy before the child is sent to instruction. A typical length of time spent in elementary education would appear to be four or five years. A high priest of Amun during the Ramesside period, for example, refers in a statue inscription to the four years he spent as a "capable child" (i.e., "good student") before beginning his advance through the ranks.[34]

These groups of elementary scribal students in the New Kingdom period, however, still cannot be regarded as "schools". There is no distinct institution in New Kingdom Egypt where instruction occurs. Groups are gathered informally at convenient places whose selection depends on the locale. Often, as at Deir el-Medinah, instruction takes place in the open air. Where an enclosed "place of instruction" (^ct $<n>$ $sb3$) is used, this is not a school building or room, but a section of a building constructed for other purposes where students are also allowed to gather. In the capital cities elementary instruction groups were gathered at temples, palaces (their administrative offices), and other state departments. In west Thebes, for example, open-air classes were held at the rear of the mortuary temple complex of Ramesses II. Similar training occurred at the temple of Mut at Karnak, and at several sites at Memphis.[35] Likewise in the main provincial towns scribal instruction must have occurred at local temples and administrative offices.

There are, moreover, no teachers by profession in New Kingdom Egypt. Students are taught by scribes who are primarily active in an administrative office or some other professional capacity.[36] In the smaller towns, where there were no bureaucratic offices, a village scribe presumably taught local boys as occasion allowed.[37]

(Chicago: University of Chicago Press, 1984) 140; cf. Lichtheim, *AEL* 2.141.

[34] Statue of Benkenkhons, see R. Williams, "Scribal Training in Ancient Egypt," 216.

[35] H. Brunner, *Altägyptische Erziehung*, 18.

[36] Cf. H. Brunner: "Berufsmässige Lehrer, also Männer, die ausschliesslich für die Erziehung der Jugend leben and dafür bezahlt werden, scheint es in Ägypten nicht gegeben zu haben" (*Altägyptische Erziehung*, 32).

[37] Cf. K. A. Kitchen, *Pharaoh Triumphant: The Life and Times of Ramesses II*, 141. Preparation for scribal office was restricted to boys, as the male orientation of the Instruction literature and the scribal miscellanies makes clear. There is some

The secondary stage of education, or advanced scribal instruction, is basically on-the-job training in the New Kingdom period. Having achieved the status of *sš*, "scribe," the student is attached as *ḥry-ꜥ*, "assistant" to a superior in the workplace (an archive, temple, store-house, etc.)[38] To mention a few examples from the Ramesside period, we find student scribe-assistants assigned to a high-level treasury official, a scribal officer of the chariotry corps, a chief clerk of the financial administration, an administrator of the cattle herds of Amun, the lector priest of an important temple, and various other officials of the army, royal bureaucracy, or temples.[39] This is a true apprenticeship system: the student helps his superior with the business of the office in exchange for continued direction in the skills of the profession. The Late Egyptian Miscellanies were written by such apprentice bureaucrats, as were the papyrus fragments of the Instruction texts which have survived from the late period.

In conclusion then, the term "school" is a misnomer for the setting of the Instruction texts, especially during the New Kingdom period. The literature does not derive from a distinct institutional setting. It is rather the property of a class of people, scribal students, whose work goes on in a variety of settings. We will dispense with the term school as a reference to the setting of the Instruction literature, and refer instead to the use of the Instruction literature in scribal education of the New Kingdom period.

It remains to be examined as a separate question whether the class of scribal students in the New Kingdom constitutes a homogeneous social and economic class, and if so, to what extent they comprise an elite. Both questions will have signficant implications for assessing the treatment of wealth and poverty in Amenemope, as well as for adjudicating the debate concerning a "wisdom school" in Israel.

---

evidence, however, of literacy among women in ancient Egypt. See H. Brunner, *Altägyptische Erziehung*, 45–48; W. Helck, "Zur Buchmalerei im alten Ägypten," in H. R. Roemer and A. North, eds., *Studien zur Geschichte und Kultur des Vorderen Orients*, fs. Bertold Spuler (Leiden: Brill, 1981) 167–70; and J. Baines and C. J. Eyre, "Four Notes on Literacy," 81–85.

[38] J. Baines, "Four Notes on Literacy," 88–89; R. Williams, "Scribal Training in Ancient Egypt," 216. For the use of the term *ḥry-ꜥ* at Deir el-Medinah see B. van de Walle, *La transmission des textes littéraires égyptiens*, 17.

[39] For the names of these individuals and the texts where they are mentioned, see Brunner, *Altägyptische Erziehung*, 36.

A Scribal Elite?

Because literacy in ancient Egypt belonged to a small segment of the population, scholars routinely refer to scribes as the elite of Egyptian society.[40] It is, however, not at all clear that Egyptian scribes belonged to a homogeneous elite class. The homogeneity of the scribal class might be inferred from the apparently hereditary nature of the profession, but a closer examination reveals that scribal office was not always passed from parent to child. It is equally uncertain that the position of a New Kingdom scribe was necessarily privileged and comfortable. In the following paragraphs I will show that the scribal class was not a closed hereditary social group; by the New Kingdom period access to scribal rank was relatively open. I will also maintain that scribes in the New Kingdom did not necessarily enjoy the good life. Their position in Egyptian society is best described as that of a "literate sub-elite".[41]

We have seen that the Egyptian standard for scribal education from the earliest period onwards was for a father to train his son as successor. The epilogue to the Instruction of Ptahhotep describes instruction passing from one generation to the next:

> A son who hears is a follower of Horus,
> It goes well with him when he has heard.
> When he is old, has reached veneration,
> He will speak likewise to his children,
> Renewing the teaching of his father.
> Every man teaches as he acts,
> He will speak to the children,
> So that they will speak to their children:
> Set an example, don't give offense,
> If justice stands firm your children will live.[42]

These verses are concerned with the inculcation of values, not just the technical skills of writing. The passage assumes, however, that the scribe-administrator will be followed in his office by his offspring. This was a powerful ideal; it survived even in the classical authors' accounts

---

[40] E.g., H. te Velde: "Scribes were the core and backbone of Ancient Egyptian civilization. They were the elite." ("Scribes and Literacy in Ancient Egypt," *Scripta Signa Vocis: Studies about Scripts, Scriptures, Scribes and Languages in the Near East*, fs. J. H. Hospers [ed. H. L. J. Vanstiphout et al.; Groningen: Egbert Forsten, 1986] 253).

[41] The phrase is from J. Baines, "Four Notes on Literacy," 67.

[42] Ptahhotep 17.10ff; Lichtheim, *AEL* 1.75.

of Egyptian society. Herodotus (2.164) and Diodorus (1.74) report that in Egypt sons were compelled to follow in the professions of their fathers.[43] If scribal office was hereditary, then scribal families would have constituted a restricted social class with a monopoly on positions of influence. But was this the case?

There is much evidence from the New Kingdom period for hereditary succession in scribal office. At Deir el-Medinah appointment to the office of "scribe of the tomb" (second in rank only to the foreman), was made by the vizier. Typically the vizier appears to have approved the succession of a son to the office of his father.[44] The family of the Ramesside scribe Thutmose is our best example of this. Thutmose left a graffito scratched on a rock in the mountain of Thebes naming his three immediate ancestors, all of whom were "king's scribes". Other texts establish that each of these individuals served as "scribe of the tomb," as did Thutmose's son and grandson. Thus there was a succession of six generations in the office, running through most of the twentieth dynasty and into the twenty-first: Amennakht—Harshire—Kha'emhedjet—Thutmose—Butehamun—Ankhefenamun.[45] M. Bierbrier has studied other official families of the nineteenth and twentieth dynasties and concluded that there was a high concentration of important offices in single families at certain periods, although none of these were able to hold on to positions for more than three generations at a time.[46]

Thus it was not rare for a father to hand down his scribal office to a son. This does not mean, however, that the scribal circles were hereditary cliques, because the ideal of hereditary succession in the scribal bureaucracy always had to compete with the practice of advancement on the basis of merit. Especially in the higher ranks, efficiency dictated the promotion of the best available individuals to open positions, irrespective of their origins. The Instruction to Merikare, for example, advises the king:

Do not prefer the wellborn to the commoner;
Choose a man on account of his skills.[47]

---

[43] See C. J. Eyre, "Work and the Organisation of Work in the Old Kingdom," 38.

[44] J. Černý, *A Community of Workmen at Thebes in the Ramesside Period*, 224.

[45] J. Černý, *A Community of Workmen at Thebes in the Ramesside Period*, 339; M. Bierbrier, *The Late New Kingdom in Egypt*, 39–42; see chart x, "The Family of the Scribe Amennakht".

[46] *The Late New Kingdom in Egypt*, 18.

Beginning in the Old Kingdom period we find biographical inscriptions of individuals who claim they were of the lowest status before the king recognized their talent and promoted them. For example Nekhebu, a high official of the 5th–6th dynasties, asserts "His Majesty found me a common builder," before he was elevated gradually to the highest position of "Overseer of all Works of the King."[48] Even though such individuals were probably literate and well-connected socially to start with, these texts emphasize the possibility of social mobility, with success being based on merit.[49]

In the New Kingdom, high-ranking individuals who claim humble origins appear with unprecedented frequency. For example, Anhurimose, high priest at Thinis under the 19th dynasty, acknowledges that he was poor (*ḥwrw*) when he was taken into the place of instruction (*ʿt-sbȝ*).[50] Anhurimose's inscription, dating to the reign of Merenptah, states:

> I was worthy as a child, clever as a lad, intelligent as a boy, able as a poor man. I was a poor person, accepted into school without trouble (?), one who was noticed and whom they marked out (for promotion).[51]

In fact Anhurimose was the son of an official of middle rank. The description of his origin as *ḥwrw* is partly a reflex of the stock references to poor origin which had become standard at the Amarna

---

[47] Lichtheim, *AEL*, 101.

[48] D. Dunham, "The Biographical Inscriptions of Nekhebu in Boston and Cairo," *JEA* 24 (1938) 1–8. Dunham's "Note on the Offices and Career of Nekhebu" is pertinent here: "The Cairo text yields interesting evidence on two matters connected with Nekhebu's professional career. In the first place he lists the offices to which he was appointed, presumably in the order of their acquisition. Secondly, in his account of his apprenticeship to his brother, he gives both the steps by which the latter rose in his profession, and the preliminary training which he himself underwent. These records not only give us an indication of the relative grades of the various professional offices, but also tend to show that they were not, at this time, acquired purely by inheritance, but were, in part at least, the rewards of training and experience" (p. 7).

[49] Cf. J. Baines, "Literacy and Ancient Egyptian Society," 585.

[50] H. Kees, "Die Laufbahn des Hohenpriesters Onhurmes von Thinis," *ZÄS* 73 (1937) 77–90.

[51] The translation is by K. Kitchen, *Pharaoh Triumphant: The Life and Times of Ramesses II*, 145; cf. Kees, "Die Laufbahn des Hohenpriesters Onhurmes von Thinis," 81.

court.[52] Anhurimose's father, however, had not attained priestly rank; he was only a military scribe. Although Anhurimose followed his father in military office, among the priests at Thinis he was parvenu. As high priest, Anhurimose is typical of the period for his acquisition of an office which formerly had been hereditary. He also belongs to a trend in which it was increasingly possible for "provincials" to attain high office as opposed to members of the powerful families of Memphis and Thebes.[53]

H. Brunner calls ancient Egypt "an open society" because of the chance that every individual had, at least in theory, for this type of advancement.[54] This is an overstatement, but on the other hand, there is no evidence that the number of literate people in ancient Egypt was ever deliberately restricted. Naturally among official families there was an urge to grasp for power and to exclude newcomers, but this was balanced by the need of the pharaonic administration to recruit the most talented individuals. The Egyptian scribal class was not a tightly controlled mandarin cadre; in fact the ideology of this class was decidedly "expansionist".[55]

For example, the oldest Instruction texts belong to the elite of the royal court, yet even here there is clear recognition of social mobility. Ptahhotep, a vizier, advises subordinates discretely to overlook the humble origins of their superiors:

> If you are lowly and serve a distinguished man,
> Be not mindful that he once was lowly.
> Do not be arrogant toward him
> Because you know his former state;
> Respect him rather for what he has received.
> Wealth and respect do not come by themselves,
> It is god who endows them.[56]

Downward mobility is an equally familiar prospect in the Instruction of

---

[52] H. Brunner, *Altägyptische Erziehung*, 42; cf. Kees, "Die Laufbahn des Hohenpriesters Onhurmes von Thinis," 83, with some examples from the biographical inscriptions of Amarna.

[53] Kitchen, *Pharaoh Triumphant: The Life and Times of Ramesses II*, 145. For a comparable stela inscription from the 19th dynasty, see Brunner, *Altägyptische Erziehung*, 169, no. xxxiii.

[54] "Schreibunterricht und Schule als Fundament der ägyptischen Hochkultur," 68. Of course Brunner has in mind only male individuals in this regard.

[55] J. Baines, "Literacy and Ancient Egyptian Society," 585.

[56] Ptahhotep maxim 10; cf. the translation in Brunner, "Schreibunterricht und Schule als Fundament der ägyptischen Hochkultur," 68; and Lichtheim, *AEL* 1.66.

Ptahhotep. Even an official who has achieved a great deal can be replaced by a competitor:

> If you are great after having been humble,
> Have gained wealth after having been poor
> In the past, in a town which you know,
> Knowing your former condition,
> Do not put trust in your wealth,
> Which came to you as gift of god;
> So that you will not fall behind one like you,
> To whom the same has happened.[57]

In the Instruction literature the hereditary ideal, for all its tenacity, is subverted by the figurative use of the terms of patrilineal succession. Already in the Old Kingdom texts the "father-son" relation of scribal teacher and student can be fictive.[58] The language of father-son succession is thus used to break the rule as much as to uphold it. For example, Ptahhotep, who says in his prologue "what age does to people is evil in everything," is so aged that his "eyes are dim, ears deaf ... the bones ache throughout."[59] Thus he is portrayed as much too old to have bodily offspring still of trainable age, yet he addresses his student as "son," *s3*.[60] Similarly it was said that at the age of 110 years the fourth-dynasty sage Djedi travelled with so many "children" that he needed an extra boat to transport them, along with his books. These "children" must have been the retinue of a great teacher rather than his family.[61] In the postscript to the Instruction to Kagemni the teacher is described as surrounded by a similar circle of "children" (i.e., students).[62]

The twelfth maxim of Ptahhotep distinguishes between "son" (*s3*, student) and "seed" (*mtwt*, progeny or offspring). The well-chosen student can bring many blessings; a son gone bad, however, means only trouble:

---

[57] Ptahhotep maxim 30; Lichtheim, *AEL* 1.71.

[58] For a survey of the use of "father" in the various ancient Near Eastern wisdom literatures to designate pedagogical relation rather than kinship, see P. Nel, "The Concept 'Father' in the Wisdom Literature of the Ancient Near East," *JNWSL* 5 (1977) 59-61.

[59] Lichtheim, *AEL* 1.63.

[60] Brunner, *Altägyptische Erziehung*, 10-11; Williams, "Scribal Training in Ancient Egypt," 215.

[61] Ibid. The story of Djedi is preserved in the Westcar Papyrus from the Middle Kingdom period, translated by Lichtheim, *AEL* 1.217-220.

[62] Lichtheim, *AEL* 1.60.

> If you are a man of maturity
> Then acquire for yourself a "son"
> [s3, i.e., "student," famulus]
> That god might be gracious.
> If he is straight and turns in your way,
> Cares well for your possessions,
> Then do all good for him.
> He is your "son," begotten by your spirit [ka].
> Do not separate your heart from him.
> But your "seed" [mtwt, i.e., "offspring"],
> If he makes trouble, goes astray,
> Rejects your counsel, resists what is said to him,
> His mouth making vile speech,
> Then disown him, he is not your son![63]

The Middle Kingdom *Kemit* book, a catalogue of scribal formulae and precepts, uses similar language for the adoption of a student:

> Ah! Open your writings, For you should take a student [s3],
> Who will be taught in the useful writings from the beginning.[64]

A New Kingdom composition in praise of great writers (Papyrus Chester Beatty IV verso 2,5–3,11) describes the same educational situation:

> The children of others are given to them [the great sages and teachers] to be heirs as their own children.[65]

The scribal terminology of paternal-filial pedagogy thus does not indicate that the scribal class was an hereditary elite. This usage of "father" and "son" describes educational adoption as readily as it denotes filiation, showing that the scribal profession was open to those outside hereditary lines. Instruction in the form of a father's teaching to his son should not be mistaken for the exclusive language of a closed group of scribal families—it is actually a flexible form which accomodates students from various backgrounds.

In the literature of the New Kingdom the language of hereditary succession is taxed to its limit, because during this period it became increasingly removed from actual practice. The Instruction of Any is cast in the traditional form of a father's teaching to his son, yet Any can also aver:

---

[63] Following the German translation of H. Brunner, "Schreibunterricht und Schule als Fundament der ägyptischen Hochkultur," 71; cf. Brunner, *Altägyptische Erziehung*, 155–56; Lichtheim, *AEL* 1.66–67.

[64] W. Barta gives the Egyptian text in transcription and a German translation, "Das Schulbuch Kemit," *ZÄS* 105 (1978) 12–13.

[65] Lichtheim, *AEL* 2.177. Cf. H. Brunner, "Die 'Weisen', ihre 'Lehren' und

> The head of the treasury has no son,
> The master of the seal has no heir,
> The scribe is chosen for his ability (ḏrt),
> His office has no children.[66]

Any clearly refers here to the displacement of hereditary succession in the bureaucracy by the principle of advancement on the basis of ability. It is probably indicative of the same trend that, as we have seen from the New Kingdom scribal miscellanies, the practice now emerges of calling a student in the scribal workplace ḥry-ꜥ, "helper," rather than sꜣ, "son".[67] The parental-filial figure of speech, in other words, is abandoned.

Only in a New Kingdom text could we find a report like that in the "Story of Truth and Falsehood," where the illegitimate son of a woman who is herself of uncertain social standing enters scribal training and excels:

> Then he was sent to school, and he learned how to write perfectly.
> He practiced all the manly arts, and surpassed all his older class-
> mates, who were at school with him.[68]

To be sure, the boy is mocked by his classmates because he has no father. His role in the story makes clear, however, that by the New Kingdom period it was conceivable that someone with no hereditary claim to scribal office could succeed.

The impression that the force of hereditary claims to scribal office weakened under the New Kingdom is confirmed by the evidence from Deir el-Medinah. As we have seen, the expectation persisted that as a rule the scribe of the tomb would be succeeded in office by his son; yet of the three scribes of the tomb whose precise date of appointment is known, none was the son of a scribe of the tomb.[69] The

---

'Prophezeiungen' in altägyptischer Sicht," *ZÄS* 93 (1966) 30.

[66] For the sense of ḏrt, literally "hand," as "ability," see H. te Velde, "Scribes and Literacy in Ancient Egypt," 253; Lichtheim renders the term literally, *AEL* 2.140.

[67] Cf. Otto, "Bildung und Ausbildung im alten Ägypten," 42.

[68] Papyrus Chester Beatty II, 4.7–5.2, translated by H. Brunner, *Altägyptische Erziehung*, 169; cf. Lichtheim, *AEL* 2.212.

[69] Ramose, year 5 of Ramesses II; Amenkha, year 32 of Ramesses III; and Amennakht, year 16 appointed by the vizier To (J. Černý, *A Community of Workmen at Thebes in the Ramesside Period*, 223). Admittedly the third of these, Amennakht, is the scribe who eventually proved to be the head of a six-generation dynasty at Deir el-Medinah, but it is significant that a scribe of obscure origin

scribe Ramose, the first of these three, was so successful that he has been called "the richest man who ever lived in Deir el-Medinah."[70] Ramose's father Amenemhab was not a scribe, but a *šms*, "runner" or "messenger." Since Amenemhab would not have been literate, J. Černý speculates that he must have been the friend of a scribe who gave lessons to Ramose, "and thus the son of a postman became a scribe."[71]

A comparable figure is the scribe Kenḥikhopshef, whose origins were outside the Deir el-Medinah community, probably in a non-scribal family, yet he stayed in office for at least 46 years, possibly as long as 54 years.[72]

There is, then, no reason to think that the scribal students for whom the Instruction of Amenemope was written belonged to a distinct social class, restricted along hereditary lines. It is important, however, to ask why entry into the scribal bureaucracy expanded during the New Kingdom. It has been a standard view of the post-Amarna period that Horemheb, in restoring government control, had difficulty finding capable individuals for the most important positions. The priesthood and bureaucracy, it is assumed, had been twice purged at the beginning and end of Akhenaten's revolution, effectively destroying the intellectual class. Horemheb thus resorted for state personnel to the army with which he had gained control of the land. This meant that access to administrative office was suddenly thrown open to whole new classes of people. Horemheb's soldiers and officers were often foreigners, not closely tied to the Egyptian scribal heritage. Their occupation of the bureaucracy, it is argued, unalterably changed the complexion of the scribal class in the New Kingdom.[73]

The infiltration of foreigners into the government of the New Kingdom, most of whom entered by way of the army, is a central aspect of the social and political development of the period, but the view described above is somewhat overdrawn. D. O'Connor gives a helpful corrective to the assertion that incursions of non-Egyptian

---

could establish himself so securely as to have this sort of posterity.

[70] K. Kitchen, *Pharaoh Triumphant: The Life and Times of Ramesses II*, 193; J. Černý, *A Community of Workmen at Thebes in the Ramesside Period*, 317.

[71] Ibid.

[72] J. Černý, *A Community of Workmen at Thebes in the Ramesside Period*, 329–337, cf. p. 223.

[73] W. Helck, *Geschichte des alten Ägypten*, 180, 196.

military personnel were the largest factor in the reshaping of the New Kingdom administration:

> The idea that Akhenaten destroyed a professional, idealistic bureaucracy which was thereafter staffed increasingly by deracinated men, frequently of foreign origin and military background, and characterized by inefficiency and corruption, must be set against the continuation of effective centralized government for a further 250 years.[74]

There was, in other words, considerable continuity in the administrative personnel of the successive regimes of the 18th and 19th dynasties. The likelihood that the Deir el-Medinah community was moved to Amarna under Akhenaten and then later returned to Thebes is an example of this.

Already in the 18th dynasty, however, the Asian and African conquests of Thutmose I and his successors had brought the need for an increased military, fiscal, and cultic administration. The need under the Empire for a larger scribal bureaucracy persisted, opening access to scribal standing not just to some foreigners from the army but also to Egyptians of relatively lower social status. The breakdown of hereditary claim to scribal standing in the New Kingdom period thus resulted from the unprecedented need for more scribes.

The theme of the praises of scribedom (with its counterpart, the mockery of other trades) becomes prominent at two points in Egyptian history: the early Middle Kingdom and the period of imperial expansion under the New Kingdom pharaohs. Both were periods when the demand of the state for an expanding scribal bureaucracy was at its highest. At the beginning of the 12th dynasty, central government in Egypt began to recover from the dissolution of the 1st Intermediate. To rebuild the collapsed administration, it was necessary for the first time in Egyptian history to recruit for the scribal bureaucracy in competition with other trades. Toward this end the Instruction of Dua-Khety, a text which has no antecedent in the literature of the Old Kingdom, was written. The humorous nature of the text has been disputed, but there is no question that the purpose of the text is to emphasize the advantages of the scribal profession over the hardships of other work.[75] G. Posener

---

[74] "New Kingdom and Third Intermediate Period, 1552–644 BC," *Ancient Egypt: A Social History* (eds. B. G. Trigger, et al.; Cambridge: Cambridge University Press) 222–23.

[75] W. Helck has argued that the text is a wholly serious composition (*Die Lehre des Dw3-Htjj* [Wiesbaden: Harrassowitz, 1970). Most interpreters still follow

first argued that the "Satire of the Trades" was promulgated as propaganda for state service in the new regime of the 12th dynasty.[76]

The Instruction of Dua-Khety was immensely popular during the New Kingdom period, and its themes recur throughout the late Egyptian miscellanies. The miscellanies, however, present a new theme: in addition to the twenty trades which are ridiculed in Dua-Khety, now the hardships of a military career are especially emphasized. For example, in Papyrus Lansing we read:

> Come, <let me tell> you the woes of the soldier, and how many are his superiors: the general, the troop-commander, the officer who leads, the standard-bearer, the lieutenant, the scribe, the commander of fifty, and the garrison-captain. They go in and out in the halls of the palace, saying: "Get laborers!" He is awakened at any hour. One is after him as <after> a donkey. He toils until the Aten sets in his darkness of night. He is hungry, his belly hurts; he is dead while yet alive.[77]

It is no accident that military life is depicted in miserable terms in this text, since during this period the army became an especially attractive route for advancement.[78] The celebration of the scribal trade which appears so frequently in New Kingdom literature thus belongs to the language of recruitment. Once we recognize the propagandistic function of these texts, it becomes necessary to reassess the picture of scribal life as privileged, comfortable, and elite, which so many scholars have adopted uncritically from this literature.

The scribe's life is described as one of unqualified ease and prestige. "It is he," we are told, "who commands the entire land. All business is under his control."[79] "One will do all you say," Any asserts, "if you are versed in writings."[80] "A scribe at whatever post in town," according to Dua-Khety, "he will not suffer in it."[81] Elsewhere in New Kingdom sources, however, the picture is not so sanguine.

Maspero in viewing the text as a deliberately humorous "Satire of the Trades". Cf. Lichtheim, *AEL* 2.184–5.

[76] *Littérature et politique dans l'Egypte de la 12e dynastie*, 3–8; cf. Brunner, "Schreibunterricht und Schule als Fundament der ägyptischen Hochkultur," 64.

[77] Lichtheim, *AEL* 2.172.

[78] Cf. H. te Velde, "Scribes and Literacy in Ancient Egypt," 258; J. Baines, "Literacy and Ancient Egyptian Society," 595 n. 34.

[79] Papyrus Chester Beatty 4.1–3; cf. te Velde, "Scribes and Literacy in Ancient Egypt," 255.

[80] Lichtheim, *AEL* 2.140.

[81] Lichtheim, *AEL* 1.185.

We may consider first the assertion of the scribal propaganda that the scribe, unlike the soldier or laborer, has no superior to harass him:

> See, there's no profession without a boss,
> except for the scribe; he is the boss.[82]

Of course this is not strictly true; the scribe always has a superior. Compare the following advice from the same text:

> When you walk behind officials,
> Follow at a proper distance.
> When you enter a man's house,
> And he's busy with someone before you,
> Sit with your hand over your mouth.
> Do not ask him for anything,
> Only do as he tells you,
> Beware of rushing to the table![83]

This is not just sapiential *Bescheidenheit*; it is dutiful subservience, which we find commended throughout the Instruction:

> Do not talk back to an angry superior,
> Let him have his way;
> Speak sweetly when he speaks sourly,
> It's the remedy that calms the heart.
> ...
> Choose silence for yourself,
> Submit to what he does.[84]

The New Kingdom miscellanies portray the manual laborer as constantly threatened by beatings from his taskmaster.[85] Yet corporal punishment was also common in the scribal guild; apprentices are frequently threatened with thrashings by their superiors. The scribe Amenemope, author of the satirical letter of Papyrus Anastasi I, writes:

> Pass no day in laziness, or you will be beaten. The ear of a lad happens to be on his back. He listens when he is beaten. ... I am fed up with offering advice. ... Should I give you one hundred strokes, and you will brush them all away. For me you are a beaten donkey who recovers in the day.[86]

---

[82] Dua-Khety, in Lichtheim, *AEL* 1.189.

[83] *AEL* 1.190

[84] Any, *AEL* 2.143.

[85] See for example the texts quoted by T. G. H. James, *Pharaoh's People: Scenes from Life in Imperial Egypt* (Chicago: University of Chicago Press: 1984) 103.

[86] Cited by James, *Pharaoh's People*, 141.

Even after advancing beyond the stage of apprentice, the scribe was not immune to arbitrary punishment. Merikare's advice to the king, "Do not kill a man whose virtues you know, with whom you once chanted the writings," illustrates this well. The narrative frame to the post-Ramesside Instruction of Ankhsheshonq portrays the composition of the teaching in prison, a vivid picture of what could happen to a sage who fell out of favor with the authorities.[87]

According to the Miscellanies, the scribe has no taxes to pay: "he who works in writing is not taxed (*ḥtr*), he has no dues (*šзyt*) to pay."[88] S. Katary, however, has checked this assertion against the data concerning land apportionment and assessment in the Wilbour Papyrus from the Ramesside period. She finds not only that scribes paid signficant assessments from the produce of their land allotments, but also that their assessments were higher, on the statistical average, than those imposed upon soldiers. The mean percentage of assessment levied upon scribes was 12.5 per cent according to the Wilbour Papyrus; military personnel paid a mean assessment of 12.007 per cent.[89] Statistically this difference is not so great, but it certainly belies the assertion that scribes were free of the levy, and it remains the case that at least in the large sample of data from the Wilbour Papyrus, scribes paid more than soldiers.

The promise of wealth, or at least material security, is common in the praises of scribedom: "Lo, no scribe is short of food and of riches from the palace."[90] "Become a scribe, so that riches become numerous for you in your time!"[91] J. J. Janssen pointed out, however, that the workers and scribes of Deir el-Medinah, while they may not have been poor, were not necessarily rich either (with the exception of a few outstanding individuals like Ramose).[92] Nor were even the best provided-for members of the community always secure. As we shall see below, at times the support given to the community by the state

---

[87] See Lichtheim, *AEL* 3. 162–63.

[88] Papyrus Anastasi 5 15.6–17.3=Papyrus Sallier 1 6.1ff.

[89] "Cultivator, Scribe, Stablemaster, Soldier: The Late-Egyptian Miscellanies in Light of *P. Wilbour*," *Egyptological Miscellanies: A Tribute to Professor Ronald J. Williams* (eds. J. K. Hoffmeier et al.; Chicago: Ares, 1983) 78.

[90] Dua-Khety, *AEL* 1.191.

[91] Černý-Gardiner, Hieratic Ostraca I, 1957, pl. VI 1; translated by H.-W. Fischer-Elfert, *Literarische Ostraka der Ramessidenzeit in Übersetzung* (Klein Ägyptische Texte; Wiesbaden: Harrassowitz, 1986) 1.

[92] *Commodity Prices from the Ramessid Period*, 533–538.

became so unreliable that the workers had to strike for their rations.

The expansion of the scribal bureaucracy under the New Kingdom resulted in a wide range of ranks within which not all were privileged. We learn from the papyri that one might remain in the status of ḥry-ꜥ until as late as age 30. Papyrus Turin 74,5 admonishes: "Don't behave like a boy, for you are already 30 years old!"[93] A scribe who remained an apprentice until age 30 without receiving an established office of his own must have faced dim prospects for the rest of his career. The lowest ranks of officialdom were undoubtedly populated by such scribes, many of whom may never have acquired more than the rudimentary skills of literacy.[94]

For these individuals the task of writing was simply labor— perhaps not back-breaking like that of the peasant farmer, but neither did it afford the elite status which is promised to the student in the professional propaganda. Despite the praise given to writing in the miscellanies, at the highest levels of Egyptian society writing was done *for* the elite, not *by* the elite. Already in the Old Kingdom the highest officials had scribe statues of themselves made, but only to show that they had attained (and surpassed) a requisite level of proficiency in literacy. In the decorated tombs of the Old Kingdom high officials are not shown writing except symbolically. "Literacy is thus necessary for high status," J. Baines observes, "but writing is delegated by those who achieve that status."[95] In the tomb paintings there are pictures of scribes, but in large numbers, performing duties which tomb-owners supervise. Numerous scribes indicate prestige for the tomb owner, "but most scribes depicted belong to different and inferior social categories to tomb owners, forming a literate sub-elite."[96]

The sub-elite status of most scribes is more apparent for the New Kingdom period than earlier, if only because the overall size of the bureaucracy is so much larger. The literate professional class of the New Kingdom was a social pyramid. Despite the expansionist ideology of this class, which broke hereditary possession of office and opened

---

[93] See A. Erman, *Die ägyptische Schülerhandschriften*, APAW, Phil.-Hist. Klasse 2 (1925) 17, 23.

[94] Cf. J. Baines, "Four Notes on Literacy," 89.

[95] "Literacy and Ancient Egyptian Society," 580.

[96] J. Baines and C. J. Eyre, "Four Notes on Literacy," 67. Cf p. 78: "As can be seen in tombs, people of high status have transcended the stage of writing, and in most cases reading, for themselves, and this will be the more true of kings. These things are done for them."

the profession to those from poor or foreign backgrounds, most belonged to relatively lower ranks, where they were exhorted to remain content:

> Attend to your position,
> Be it low or high;
> It is not good to press forward,
> Step according to rank.[97]

Through the periods of Egyptian history from the Old Kingdom to the New, the broadening of the scribal class and resultant lowering of the status of most of its members is reflected in the status of the authors to whom the Instruction literature is attributed. The social-class orientation of the Instruction texts, in other words, becomes steadily lower as the genre develops.[98] Even if most Instruction texts are pseudepigraphical (this is a likelihood), the gradually lowering status of the figures to whom the Instruction is attributed reflects a broadening audience, a lower assumed status for the class of people to whom the Instruction is addressed. Thus the Old Kingdom Instruction of Ptahhotep is attributed to a prince and vizier. Kagemni likewise was vizier, and the Instruction to Hardjedef purports to be from the son of king Khufu (Cheops). The Middle Kingdom Instructions of Merikare and Amenemhet still derive from the royal court, but alongside these appear texts such as the Instruction of Dua-Khety, whose outlook suggests the middle administrative echelons. At the beginning of the New Kingdom we find the Instruction of Any, whose author is a minor official. He bears simply the title "scribe of the palace of the Queen," and his concerns have often been referred to as "middle-class".[99]

The titles invoked by Amenemope all represent mid- to lower-level bureaucratic positions. Like most of the Egyptian Instruction literature, the Wisdom of Amenemope is probably a pseudepigraphical text.[100] According to the prologue (2.7–13) the author Amenemope

---

[97] Instruction of Any, *AEL* 2. 142.

[98] J. Leclant, "Documents nouveaux et points de vue recents sur les Sagesses de l'Egypte ancienne," *Les sagesses du Proche-Orient ancien, Colloque de Strasbourg, 1962* (Paris: Presses universitaires, 1963) 14–15; I. Grumach, *Untersuchungen zur Lebenslehre des Amenope*, 19.

[99] M. Lichtheim, *AEL* 2.135; H. H. Schmid, *Wesen und Geschichte der Weisheit: Eine Untersuchung zur altorientalischen und Israelitischen Weisheitsliteratur* (BZAW 101; Berlin: Toepelmann, 1966) 54; W. McKane, *Proverbs: A New Approach* (OTL; Philadelphia: Westminster, 1970) 99.

[100] B. van de Walle, *La transmission des textes littéraires égyptiens*, 35–37; I. Grumach, *Untersuchungen zur Lebenslehre des Amenope*, 17–21. In the earlier

lived in the indeterminate past in the town of Akhmim, and wrote the text for the instruction of his son. In fact the author was probably a Theban scribe who wrote the text for scribal students destined for various levels of state service.[101]

Of the titles attributed to Amenemope in the prologue, only two are attested elsewhere: "Overseer of the Fields," *imy-r s3ṯw* (1.13); and "Scribe who Determines the Offerings for All the Gods," *sš w3ḥ ḥtp nṯr n nṯrw nbw* (2.3).[102] The remainder of the titles are apparently literary paraphrases of various duties of scribes in the pharaonic administration:[103]

> The overseer of grains who controls the measure,
> Who sets the harvest-dues for his lord,
> Who registers the islands of new land,
> ...
> Who records the markers of the borders of fields,
> Who acts for the king in his listing of taxes,
> Who makes the land-register of Egypt;
> ...
> Who gives land-leases to the people,
> The overseer of grains, [provider of] foods.
> (1.15–2.5; *AEL* 2.148–9)

A single scribe would not have fulfilled all these duties; the titles show rather that the text is meant to instruct members of the scribal profession who work in a wide range of capacities. Amenemope is a sophisticated text, but it addresses the vast sub-elite of the scribal class along with the few who could really appreciate its theological and literary sophistication.

Egyptologists and biblical scholars have long debated the question whether the Instruction literatures of ancient Egypt and Israel

---

discussion the historicity of both figures, Amenemope and his father, Kanakht, was often assumed (e.g., A. Wiedemann, review of Budge, *The Teaching of Amen-em-apt*, *OLZ* 28 [1925] 300). H. Brunner thinks that the authorship of the Instructions of Dua-khety, Any, and Amenemope is authentic ("Die Weisheitsliteratur," *Handbuch der Orientalistik*, vol. 1, pt. 2, *Ägyptologie*; [ed. B. Spuler; Leiden: Brill, 1952; 92–93).

[101] See I. Grumach, *Untersuchungen zur Lebenslehre des Amenope*, 19–21. Theban provenance is indicated by close literary affinities of the text to the memorial inscriptions of the Theban necropolis.

[102] Cairo stat. no. 36919, from the late period; and Cairo stat. no. 42211, Lange, *Das Weisheitsbuch des Amenemope*, 27,29.

[103] Cf. F. L. Griffith, "The Teaching of Amenophis," 226.

reflect a "class ethic" (*Standesethik*). For Egypt, the verdict has been negative in the main. H. Gese and H. Brunner maintain that the Egyptian Instruction literature commends models of behavior for all levels of society, not just the elite.[104] Schmid has characterized the theological development which accompanied this lowering of social-class orientation in the Instruction genre as the "democratizing of Maat."[105]

I will argue that a similar democratizing of ethical outlook with regard to wealth and poverty is exhibited in the Wisdom of Amenemope. This is not just the reflection of a literary trend, however. Amenemope's outlook differs from the earlier Instruction literature because its audience belongs to a lower socio-economic level. The scribes of the New Kingdom were not cloistered in a school; they were not a closed hereditary class, nor were they sheltered from the economic vicissitudes of the period. As the Instruction of Amenemope was not written for an elite class, we are not suprised to find it does not reflect an elite outlook. Before turning to Amenemope, however, we must examine the broader social and economic background against which the text was written.

ASPECTS OF THE ECONOMIC AND SOCIAL HISTORY OF RAMESSIDE EGYPT

The International Context

Egypt first became an imperial power under the New Kingdom pharaohs, and the Instruction texts of the period reflect clearly the changes wrought upon Egyptian society by that development. While the 18th-dynasty Instruction of Any reflects Egypt at the height of its imperial power,[106] the author of Amenemope is a witness to the decline of the Egyptian empire. Thus we begin our account of the historical background to Amenemope by sketching briefly the course of Egyptian imperial expansion and its ultimate failure.

---

[104] H. Gese, *Lehre und Wirklichkeit in der alten Weisheit: Studien zu den Sprüchen Salomos und zu dem Buche Hiob* (Tübingen: Mohr, 1958) 30; and Brunner, *Altägyptische Erziehung*, 116–17.

[105] *Wesen und Geschichte der Weisheit*, 38,54.

[106] Cf. for example the mention in the epilogue to Any that "one teaches the Nubian to speak Egyptian,/the Syrian and other strangers too" (Lichtheim, *AEL* 2.144).

Before the New Kingdom period, when Egypt was confident of its superiority, it viewed foreign lands with indifference. This attitude changed, however, after the humiliation of Hyksos occupation. For the first time, Egypt had been dominated by foreign conquerors. Combining military superiority (above all through the use of horse and chariot) with disregard for Egyptian culture, the Hyksos ruled from heavily fortified compounds in the Delta where their main interest was in exacting tribute from the native Egyptians to the south.[107] Centuries later Egyptian rulers would continue to denounce the Hyksos as those who "ruled without Re" and "those whom the gods abominate".[108]

With the expulsion of the Hyksos from Egypt in the mid-sixteenth century, Ahmose I (1552-1527 BCE), founder of the 18th dynasty, launched Egypt on an unprecedented program of imperial expansion. Moreover, for the remaining half of the second millennium, Egypt always had to remain on guard against new waves of invaders from the eastern Mediterranean. The military buildup which this required changed fundamentally the character of Egyptian society internally, and toward its neighbors Egypt became vigorously expansionist.[109]

In addition to national pride and security, a prime motive of the developing imperial ideology was economic return. To the south there was the lure of gold ready to be exploited, unimpeded by levies from competing states. In Syria-Palestine the incentive for expansion was booty from military campaigns and tribute imposed in those regions where control was possible.[110]

Ahmose I, after destroying Hyksos bases in Palestine (including Tell el-ʿAjjûl, Beth-Shemesh, Shiloh, and Beth-Zur), took control of territory south of Egypt between the first and second cataracts. His

---

[107] See J. Wilson, *The Burden of Egypt: An Interpretation of Ancient Egyptian Culture* (Chicago: University of Chicago Press, 1951), chapter 7, "The Great Humiliation," 154-165.

[108] From an inscription of Hatshepsut (1490-1468 BCE), in Pritchard, *ANET* 231.

[109] The militarization of New Kingdom society is traced by W. Helck, *Der Einfluss der Militärführer in der 18. ägyptischen Dynastie* (Leipzig: J. C. Hinrichs, 1939); and A. Kadry, *Officers and Officials in the New Kingdom*, Studia Aegyptiaca, 8 (Budapest: Université Loránd Eötvös de Budapest 1982).

[110] B. J. Kemp, "Imperialism and Empire in New Kingdom Egypt (c. 1575-1087 BC)," *Imperialism in the Ancient World* (eds. P. D. Garnsey and C. R. Whittaker, Cambridge: Cambridge University Press, 1978) 19.

successor Amenhotep I (1527-1506) consolidated the conquest of Nubia proper (Wawat). Tuthmosis I (1506-1494) then extended Egyptian control deep into the Sudan (Kush), occupying the region just below the fourth cataract, where he founded the important town of Napata. By 1500 Tuthmosis I had campaigned all the way to Naharin in northern Syria, leaving a victory stela on the bank of the Euphrates.[111]

Tuthmosis III (1490-1436 BCE) was the most energetic empire builder of the 18th dynasty. He expanded and consolidated control over Nubia and the northern Sudan and carried out an extended series of Syrian campaigns.[112] A major victory at Megiddo early in his reign gave Tuthmosis III claim to Syria; then in his thirty-third year he successfully crossed the Euphrates and repulsed the king of Mitanni.[113] These military successes caused the wealth of empire to flow into Thebes. In the course of his reign Tuthmosis III is estimated to have donated approximately 15,000 kilograms of gold to the temple of Karnak.[114] Tuthmosis III also undertook huge building projects at home with the profit of his victories abroad.

The Amarna correspondence shows, however, how easily the Egyptian hegemony of Syria could slip away. Already under Amenhotep III (1402-1364 BCE) some local Syrian rulers had withdrawn from Egyptian control. In the subsequent decades while the Akhenaten regime was preoccupied with domestic revolution, the Hittite king Suppiluliumas overwhelmed Mitanni and assumed control of most of Syria and northern Phoenicia. By the time of the reigns of Smenkhare (1351-1348 BCE) and Tutankhamen (1347-1337 BCE), the entire Syro-Palestinian domain was lost for Egypt.[115] Horemheb (1333-

---

[111] J. Wilson, *The Burden of Egypt*, 167; B. J. Kemp, "Imperialism and Empire in New Kingdom Egypt," 44.

[112] G. Steindorff and K. C. Seele, *When Egypt Ruled the East*; rev. ed. (Chicago: University of Chicago Press, 1957) 53-66.

[113] For the account of the battle of Megiddo from the annals of Tuthmosis III, see Lichtheim, *AEL* 2.29-35. Accounts of the eighth campaign against the Mitanni are collected in Pritchard, *ANET* 239-41.

[114] J. Janssen, "Prolegomena to the Study of Egypt's Economic History during the New Kingdom," 154; cf. estimates of gold imports from Nubia and Sudan at around 28.35 kilograms yearly for the later years of the reign of Tuthmosis III: T. Säve-Söderbergh, *Ägypten und Nubien: Ein Beitrag zur Geschichte altägyptischer Aussenpolitik* (Lund: 1941), 201-11; Vercoutter, J. "The Gold of Kush. Two Gold-Washing Stations at Faras East." *Kush* 7 (1959) 129-35.

[115] J. Wilson, *The Burden of Egypt*, 230-31; C. Aldred, "Egypt: The Amarna Period and the End of the Eighteenth Dynasty," *Cambridge Ancient History*, 3rd ed.; vol. 2, part 2; *History of the Middle East and the Aegean Region c. 1380-*

1305 BCE) managed to reestablish order on the domestic front but was unable to recover Egypt's foreign holdings.

Thus when Ramesses I (1305-1303 BCE) inaugurated the 19th dynasty, Egypt's standing in the world arena had diminished greatly. As the rulers of the 19th dynasty set out to regain Egypt's advantage in Asia, war with the Hittites was unavoidable. Seti I (1303-1289 BCE) had some success in northern Palestine, as his stela at Beth-Shan attests.[116] The major clash with the Hittites came in the fifth year of Ramesses II (1289-1224 BCE) in the battle at Kadesh. Ramesses celebrated victory, but the battle was actually a standoff from which Ramesses was lucky to have escaped alive.[117]

If monumental building programs are any gauge of national prosperity, Egypt flourished under Ramesses II. He built more than any other pharaoh, previous or subsequent.[118] Under his rule, however, Egyptian external power reached its limit. Although the treaty which Ramesses II concluded with Hattusilis 16 years after the battle of Kadesh drew no formal boundary lines, it effectively ratified Hittite control of most of Syria.[119] The Egyptian-Hittite detente which this treaty established was motivated by greater threats looming over each of the two states. Through the first half of the thirteenth century the Hittites watched Assyria grow and begin to contest Hittite control of Mitanni; during the same period the Sea Peoples began threatening to overrun the Egyptian delta.

Skirmishes with the Sea Peoples occurred already early in the reign of Ramesses II. By the time of the battle of Kadesh Ramesses

---

1000 B.C. (eds. I. E. S. Edwards, C. J. Gadd, N. G. L. Hammond, and E. Sollberger; Cambridge: Cambridge University Press, 1975) 81-84; cf. A. Goetze, "The Struggle for the Domination of Syria (1400-1300 BC)," *Cambridge Ancient History*, 3rd ed.; vol. 2, part 2; 17; K. A. Kitchen, *Suppiluliuma and the Amarna Pharaohs* (Liverpool: Liverpool University Press, 1962).

[116] See Pritchard, *ANET* 253-55.

[117] For the Kadesh battle inscriptions of Ramesses II, see Lichtheim *AEL* 2. 57-71.

[118] R. O. Faulkner, "Egypt: From the Inception of the Nineteenth Dynasty to the Death of Ramesses III," *Cambridge Ancient History*, 3rd ed.; vol. 2, part 2; *History of the Middle East and the Aegean Region c. 1380-1000 B.C.* (eds. I. E. S. Edwards, C. J. Gadd, N. G. L. Hammond, and E. Sollberger; Cambridge: Cambridge University Press, 1975) 230.

[119] B. J. Kemp, "Imperialism and Empire in New Kingdom Egypt," 44. The Egyptian and Hittite versions of the treaty are translated in Pritchard, *ANET* 199-203.

claims to have incorporated into his army "Sherden ["Sardinians"?] in his majesty's captivity whom he had brought back in the victories of his strong arm."[120] It was, however, Ramesses II's successor Merenptah (1224–1204 BCE) who faced the full attack of the Sea Peoples. In Merenptah's fifth year a coalition of Libyans and various Sea Peoples, having plotted with the Nubians to incite revolt in the south, invaded from the west.[121] Merenptah lost no territory to the invaders; his victory is recounted on the temple reliefs at Karnak and on the poetic stela famous for its mention of Israel.[122] Merenptah's successors, however, would have greater difficulty in securing the western frontier.

Entering the period of the 20th dynasty, when the Instruction of Amenemope was written, Egypt's international situation deteriorated precipitously. During the reign of Ramesses III, second ruler of the 20th dynasty (1184–53 BCE), waves of Sea Peoples surged along the eastern Mediterranean coast, while from the west Libyans invaded the Egyptian Delta. Ramesses III's funerary temple at Medinet Habu records three major wars during his reign.[123] In year 5 of Ramesses III the Libu and Meshwesh tribes, having recovered from their defeat by Merenptah, invaded again. Once again they were repulsed. In year 8 a wave of Sea Peoples approached (Ramesses names the Peleset, Tjekker, Sheklesh, Sherden, Weshesh, and Denyen). These groups, having felled the Hittite capitals, marched on the north Syrian coastal region of Amurru, then advanced down the Syrian coast. Ramesses III managed to stop the land movement from his coastal outpost at Djahi and destroyed an enemy fleet apparently at the mouth of the Nile. Then in year 11 the Libyans attacked again. This time the Libu and

---

[120] From the Kadesh battle inscription, Lichtheim, *AEL* 2.63; cf. J. Wilson, *The Burden of Egypt*, 245.

[121] Accounts of the battle in A. Gardiner, *Egypt of the Pharaohs* (Oxford: Oxford University Press, 1961) 270–74; K. A. Kitchen, *Pharaoh Triumphant: The Life and Times of Ramesses II*, 215; J. Wilson, *The Burden of Egypt*, 254. It is widely thought that the Sea Peoples named by Merenptah were the forerunners of the settled peoples later known as the Lycians, Achaeans, Sardinians, Etruscans, and Sicilians. See W. F. Albright, "Some Oriental Glosses on the Homeric Problem," *AJA* 54 (1950) 162–76; A. Strobel, *Der spätbronzezeitliche Seevölkersturm*; (BZAW 145; Berlin/New York: de Gruyter, 1976).

[122] Lichtheim, *AEL* 2.73–78.

[123] W. Edgerton and J. A. Wilson, *Historical Records of Ramses III* (Chicago: Oriental Institute, 1936).

Meshwesh were supported by five additional tribes. The Harris Papyrus, dated at the death of Ramesses III, indicates that on this occasion the Libyan invaders had some initial success before they were finally expelled by Ramesses III, who claims to have taken over two thousand Libyan captives.[124]

Ramesses III's accounts of his victories over the Libyans give the impression that he had turned them back forever, but this was far from true. By the mid-20th dynasty numerous texts attest to incursions of Libu and Meshwesh far into upper Egypt, with frequent attacks on Thebes itself. Laborers at Deir el-Medinah during this period cited fear of roaming Libyans as a reason for staying home from work. These Libyan raids in upper Egypt were the spillover from major infiltrations in the Delta and below Memphis at Heracleopolis. Toward the end of the 20th dynasty the Libyans were able to penetrate lower Egypt peacefully, as the Theban government was no longer capable of offering resistance. Libyans gradually occupied the whole western Delta and founded principalities of their own, each served by an important town as its center.[125]

When Ramesses III died, the last imperial pharaoh was gone. After the reign of Ramesses III there is no clear evidence that Egypt controlled any regions of Palestine or Syria. As Černý points out, although a few scarabs of later Ramesside date have been found at Syro-Palestinian sites (Ramesses IV at Tell eṣ-Ṣâfi, Tell Zakarîya, and at Tell Jazari [Gezer]; Ramesses VI at Alalakh), scarabs were widely traded in the eastern Mediterranean; their presence at a site is no indication of Egyptian control of the region.[126]

The mining of turquoise and copper in the Sinai peninsula and the ʿArabah ended with Ramesses V (1146–1142 BCE) and Ramesses VI (1142–1135 BCE), so that by 1135 BCE the eastern frontier of Egypt was probably the shortest possible line from the Mediterranean to the Red Sea.[127] Sudanese gold was still exploitable, but gold production

---

[124] The wars of Ramesses III are reviewed by R. O. Faulkner, "Egypt: From the Inception of the Nineteenth Dynasty to the Death of Ramesses III," *Cambridge Ancient History*, 3rd ed.; vol. 2, part 2; 241–43; J. A. Wilson, *The Burden of Egypt*, 259–60; and W. Helck, *Geschichte des Alten Ägypten*, 193–95.

[125] J. Černý, "Egypt: From the Death of Ramesses III to the End of the Twenty-First Dynasty," *Cambridge Ancient History*, 3rd ed.; vol. 2, part 2; 616–619.

[126] J. Černý, "Egypt: From the Death of Ramesses III to the End of the Twenty-First Dynasty," *Cambridge Ancient History*, 3rd ed.; vol. 2, part 2; 614.

[127] J. Černý, "Egypt: From the Death of Ramesses III to the End of the

was significantly lower under the Ramessides. The Harris Papyrus records Ramesses III's gifts to the Egyptian temples at a total volume of 232.7 kilograms of gold. Compared with the figures mentioned earlier for Tuthmosis III (donation of approximately 15,000 kilograms of gold at Karnak), this indicates much lower total gold production under the 20th dynasty.[128]

Because of the serious decline in foreign income in the form of trade, booty, tribute, and mining, there was a marked diminution of building activity under the 20th dynasty, even during the longer reigns of Ramesses III, IX, and XI.[129] The second half of the 20th dynasty witnessed a political contest between the pharaonic court and the priesthood of Amun, in which the Theban monarchy steadily lost ground until finally unified pharaonic rule dissolved. Smendes, who founded the 21st dynasty at Tanis in 1069 BCE, was compelled to share rule of Egypt with Herihor and the priesthood of Amun who had controlled Thebes since the close of the reign of Ramesses XI.[130]

The decline of Egypt's international prestige and economic viability at the end of the 20th dynasty is reflected in the late Egyptian narrative known as the "Report of Wenamun."[131] Wenamun is depicted as a Theban official during the final decade of the reign of Ramesses XI. He is sent to Byblos to acquire timber for the sacred bark of Amun. Although Byblos had been a trading partner of Egypt since the Old Kingdom period, in this narrative the prince of Byblos refuses to supply the timber without first being paid in cash. Wenamun is reduced to the indignity of quarreling with the prince of Byblos over the authority of his mission, and suffers numerous other embarrassments.

Twenty-First Dynasty," *Cambridge Ancient History*, 3rd ed.; vol. 2, part 2; 615; D. O'Connor, "New Kingdom and Third Intermediate Period," *Ancient Egypt: A Social History*, 226.

[128] J. Janssen, "Prolegomena to the Study of Egypt's Economic History during the New Kingdom," 155; cf. A. Kadry, *Officers and Officials in the New Kingdom*, 186.

[129] D. O'Connor, "New Kingdom and Third Intermediate Period," *Ancient Egypt: A Social History*, 226; cf. J. Černý, "Egypt: From the Death of Ramesses III to the End of the Twenty-First Dynasty," 3rd ed.; vol. 2, part 2; 614.

[130] See W. Helck, "Der Zerfall des Staates," in *Geschichte des Alten Ägypten*, 217–230; Černý, "Egypt: From the Death of Ramesses III to the End of the Twenty-First Dynasty," *Cambridge Ancient History*, 3rd ed.; vol. 2, part 2; 638, 643–57.

[131] Lichtheim, *AEL* 2.224–230.

In the context of this story it is clear that the once considerable imperium of Egypt has faded.[132]

The external conditions of the crumbling empire were mirrored domestically by a series of economic and social crises under the Ramesside administration. We turn now to these circumstances, which form the immediate backdrop to the composition of Amenemope.

The Grain Crisis

The Genesis story of Joseph and his brothers depicts Egypt as a breadbasket to the world, managing its own harvests so well that it could sustain other peoples through periods of famine (cf. also Gen 12:10). During many periods in the history of Egypt this picture was basically true. In the Amarna correspondence we find Syrian princes appealing not just for Egyptian gold and troops, but also for Egyptian shipments of grain in order to survive.[133] Merenptah reports that early in his reign he sent grain to relieve famine in Hatti.[134] In Ramesside Egypt, however, the fabled grain administration system of the pharaohs faltered. One of the clearest indexes of economic deterioration under the Ramesside pharaohs is the sharp rise in grain prices at Thebes which is attested for the middle period of this dynasty.

We can speak of the "price" of grain in ancient Egypt only in qualified terms, because there was no proper monetary system. As early as the Old Kingdom period metal had been used as a means of expressing the value of goods and services, but coinage was not introduced until the 26th dynasty.[135] Trade was carried out by a complicated process now referred to by ethnographers as "money barter". In such a system the value of goods is fixed in quantities of

---

[132] Cf. J. Černý, "Egypt: From the Death of Ramesses III to the End of the Twenty-First Dynasty," *Cambridge Ancient History*, 3rd ed.; vol. 2, part 2; 642; A. Kadry, *Officers and Officials in the New Kingdom*, 187.

[133] W. Helck mentions Rib-Addi of Byblos in this connection (*Wirtschaftsgeschichte des alten Ägypten im 3. und 2. Jahrtausend vor Chr.* [Leiden: Brill, 1975], 203), although we may note that Rib-Addi's problems were military not agricultural.

[134] W. Helck, *Geschichte des alten Ägypten*, 190. Helck notes that the famine is also mentioned in a letter from the last Hittite king, Suppiluliumas II, to Ammurapi of Ugarit.

[135] J. Černý, "Prices and Wages in Egypt in the Ramesside Period," 904; J. W. Curtis, "Coinage of Pharaonic Egypt," *JEA* 43 (1957) 71–76.

other commodities (in ancient Egypt, copper, silver, or grain). The commodities used to express the value of goods, however, are not used as money. They serve as reference values only and are not necessarily exchanged in a given transaction.[136] For example, in the purchase of a Syrian slave girl attested in a legal papyrus from the 15th year of Ramesses II, the value of the transaction was fixed at a certain amount of silver and copper. In reality the girl was purchased, however, with an assemblage of bronze vessels, garments and pieces of cloth, a pot of honey, and scrap copper, which was reckoned to approximate the required value of precious metal.[137] Although this type of bargaining is complex, it affords trading parties with mutually recognized standards of value.

In the New Kingdom period the value of grain was commonly fixed in terms of copper. The standard unit was the *deben*, a weight of copper (sometimes silver, rarely gold) equivalent to 91 grams. The smallest fraction by which copper was reckoned was ½ *deben*. A smaller unit called the *kitē*, equivalent to one-tenth *deben* (9.1 grams), was used for the more precious metals. The *sniw* was a weight of silver. For prices from the end of the 19th dynasty, 1 *sniw* silver equaled 5 *deben* copper. The *hin*, a measure of capacity (0.48 liters, typically of oil) equaled ⅙ *sniw* or about 1 *deben* copper. The basic grain measure was the *khar*, which amounted to 76.88 liters. A unit of ¼ *khar* (19.22 liters) was called the *oipē* (*ipt*, cf. BH אֵיפָה).[138]

In 1934 J. Černý published a study based on data from Deir el-Medinah in which he traced increases in the price of emmer wheat (*bdt*), the grain used for baking bread, and barley (*it*), from which beer was made.[139] Summarizing his conclusions, Černý suggested a connection between the extraordinary inflation of grain prices and the social upheavals which characterized the latter half of the 20th dynasty:

---

[136] J. J. Janssen, "Prolegomena to the Study of Egypt's Economic History during the New Kingdom," 177; cf. J. Janssen, *Commodity Prices from the Ramessid Period*, 545, where he cites examples of money barter economies among the indigenous peoples of the Philippines, Gambia, and Sierra Leone.

[137] A. H. Gardiner, "A Lawsuit arising from the Purchase of Two Slaves," *JEA* 21 (1935) 140–6; cf. J. Černý, "Prices and Wages in Egypt in the Ramesside Period," 907.

[138] J. J. Janssen, *Commodity Prices from the Ramessid Period*, 101–109.

[139] J. Černý, "Fluctuations in Grain Prices During the Twentieth Egyptian Dynasty," *Archiv Orientální* 6 (1934) 173–78; cf. J. A. Wilson, *The Burden of Egypt*, 274.

The enormous ascent of both spelt and barley prices towards the middle of the XXth Dynasty is quite conspicuous. It reflects, without any doubt, the decay which took place in Egypt at the end of the reign of Ramesses III and under his immediate successors, a period into which fell the repeated strikes of the Royal Necropolis workmen (under Ramesses III, an unnamed king of the XXth Dynasty, probably Ramesses IX, and Ramesses X), the invasions of the Libyans and other foreigners, a revolt against the high-priest Amenhotep, as well as the systematic robberies of the Royal tombs in the year 13 and 17 of Ramesses IX.[140]

Since Černý's study much additional information has become available, but the basic picture remains the same. J. Janssen's comprehensive study of *Commodity Prices in the Ramessid Period* provides the following figures: For emmer wheat in the late 19th and early 20th dynasty none of the price calculations is certain, but levels are low compared to later. A price of 1 *deben* of copper per *khar* of grain is typical. Texts of the mid-20th dynasty, from the reigns of Ramesses IV to VII, show prices in basically the same range, fluctuating between 1¼ and 2 *deben* per *khar*. From the reign of Ramesses VII onwards prices rise steeply. A papyrus from Ramesses VII's reign shows emmer wheat at 4 *deben* and then at 8 *deben* per *khar*. Another text, dated tentatively to the reign of Ramesses IX, shows a price of 12 *deben*. By the end of the 20th dynasty the ordinary upper level of 2 *deben* once again appears.[141]

Barley prices show a comparable pattern. Under Ramesses III a stable price of 2 *deben* holds. Thereafter are increases up to 5 *deben* per *khar*; then sharp inflation under Ramesses VII brings barley prices to 8 *deben* and in one instance 24 *deben* per *khar*, followed by a return to lower prices at the end of the dynasty.[142] Oil prices during the mid-

---

[140] "Fluctuations in Grain Prices During the Twentieth Egyptian Dynasty," 176-777.

[141] Janssen, *Commodity Prices from the Ramessid Period*, 112–116. Janssen adduces altogether 30 examples of emmer wheat prices under the Ramessides.

[142] Janssen, *Commodity Prices from the Ramessid Period*, 119–122. These ranges are based on 24 examples of barley prices during the period. Cf. the charts in D. O'Connor, "New Kingdom and Third Intermediate Period," *Ancient Egypt: A Social History*, 228, fig. 3.10; but note that these do not reflect the high end of the price ranges recorded by Janssen, due to the ommission of "certain doubtfully dated examples, or atypically high values" (ibid.) M. Gutgesell differs from Janssen on the interpretation of a few ostraca, but his conclusions do not alter the economic picture in any essentials (see "Die Entwicklung des Getreidewertes als Datierungskriterium," in *Die Datierung der Ostraka und Papyri aus Deir el-Medineh und ihre ökonomische Interpretation, Teil I: Die 20. Dynastie* (HÄB 18;

20th dynasty showed some agreement with this pattern; generally the prices of other commodities seem to have been unaffected.

These steep increases in the price of the staple grains clearly represent a major economic disruption. In a modern market economy where prices are sensitive to changes in supply and demand, inflation on this scale would be considered severe. In the ancient Egyptian economy, whose price structure was highly traditional and conservative, it is even more exceptional for prices of the basic foodstuff to have increased twelve-fold within a few decades.[143]

Although the data for these price increases come from Deir el-Medinah, we can be sure that the economic crisis affected not just the workers' settlement but the whole population, which was dependent upon the pharaonic grain administration system. The social cost of this grain crisis must have been high. One text from late during the 20th dynasty refers to this period as "the year of the hyenas, when people starved."[144]

The cause of these price increases was apparently not inadequate harvest.[145] Despite the rich documentation we have for the period, there is no indication of inadequate Nile inundation (as we do have, for example, for the first one hundred years of the first Intermediate period, when famine was rampant).[146] Some of the fluctuation in prices may be seasonal, but as a whole the data do not sustain such an

---

Hildesheim: Gerstenberg, 1983) 2.522–31.

[143] On the nature of the ancient Egyptian economy, and the inadequacy of modern market economy models for describing it, see J. J. Janssen, "Prolegomena to the Study of Egypt's Economic History during the New Kingdom," 178–80; S. Morenz, *Prestige-Wirtschaft im alten Ägypten* (Bayerische Akademie der Wissenschaften, Philosophisch-Historische Klasse, Sitzungsberichte 4; Munich: Bayerische Akademie der Wissenschaften, 1969); and especially M. Gutgesell, *Die Datierung der Ostraka und Papyri aus Deir el-Medineh und ihre ökonomische Interpretation*, 2.571–74.

[144] British Museum no. 10052, 11,8 see Peet, *JEA* 12 (1926) 248; Černý, "Fluctuations in Grain Prices During the Twentieth Egyptian Dynasty," 177; Gutgesell, *Die Datierung der Ostraka und Papyri aus Deir el-Medineh*, 152, 556.

[145] D. O'Connor, "New Kingdom and Third Intermediate Period," *Ancient Egypt: A Social History*, 229.

[146] See J. Vandier, *La famine dans l'Egypte ancienne* (Recherches d'archéologie, de philologie et d'histoire 7; Cairo: Institut français d'archéologie orientale, 1936), 3–20, 45–47; B. J. Kemp, "Old Kingdom, Middle Kingdom and Second Intermediate," in B. G. Trigger et al., eds. *Ancient Egypt: A Social History* (Cambridge: Cambridge University Press) 180–181.

interpretation. It is clear that seasonal variances cannot explain the sharp changes at the middle of the dynasty.[147]

Administrative Corruption

Rather than natural causes, the more likely reason for the grain crisis was administrative inefficiency and corruption, which grew increasingly rife in the vast Pharaonic grain collection and redistribution system. Earlier New Kingdom rulers had been forced to take strong measures against corruption in their administrations. Graft appears to have become a serious problem during the Amarna years, in response to which Horemheb issued an edict around the year 1330 BCE aimed at securing the delivery of grain and other produce taxes to the pharaoh.[148] The edict catalogs various offenses of embezzlement and extortion, stipulating penalties of unprecedented severity. For example, the penalty for interfering with a boat used to transport taxes to the royal stores is mutilation (*viz.*, removal of the nose) and exile to the border fortress of Sile.[149] A soldier who steals an animal hide belonging to the royal levy is treated thus:

> Starting from today, the law shall be applied against him by inflicting upon him a hundred blows, causing five open wounds, and taking from him the hide which he has seized as (being) something that has been unlawfully acquired.[150]

Of the ten enactments in Horemheb's decree, five cite royal officials or soldiers as the offenders. The remaining enactments prohibit crimes likely to be committed by people of similar status.[151] The decree thus is enacted not against resistant tax-payers, but against official abuses in the taxation administration.

A few decades later Seti I (1303–1829 BCE) issued a similar

---

[147] Helck, *Wirtschaftsgeschichte des alten Ägypten*, 279; cf. Janssen, *Commodity Prices from the Ramessid Period*, 117–18, 125–127.

[148] For the text in translation with notes, see K. Pflüger, "The Edict of King Haremhab," *JNES* 5 (1946) 260–276; cf. J. Wilson, *The Burden of Egypt*, 237–239; C. Aldred, "Egypt: The Amarna Period and the End of the Eighteenth Dynasty," *Cambridge Ancient History*, 3rd ed.; vol. 2, part 2; 76.

[149] Pflüger, "The Edict of King Haremhab," 261.

[150] Pflüger, "The Edict of King Haremhab," 263; on the harshness of the penalties in comparison with earlier decrees, see Wilson, *The Burden of Egypt*, 241–242.

[151] Pflüger, "The Edict of King Haremhab," 267.

decree, designed to protect the revenues of a religious foundation at Abydos from misappropriation by officials.[152] Again the penalties seem disproportionately harsh compared to those of earlier decrees:

> Any person sent on mission to Kush, who shall detain any boat belonging to the Foundation, likewise any boat belonging to any agent of this estate, and moor it even for one single day,... punishment shall be done to him by [beating him] with two hundred blows (and) five pierced wounds together with exacting the work of the boat from him for every day that it shall spend moored, to be given to the Foundation (I.B.2.a-b). ... Likewise the one who shall be found taking any animal belonging to the Foundation, punishment shall be done to him by cutting off his nose (and) his ears, he being put as a cultivator in the Foundation, [in exchange(?) for his crime(?)] and putting his wife and children as serfs of (the) steward of this estate (II.B.2.a-b).[153]

One suspects that the severity of these penalties reflects the anticipated difficulty with which the decrees could be actually enforced. As the Pharaoh's word no longer carried absolute authority, cruel penalties were required to protect the property under Pharaoh's care.[154] This trend worsened under the ineffectual rulers of the 20th dynasty. The grain redistribution system became so poorly regulated that the later Ramesside period is regularly referred to as the heyday of corruption in official Egyptian society.[155]

A notorious example is the case of a ship captain named Khnumnakht during the reigns of Ramesses IV and V. This official was responsible for transporting grain from estates in the Delta to the temple of Khnum at Elephantine. A papyrus from the Elephantine temple archives (P. Turin 1887) records an indictment against Khnumnakht for prolonged embezzlement of the temple's grain.[156] According to this document, 700 *khar* of barley per year were due to

---

[152] F. L. Griffith, "The Abydos Decree of Seti I at Nauri," *JEA* 13 (1927) 193–208; W. F. Edgerton, "The Nauri Decree of Seti I: A Translation of and Analysis of the Legal Portion," *JNES* 6 (1947) 219–230; cf. J. Wilson, *The Burden of Egypt*, 241.

[153] W. F. Edgerton, "The Nauri Decree of Seti I," 223–224. The section numbers for these quotations are Edgerton's.

[154] Cf. Wilson, *The Burden of Egypt*, 142.

[155] "die Blütezeit der Korruption" (H. Brunner, "Die religiöse Antwort auf die Korruption in Ägypten," *Korruption im Altertum* [ed. W. Schuler; Munich/Vienna: Oldenbourg, 1982] 72).

[156] T. E. Peet, "A Historical Document of Ramesside Age," *JEA* 10 (1924) 116–27; A. H. Gardiner, "Ramesside Texts Relating to the Taxation and Transport of Corn," *JEA* 27 (41) 60–62.

the temple. Khnumnakht's deliveries (and the amounts missing) according to the papyrus are given in Table 2 below:[157]

TABLE 2. GRAIN EMBEZZLEMENT EVIDENCED BY P. TURIN 1887

Year	Amount Delivered	Amount Embezzled
1 of Ramesses IV	100 khar	600 khar
2 of Ramesses IV	130 khar	570 khar
3 of Ramesses IV	"He brought none of them"	700 khar
4 of Ramesses IV	20 khar	680 khar
5 of Ramesses IV	20 khar	680 khar
6 of Ramesses IV	"He did not deliver them"	700 khar
1 of Ramesses V	"He did not deliver them"	700 khar
2 of Ramesses V	186 khar	514 khar
3 of Ramesses V	120 khar	580 khar

Total Amount Embezzled: 5004 khar

Despite a slight discrepancy between the total theft listed in the papyrus and the individual amounts for each year, it is clear that for a period of nine years the temple of Khnum received less than ten per cent of the prescribed deliveries by this ship's captain.[158] J. Černý remarks concerning the case of Khnumnakht:

> The fact that his activities could have gone on for so many years, and have been tolerated, must necessarily throw an unfavorable light on the administration and on justice during the two reigns even if it is assumed that an event of this type was an exception rather than a common phenomenon.[159]

It is unlikely, however, that the habitual stealing of Khnumnakht was an isolated offense. The same papyrus charges Khnumnakht with extorting from two individuals the amount of 50 khar of barley annually for 10 years, "making 1000 khar: he appropriated them to his own use and brought none of them into the temple of Khnum."[160] Khnumnakht

---

[157] Source for Table 2: T. E. Peet, "A Historical Document of Ramesside Age," 123. Peet observes: "The total, 5004 khar, is incorrect; it should be 5724. The common error of taking a 60-sign in hieratic for an 80 may account for the 20, and the 700 is perhaps to be explained by the fact, obvious on the original, that the scribe first missed out Year 1 of Ramesses IV and crowded it in afterwards" (p. 126).

[158] Cf. Wilson, The Burden of Egypt, 280.

[159] "Egypt: From the Death of Ramesses III to the End of the Twenty-First Dynasty," Cambridge Ancient History, 3rd ed.; vol. 2, part 2; 611.

[160] T. E. Peet, "A Historical Document of Ramesside Age," 124.

is accused also of having burned a boat belonging to the temple of Khnum, and then bribing inspectors of the temple to make no report of it.[161]

The papyrus from Elephantine records the corruption of several other officials besides the ship captain Khnumnakht. A scribe of the treasury Menthuherkhepeshef, as acting mayor of Elephantine, accepted bribes for the release of thieves caught with garments stolen from a temple.[162] Also detailed are the charge that an unnamed w^cb priest stole sacred calves belonging to the temple, selling them for his own profit, and various other instances of theft and bribery.

More evidence of abuses in the grain administration comes from Deir el-Medinah. During the reign of Ramesses XI the scribe of the necropolis Tuthmose was responsible for collecting grain taxes from settlements south of Thebes for delivery to the necropolis workers. A papyrus containing the scribe Tuthmose's accounts (Papyrus Turin 1895+2006) discloses significant discrepancies.[163] For example, Tuthmose's account of grain from the town of Esna reports a total of 343¼ *khar* collected. Of this, 6¼ *khar* were immediately "given for the expenses" at Esna, leaving a total "placed to the credit of Pharaoh, 337 *khar*." Of these 337, however, Tuthmose reports 110¼ to have been delivered on one boat and 203¾ on another. Thus a total of 314 *khar* was delivered, reflecting shrinkage *en route* of 13 *khar*. The scribe's explanations for various portions of the missing grain merely provide "unmistakable evidence that the accounts have been faked."[164]

The amount of missing grain in this case is not as great as that in the Elephantine scandal, but the documentation gives the impression that petty dishonesty in grain transport was routine.[165] Elsewhere in the accounts of Tuthmose we find one shipment of grain from the town of Imiotru, 12 *khar* of wheat and 6½ *khar* of barley, listed as having been stored (simultaneously?) in two different places. As A. Gardiner remarks: "Strange are the ways of Egyptian book-keeping!"[166]

---

[161] Ibid.

[162] T. E. Peet, "A Historical Document of Ramesside Age," 122, 126.

[163] A. H. Gardiner, "Ramesside Texts Relating to the Taxation and Transport of Corn," 22–37.

[164] A. H. Gardiner, "Ramesside Texts Relating to the Taxation and Transport of Corn," 31. Gardiner gives here the details of the falsification.

[165] Cf. J. Wilson: "It is quite clear that the reckoning has been falsified and that Thut-mose expected no punishment for his laxness" (*The Burden of Egypt*, 279).

[166] A. H. Gardiner, "Ramesside Texts Relating to the Taxation and Transport of Corn," 34.

An ostracon from Deir el-Medinah records proceedings against an official and his wife who apparently schemed to embezzle goods from the royal stores at Thebes.[167] When the official, who had been in charge of several storehouses under Ramesses II, was transferred to new duties inspecting Pharaoh's flocks and herds in the north Delta, he left a wife and daughter behind. They acted in his name, and continued to transfer goods from the state magazines into the official's private store. When the racket was finally uncovered in the thirtieth year of Ramesses II, the family was charged with the misappropriation of a variety of commodities, including grain, salt, copper, various wines, oil, clothing, yarn, slaves, livestock, chariots, and bricks.

The amounts of goods listed as stolen are prodigious: for example, 20,000 *khar* of grain, 1200 *khar* of salt, 440 leather sandals, 30 chariots with harnesses, 40 cows, 30 bulls, and 300 goats. These amounts suggest that the theft did not occur at Deir el-Medinah, but in Thebes where stores of this size would have been found.[168] The scale of the theft clearly exceeds the capacity for consumption of a single family. It is, moreover, hard to believe that two people alone could move such a volume of goods. The official must have conducted a regular business in stolen goods, involving the complicity of many individuals. The outcome of this case is unknown. Although records of the embezzlements were found in the official's own file boxes, he denied all when confronted, and unfortunately our account breaks off before the matter is settled.

Also from Deir el-Medinah comes evidence of the corruptibility of the pharaoh's vizier. The famous Salt Papyrus 124, a judicial record from the end of the 19th dynasty reports the charge of a necropolis worker Amennakht that his rival Paneb achieved the position of chief-workman at the necropolis by bribing the vizier:

> [The workman] Amennakht [says]: I am the son of the chief-workman Nebnufer. My father died [and the chief-workman] Neferhotep, my brother, [was put] in his place. And the enemy killed Neferhotep [and (although) I am (?)] his brother, Peneb gave

---

[167] S. Allam, *Hieratische Ostraka und Papyri aus der Ramessidenzeit* (Urkunden zum Rechtsleben im alten Ägypten 1; Tübingen: S. Allam, 1973) 20–24; cf. K. A. Kitchen, *Pharaoh Triumphant: The Life and Times of Ramesses II,* 133–35.

[168] S. Allam, *Hieratische Ostraka und Papyri aus der Ramessidenzeit,* 24.

five servants of my father to Preemheb who was then Vizier ...
[and he put him in the place of?] my father, although, indeed, it
was not his place.[169]

The case is not as clear-cut as the aggrieved Amennakht would have it.
Paneb seems to have had some tenuous claim to the office, having been
adopted by Neferhotep, as is indicated in Amennakht's account of a
quarrel between the two:

> Charge [against Paneb] concerning his running after the chief-
> workman Neferhotep, my brother, although it was he who reared
> him.[170]

Nonetheless, as W. Helck observes, so far as we can tell it was always
considered unjust in ancient Egypt to attempt to buy an office.[171] The
Salt Papyrus gives an unsavory picture of official misconduct in the late
New Kingdom, both on the part of the vizier for accepting a bribe, and
on the part of Paneb who, according at least to Amennakht, was also
guilty of murder, robbery, rape, and other offenses.

We will see a great emphasis in the Instruction of Amenemope
against official misconduct and unjust gain. Morale among the official
classes of Ramesside Egypt, both petty and elite, must have been low.
The ideal of *Maʿat* as the guiding principle for officials became
increasingly corrupt during the Ramesside age.[172]

Strikes at the Theban Necropolis

Both the severity of the grain crisis and the degree to which
official mismanagement was responsible for it are illustrated by a series
of strikes among the royal necropolis workers at Deir el-Medinah
during the 20th dynasty.[173] The workers were paid a monthly ration

---

[169] J. Černý, "Papyrus Salt 124 (Brit. Mus. 10055)," *JEA* 15 (1929) 244; for
the date of the Salt Papyrus see now M. Bierbrier, *The Late New Kingdom in
Egypt*, 22–23.

[170] J. Černý, "Papyrus Salt 124," 245; cf. M. Bierbrier, *The Tomb-Builders of
the Pharaohs*, 108.

[171] W. Helck, "'Korruption' im Alten Ägypten," *Korruption im Altertum* (ed.
Schuler. Munich/Vienna: Oldenbourg, 1982) 68.

[172] On this point W. Helck and H. Brunner agree in their discussions of
corruption in ancient Egypt (Helck, "'Korruption' im Alten Ägypten," 68–70;
Brunner, "Die religiöse Anwort auf die Korruption in Ägypten," 74).

[173] First described by W. Spiegelberg, *Arbeiter und Arbeiterbewegung im
Pharaonenreich unter den Ramessiden (ca. 1400–1100 v. Chr.) eine Kultur-*

(*djw*) of wheat and barley from the royal granaries. This grain derived from taxes paid by growers in the region of Thebes. Compared to the basic ration of an agricultural worker (1½ *khar* a month), the wage of the necropolis workers was ample: 4 *khar* of emmer wheat and 1½ *khar* of barley each month. Foremen and scribes received a higher wage of 5½ *khar* of wheat and 2 *khar* of barley.[174]

These wages, however, were not always paid reliably, even outside times of crisis. There is evidence of administrative irregularity already in the 19th dynasty. One text records rations paid two weeks late during the first year of Amenmesses (1204 BCE); another from the first year of Siptah (1194 BCE) reports a delivery of rations to Deir el-Medinah six months late.[175]

Under the 20th dynasty provisions became increasingly unreliable, until on some occasions supplies in the village apparently ran out entirely. Faced with the threat of starvation, the workers marched *en masse*, sometimes in a most unruly manner, from their village to protest to the authorities. Although these protests are usually referred to by scholars as "strikes"—clearly the workers were off the job when they marched out of the necropolis and heckled their superiors—C. J. Eyre suggests:

> their actions were more, however, in the nature of a hunger march, "seeking for their grain rations" [e.g. HO XXV 2:vs.2–3] than a strike. Indeed their demonstrations frequently began at the weekend, when they would not have been working.[176]

Evidence of protests first appears in the same period that the data

---

geschichtliche Skizze (Strassburg: K. J. Trübner, 1895).

[174] C. J. Eyre, "Work and the Organisation of Work in the New Kingdom," 178, 201. Other rations, such as fish, firewood, and vegetables were given, but not as regularly. Meat and wine were provided for festivals, and clothing was issued once a year. Also tools were provided as needed. Cf. J. Janssen, "Prolegomenon to the Study of Egypt's Economic History during the New Kingdom," 169; J. Černý, "Egypt: From the Death of Ramesses III to the End of the Twenty-First Dynasty," *Cambridge Ancient History*, 3rd ed.; vol. 2, part 2; 622; W. Helck, *Wirtschaftsgeschichte des alten Ägypten*, 232.

[175] Year 1 of Amenmesses: Ostracon DeM 621.1; year 1 of Siptah: Ostracon DeM 611.1–2 (J. Janssen, *Commodity Prices from the Ramessid Period*, 464). Janssen summarizes: "The data show that regular payment of the rations was not at all usual.... Arrears of half a month seem to have been the rule rather than the exception" (p. 465).

[176] "Work and the Organisation of Work in the New Kingdom," 180.

for grain prices begins to reflect a crisis, in the latter years of Ramesses III.[177] It is unknown how long the workers had been suffering shortages, although an ostracon from some four months before the initial protest already attests to arrears in grain payments:

> Year 29, II, 21. This day, the scribe Amennakht announced to the crew saying, "Twenty days have elapsed in the month, and rations have not been given us."[178]

Then in the 6th month of Ramesses III's 29th year, with grain rations two months in arrears, the laborers demanded redress. We possess the detailed record of the scribe Amennakht, who was witness to the events.[179] According to the papyrus, the laborers marched out of the necropolis, announced their grievance, and staged a sit-in at the mortuary temple of Tuthmosis III:

> [Year] 29, VI, 10. This day, passing of the five walls of the Necropolis by the crew, saying, "We are hungry: eighteen days have passed in this month." And they sat down [at] the rear of the Mansion of *Mn-ḫpr-rᶜ*.[180]

Three officials swore assurances of redress to the workers, but they remained for the day and only returned to their homes that night.

The journal entries of Amennakht depict the workers marching again on the following two days, this time invading the Ramesseum:

> Year 29, VI, 11. They passed again. Reaching the gate of the southern boundary of the Mansion of *Wsr-m3t-rᶜ-stpn-rᶜ*. Year 29, VI, 12. Reaching the Mansion of *Wsr-m3t-rᶜ-stpn-rᶜ*. Spending the night in disorder in its gate. Entering into its interior ... They said to them, "It was because of hunger and because of thirst that we came here. There is no clothing, no ointment, no fish, no vegetables. Send to Pharaoh our good lord about it, and send to the vizier our superior, that sustenance may be made for us." And the rations of the fifth month were issued to them on this date.[181]

---

[177] Cf. J. Wilson, *The Burden of Egypt*, 275.

[178] O. Berlin 10633=Allam, *Hieratische Ostraka und Papyri aus der Ramessidenzeit*, no. 8.

[179] The "Turin Strike Papyrus," published in A. Gardiner, *Ramesside Administrative Documents* (Oxford: Oxford University Press, 1948) no. 18, pp. xiv–xvii and 45–48; translation and commentary in W. F. Edgerton, "The Strikes in Ramses III's Twenty-Ninth Year," *JNES* 10 (1951) 139–45; and see the summaries of the events in J. Wilson, *The Burden of Egypt*, 276–278; C. J. Eyre, "Work and the Organisation of Work in the New Kingdom," 180, A. Eggebrecht, "Die frühen Hochkulturen: Das Alte Ägypten," in *Geschichte der Arbeit: Vom Alten Ägypten bis zur Gegenwart*, 89.

[180] W. F. Edgerton, "The Strikes in Ramses III's Twenty-Ninth Year," 139.

During the following the month after more missed payments the workers renewed their protest:

> Year 29, seventh month. Passing of the walls by the crew. Settling in the Necropolis.[182]

This time, however, they added to their complaint the charge that their deprivations were due to fraud:

> We will not come. So tell your supervisors, as they stand at the head of their companions, that we certainly did not cross over (the walls) because of our hunger (alone, but) we have an important accusation to make, that crimes are certainly being committed in this place of Pharaoh![183]

During the next month the vizier To, who had himself started out as a scribe among the necropolis workers, carefully stayed on his side of the river to avoid facing the protesters. He sent instead a police chief with his message to the workers:

> Year 29, VIII, 28. Faring downstream by the vizier To.... Returning by the chief of police Nebsemen son of Pinḥasy to say to the three chiefs of the crew, as they were standing at the fortress of the Necropolis, "Thus saith the vizier To: 'It was not because there was nothing to bring to you that I did not come. Now as for your saying, 'Do not take away our ration,' do I, the vizier, give in order to take away? Have I not given what the one like me has done? If it happened that there was nothing even in the granaries, I have given you that which I have found.'" And the scribe Hori of the Tomb said to them, "There is given to you a half-ration. I will distribute it to you myself."[184]

The vizier's words are defensive. Moreover, while the charges of the workers against him are veiled, the vizier To confronts openly—if none too successfully—their suspicion that he has misappropriated their grain ("Now as for your saying, 'Do not take away our grain'"). We also see here the vizier justifying himself on the grounds that the grain stores are empty, and we learn that he finally manages to gather only a half-ration of grain for the workers.

During the final protest of Ramesses III's 29th year, the workers occupied the mortuary temple of Merenptah, and heckled the mayor of

---

[181] W. F. Edgerton, "The Strikes in Ramses III's Twenty-Ninth Year," 139–40.

[182] W. F. Edgerton, "The Strikes in Ramses III's Twenty-Ninth Year," 140.

[183] Following here the translation of Wilson, *The Burden of Egypt*, 277; cf. W. F. Edgerton, "The Strikes in Ramses III's Twenty-Ninth Year," 140.

[184] W. F. Edgerton, "The Strikes in Ramses III's Twenty-Ninth Year," 140–

Thebes once again with the cry, "We are hungered!" He sent word to them "Lo, I have given you these fifty bushels of emmer for sustenance until Pharaoh shall give you rations," but later he was accused of misusing offerings belonging to the Ramesseum in order to feed the workers.[185]

Edgerton expressed doubt whether the plight of the workers was as serious as they maintained:

> It is at least as likely, I think, that the artisans of the royal tomb were exploiting their eminent relative, the vizier To, as that they were genuinely hungry.[186]

More recently however, a text has come to notice which verifies the worker's complaints.[187] This text records wages received and deficits in provisions to an unnamed worker during years 28–30 of Ramesses III. The data of this text suggest that there was a general trend of worsening deficiencies in wheat rations during these years. For a five month period in year 28 wheat rations were 20 per cent short, by the same period of the following year they were over 35 per cent deficient.[188] Unfortunately the text does not preserve data for the dates of all the protests described in the Turin Strike Papyrus. The period of the final protest of the papyrus, however, is covered by this ostracon. J. Janssen observes:

> In that month, in which the workmen complained of being hungry, the author has received 3 instead of 5½ khar, in the month preceding even only 2 khar; thus in two months less than one full monthly ration. If all members of the gang were in the same position their complaints were certainly not unfounded.[189]

Although the Turin Strike Papyrus is our fullest account of worker protests under the Ramesside pharaohs, numerous references in other texts make clear that the trouble continued after the reign of Ramesses III. Ramesses IV appears to have tried to restore regular payments, but according to O. DEM 44 in his first year 2 months

---

41.

[185] W. F. Edgerton, "The Strikes in Ramses III's Twenty-Ninth Year," 141, 144; J. Wilson, *The Burden of Egypt*, 277.

[186] "The Strikes in Ramses III's Twenty-Ninth Year," 145.

[187] O. Turin 57072; see J. Janssen, "Background Information on the Strikes of Year 29 of Ramesses III," *OrAnt* 18 (1979) 301–308.

[188] "Background Information on the Strikes of Year 29 of Ramesses III," 304.

[189] "Background Information on the Strikes of Year 29 of Ramesses III," 305.

rations were missed.[190] An ostracon dated by onomastic evidence to the reign of Ramesses IV, V, or VI uses language similar to the Turin Strike Papyrus, referring to

> the Crew having gone out, being hungry, [saying] "We have gone out because we are hungry: there is no wood, (nor) vegetables, (nor) fish."[191]

An ostracon of the Cairo collection (O. Cairo 25533) belongs to the period of a foreman Nekhemmut, who must be either earlier or later than the foreman Khonsu named in the Turin papyrus. This text reports a protest lasting eleven days until rations are finally given, followed by a later unspecified incident which also lasted eleven days.[192]

From about a half-century later than these events of the 29th year of Ramesses III there has survived a journal of work at the necropolis recorded by a paymaster scribe.[193] Under Ramesses IX the workers are reported to have been idle for long periods, with the scribe noting that rations were 95 days late. Four years later the work crews raise the familiar complaint, "We are weak and hungry, for we have not been given the rations that Pharaoh gave for us!" The protests recur in year 3 of Ramesses X. Similar troubles are recorded in a Deir el-Medinah ostracon of year 9 of an unnamed king. W. Helck dates the text to Ramesses IX or XI.[194].

Although the "strike texts" themselves do not explain the reasons for the missed payments, the other evidence for the period makes clear that a combination of inept and dishonest handling of the royal grain

---

[190] W. Helck, *Wirtschaftsgeschichte des alten Ägypten*, 232; J. Černý ("Egypt: From the Death of Ramesses III to the End of the Twenty-First Dynasty," *Cambridge Ancient History*, 3rd ed.; vol. 2, part 2; 623), cites also O. Berlin 12631, 15 (unpublished) in year 1 of Ramesses IV in connection with workers' strikes.

[191] Nicholson Museum (Sydney) R. 97: C. J. Eyre, "A 'Strike' Text from the Theban Necropolis," *Glimpses of Ancient Egypt: Studies in Honour of H. W. Fairman* (eds. J. Ruffle, G. A. Gaballa and K. A. Kitchen; Warminster: Aris & Phillips, 1979) 80.

[192] C. J. Eyre, "A 'Strike' Text from the Theban Necropolis," 85; W. F. Edgerton, "The Strikes in Ramses III's Twenty-Ninth Year," 137.

[193] G. Botti and T. E. Peet, *Il Giornale della Necropoli di Tebe* (Turin: Fratelli Bocca, 1928). I have not seen this publication; the details given here are taken from J. Wilson, *The Burden of Egypt*, 278.

[194] O. DEM 571: C. J. Eyre, "A 'Strike' Text from the Theban Necropolis," 85; H. W. Helck, *Materialien zur Wirtschaftsgeschichte des Neuen Reiches* (Wiesbaden: Harrassowitz, 1961–70) 585.

stores was responsible. Embezzlement by the highest officials, who would have had greatest access to manipulating resources in the black market, is most likely.[195]

Likewise the gravity of the problems in the necropolis can not be discounted. Their frequency and severity from the workers' perspective is clear. From the rulers' point of view, the troubles were also serious. Officially at least, a central purpose of Egyptian society was still to perpetuate the life of the pharaoh as a god after his earthly death. No pharaoh could afford to neglect providing for his mortuary cult.[196] Hence the frequent abandonment by Ramesside pharaohs of their necropolis workers must be viewed as symptomatic of the breakdown of the whole pharaonic administrative system.

Tomb and Temple Robberies

The most notorious consequence of the economic distress during the twentieth dynasty was the dramatic increase of tomb robberies in the Theban necropolis. As the royal grain administration deteriorated, people were forced to buy food on a burgeoning black market. As we have seen, the values of staple grains skyrocketed during this period; hence in Thebes it appears that many could get the necessary payment only through grave robbery. The officials of the necropolis were corrupt, allowing much illegal activity to be covered by bribes. Despite the threat of severe penalties, including death, theft finally escalated to the point of open looting of temples in west Thebes by their own priests. The extent of these activities suggests, as W. Helck observes, that "economic misery must have been very great during this period."[197]

Grave robbing had always been a problem in ancient Egypt; as early as the 4th dynasty the tomb of Khufu's mother appears to have been robbed.[198] The Admonitions of Ipuwer describe plundering of the royal pyramids:

> Behold now, something has been done which never happened for a long time: the king has been taken away by poor men. Behold, he who was buried as a falcon (now lies) on a (mere) bier. What the pyramid hid has become empty.[199]

---

[195] Cf. Helck, *Wirtschaftsgeschichte des alten Ägypten*, 232.

[196] W. F. Edgerton, "The Strikes in Ramses III's Twenty-Ninth Year," 137.

[197] Helck, *Geschichte des alten Ägypten*, 201.

[198] J. Wilson, *The Burden of Egypt*, 282, with further bibliography.

This text is difficult to date, but it makes clear that until the period of the late New Kingdom, tomb robbery was regarded as an extraordinary offense which signaled the breakdown of the Egyptian social fabric.[200] We know that tomb robbers were active early in the reign of Horemheb, violating tombs which included those of Tuthmosis IV and Tutankhamen. This was one of the types of offenses which led Horemheb to issue his edict.[201] Under the later Ramesside rulers these activities reached an unprecedented scale.

A series of well-preserved papyri attest to important state trials which began in the sixteenth year of Ramesses IX and continued as long as a generation later.[202] These records are important not only for their evidence of the thieves' activity; by reading between the lines we can also discern the corruption of high-level officials who condoned abuses in the necropolis. The instigator of these trials was the mayor of

---

[199] *ANET* 442; cf. Lichtheim, *AEL* 1.155-6.

[200] In his original publication of the text, A. Gardiner interpreted the Admonitions as historical remembrances of the disorders of the First Intermediate period, composed by an author of the 12th dynasty (*The Admonitions of an Egyptian Sage*, Leipzig: J. C. Hinrichs, 1909). A later date has been proposed, however by J. van Seters, "A Date for the 'Admonitions' in the Second Intermediate Period," *JEA* 50 (1964) 13-23. Moreover several scholars question whether the text describes the events of any historical period. S. Luria studied the theme of "national distress" portrayed by Ipuwer and other texts, and concluded that the genre is entirely unhistorical ("Die Ersten werden die Letzten sein," *Klio* 22 [1929] 405-431). M. Lichtheim follows Luria's analysis, concluding that the Admonitions of Ipuwer is "a work of the late Middle Kingdom and of purely literary inspiration" (*AEL* 1.149). If this is the case, then the troubles recounted by the Admonitions of Ipuwer, including tomb robbery, illustrate the author's typical conception of the threat of social deterioration.

[201] Aldred, "Egypt: The Amarna Period and the End of the Eighteenth Dynasty," *Cambridge Ancient History*, 3rd ed.; vol. 2, part 2; 75.

[202] The primary text material is assembled in T. E. Peet, "Fresh Light on the Tomb Robberies of the Twentieth Dynasty at Thebes: Some New Papyri in London and Turin," *JEA* 11 (1925) 37-55, and *The Great Tomb-Robberies of the Twentieth Egyptian Dynasty* (Oxford: Oxford University Press, 1930); and J. Capart, A. Gardiner, and B. van de Walle, "New Light on the Ramesside Tomb-Robberies," *JEA* 22 (1936) 169-93. For an overview, see Gardiner, *Egypt of the Pharaohs*, 299-300. The trials are recounted in some detail also by J. Wilson, *The Burden of Egypt*, 282-88; and M. Bierbrier, *The Tomb-Builders of the Pharaohs*, 111-116. Selections from the papyri below are taken from the translations of Wilson and Bierbrier, when available, to avoid the archaic English of Peet and his contemporaries.

the city of Thebes, Paser. His charges were directed primarily against the mayor of West Thebes, named Pawero, who by virtue of his office was responsible for the security of the graves. The proceedings appear at times to have been simply the vehicle for a personal vendetta between Paser and Pawero. The two rivals maneuvered much more energetically to discredit one another than to secure the necropolis.

According to the trial records, when word of repeated violations of the tombs in West Thebes reached Paser's office, he publicly denounced the break-ins and thus forced Pawero to request an investigation. The vizier Khaemwaset convened a tribunal which included the vizier himself, the high priest of Amon, Amenhotep, and other important officials. These dignitaries sided quickly with Pawero and made clear that they resented Paser's criticism of the administration under Pawero.[203]

Paser had charged that ten royal tombs were violated, but the investigation revealed that only one, the tomb of the 17th-dynasty ruler Sobekemsaf, had been entered:

> The burial chamber of the king was found empty of its lord and likewise the burial chamber of the great royal wife Nubkas, his wife, the robbers having laid hands upon them.[204]

Also in the valley of the Queens two "tombs of the singing-women of the House of the Divine Votaress of Amon-Re, king of the Gods," had been robbed. The tomb of Amenhotep I, however, which Paser had specifically charged to have been entered, was found undisturbed.[205] Thus technically the accuser Paser was discredited, since only one royal tomb was proved to have been robbed. An inspection of the tomb of the queen Isis, wife of Ramesses III, also disclosed no robbery, but this investigation may have been manipulated so as to cover an actual violation. A coppersmith by the name of Peikhal had confessed to breaking into the tomb of Isis, but an on-site interrogation by the vizier Khaemwaset and the royal butler Nesamun failed to reveal any damage. The circumstances of the investigation have been called "suspicious":

> It is noticeable that Pesiur was not asked to accompany Khaʿemwese and Nesamun, and it seems ominous that exactly fifteen months and a day later the vizier Khaʿemwese, making a fresh

---

[203] J. Capart, A. Gardiner, and B. van de Walle, "New Light on the Ramesside Tomb-Robberies," 186.

[204] Bierbrier, *Tomb-Builders of the Pharaohs*, 113.

[205] Peet, "Fresh Light on the Ramesside Tomb-Robberies," 38.

investigation, found the very same tomb which Peikhal said he had plundered with its granite portcullis smashed to atoms and all its contents removed.[206]

With Paser's charges ostensibly refuted, there ensued a raucous demonstration by the manifestly corrupt Pawero and his followers on the west bank, including workers from Deir el-Medinah, in which Paser was denounced for having accused them:

> The high officials let the supervisors, the agents, the necropolis workmen, the chiefs of police, the police, and all the necropolis serf-laborers go around the west of Thebes in a great demonstration (reaching) as far as Thebes (across the River).[207]

The demonstrators presumed themselves to be vindicated, but besides the ruined tomb of Sobekemsaf, the tribunal had also inspected a number of private tombs, finding that

> the thieves had robbed them all, dragging their owners out from their inner coffins and outer coffins ... and stealing their funerary equipment which had been given to them with the gold, silver, and the fittings which were in their inner coffins.[208]

In the confrontation between Paser and the west bank crowd, the chief workman of the necropolis Userkhepesh clearly lied in asserting

> all the kings with their royal wives and royal mothers and royal children who rest in the great and noble necropolis together with those who rest in the Place of Beauty [Valley of the Queens] are intact. They are protected and ensured for eternity.[209]

This spurred Paser to claim that he had five additional accusations to report to Pharaoh. Paser's new charges were not proved, but again it appears that the inquiries were not conducted honestly. Peet observes,

> there is clearly a coalition of Pewer'o and his workmen with the vizier against Pesiur, and what more likely than that they avoided investigation of those of Pesiur's charges which were well-founded by concentrating the attention of the Court on those which happened to be incorrect.[210]

Since the destruction of Sobekemsaf's tomb was undeniable, the authorities were obliged to pursue this matter further. After a roundup

---

206 Capart, Gardiner, and Van de Walle, "New Light on the Ramesside Tomb-Robberies," 188.

207 Wilson, *The Burden of Egypt*, 285.

208 Bierbrier, *Tomb-Builders of the Pharaohs*, 113.

209 Bierbrier, *Tomb-Builders of the Pharaohs*, 114.

210 T. E. Peet, "Fresh Light on the Tomb Robberies," 39.

of known or suspected tomb robbers (apparently this was a population of considerable number), interrogation focused on a worker named Amenpanufer, who confessed that he robbed the tomb along with seven accomplices. The lengthy testimony of Amenpanufer discloses key aspects of the situation. Following is an excerpt of essential portions:

> [There was brought] Amen[panufer, the son of Anḥer-nakhte], a stone-mason ... He said: 'I was employed upon work ... together with the fellow stone masons who were with me, and I fell into the habit of robbing the tombs in company with the stone-mason Ḥaꜥpiwer, ... four years ago I joined with [the carpenter] Setekhnakhte, ... also with the decorator Haꜥpiꜥo of the house of Amun, with the field-laborer Amenemḥab ... with the carpenter Irenamun ... with the water-pourer Kaemwese ... and with the boatman of the mayor of Thebes ꜥAḥay ... in all 8 men. We went to rob the tombs in accordance with our regular habit, and we found the pyramid of king Sekhemreꜥ-shedtaui, the son of Reꜥ, Sebkemsaf, this being not at all like the pyramids and tombs of the nobles which we habitually went to rob ... [We] found this god lying at the back of his burial place. And we found the burial place of Queen Nubkhaꜥaꜥs his queen situated beside him. ... We opened their sarcophagi and their coffins in which they were, and found the noble mummy of this king equipped with a falchion; a large number of amulets and jewels of gold were upon his neck, and his headpiece of gold was upon him. The noble mummy of this king was completely bedecked with gold, and his coffins were adorned with gold and silver inside and out and inlaid with all kinds of precious stones. We collected the gold we found on the noble mummy of this god, together with (that on) his amulets and jewels which were on his neck and (that on) the coffins in which he was resting, [and we] found [the] queen in exactly the same state. We collected all that we found upon her likewise, and set fire to their coffins. We took their furniture which we found with them consisting of articles of gold, silver, and bronze, and divided them amongst ourselves. And we made into eight portions the gold which we found on these two gods coming from their mummies, amulets, jewels, and coffins, and 20 *deben* of gold fell to each of the eight of us, making 160 *deben* of gold, the fragments (?) of the furniture not being included. Then we crossed over to Thebes. And after some days, the district superintendents of Thebes heard that we had been stealing in the West, and they seized me and imprisoned me in the office of the mayor of Thebes. And I took the 20 *deben* of gold that had fallen to me as (my) portion, and gave them to Khaꜥemope, the scribe of the quarter attached to the landing-place of Thebes. He released me, and I rejoined my companions, and they compensated me with a portion once again. Thus I, together with the other thieves who are with me, have continued down to this day in the practice of robbing the tombs of the nobles and people of the land who rest in the west of Thebes. And a large number of the people of the land rob them as well, and are (as good as) partners (of ours).[211]

---

[211] Papyrus Leopold 1,8–3,7; in Capart, Gardiner, and van de Walle, "New

We learn from the testimony in this case that the robbers all belonged to the socio-economic class of manual laborers. The defendant was a stone mason. His partners in crime included other masons, two carpenters, a "decorator" (draftsman) in the temple of Amun, a field-laborer, a water-pourer, and a boatman of the mayor of Thebes. The aim of the thieves was to acquire precious metals: gold, silver, and bronze. Their destructive methods included the burning of wooden sarcophagi to extract these metals.

The testimony of this case indicates that tomb-robbery was a chronic and widespread practice during this period. By the time of his arrest in the 16th year of Ramesses IX, Amenpanufer had been working with his current gang for four years, and he had already been involved in tomb-robbery before forming that association. He repeatedly refers in the testimony to the tomb robbery activities as habitual. Amenpanufer had been arrested at least once before for robbing tombs. He asserts, apparently in a weak attempt to excuse himself, that "a large number of the people of the land rob them as well, and are (as good as) partners (of ours)."

At the end of his testimony Amenpanufer implicitly incriminates the administration of the mayor of Thebes, indicating that with sufficient resources for bribery, one could expect to rob tombs with impunity. When he had been previously arrested and imprisoned by the mayor's office, Amenpanufer had simply given his share of the loot to the scribe in charge, and he was then freed to resume his activities. We might ask how it happened that the thief was allowed to keep his stolen gold long enough to make this transaction. The amount of 20 *deben*, almost 2 kilograms, would be too large a volume to conceal in jail from the authorities until he could make a secret bribe. It is perhaps significant that the defendant had not been caught in the act of robbing tombs; he was taken into custody only "after some days" when officials had heard of the success of the operation. It is likely therefore that Amenpanufer's purchase of his release was not an isolated case of bribery, but exemplified the systematic extortion of the tomb-robbers which enriched Theban officials at many levels.[212]

Light on the Ramesside Tomb-Robberies," 171-72.

[212] Cf. J. Wilson, *The Burden of Egypt*, 287: "What happened to the record of his [Amenpanufer's] arrest? Probably the District Clerk of the Theban harbor did not retain all of the twenty *deben*; the bribe went on up high enough to choke off any inquisitiveness about the failure of legal procedure."

In investigations which continued into the year following this first series of trials, members of the workers' village of Deir el-Medinah were accused. It is not surprising to find necropolis workers among the apprehended robbers. They knew the locations best and had the technical expertise necessary to exploit the tombs successfully. We know from the strike papyri that the necropolis workers suffered privations during this period. Ramesses IX caught a band of eight, all of whom lived in the workers' settlement at Deir-el-Medinah. Large amounts of stolen goods were recovered from homes of the robbers and of others who had received stolen goods. The loot amounted to 236 *deben* gold and silver and 1000 *deben* copper. Considering the basic wage at the time of an equivalent to 11 *deben* monthly, this was a significant sum even if divided by eight.[213]

Also during this year the new inspection of the tomb of Isis, queen of Ramesses III, showed that a robbery had indeed taken place as Paser had charged. It appears, however, that the battle of wits between Paser, who sought to expose the corrupt network that allowed the tomb robberies to go on, and Pawero, the ring leader, finally tilted in favor of the latter. Paser drops out of the record while Pawero manages to stay in office and is still attested 30 years later.[214]

Simple greed may have motivated some tomb robbers during the late twentieth dynasty, but many were driven by economic deprivation or even the threat of starvation. In some trial records the accused refer to their actions as "furnishing bread".[215] This must reflect the necessity of getting food on the local market by negotiating precious metal. Papyrus BM 10052, which dates to the reign of Ramesses XI, contains numerous instances of this usage. In the examination of an incense-burner named Shedsukhons, for example, the witness tells how a party of tomb robbers came in the night and invited him: "They said to me, 'Come out; we are going to fetch some of the bread [ˤkw] and eat it.'"[216] Similarly the herdsman Bukhaaf testifies:

---

[213] A. Eggebrecht, "Das Alte Ägypten," in *Geschichte der Arbeit*, 89; Peet, *The Great Tomb Robberies*, 104–104.

[214] Wilson, *The Burden of Egypt*, 287; Bierbrier, *Tomb-Builders of the Pharaohs*, 116; Capart, Gardiner, and van de Walle, "New Light on the Ramesside Tomb-Robberies," 190.

[215] Helck, *Wirtschaftsgeschichte des alten Ägypten*, 259; A. Eggebrecht, "Das Alte Ägypten," in *Geschichte der Arbeit*, 89.

[216] Peet, "Fresh Light on the Tomb Robberies at Thebes," 41; *The Great Tomb-Robberies*, 142.

> The citizeness <Nesmut> came to the place where I was and she
> said to me, "Some men have found something that can be sold for
> bread [*šsp n ʿk̠*]; let us go that you may eat it [*wnm=k*] with
> them."[217]

Peet does not think that the thieves were hungry; he compares the
usage to modern slang in which a "haul of dough" would refer to a
load of money or loot collected by thieves.[218] This is a possible
reading, since Egyptian *ʿk̠* can have the sense of "income, revenue"
and *wnm* can refer to the usufruct of property.[219]

Other passages in Papyrus BM 10052, however, show that
getting food was the concern of the grave robbers. For example, the
examination of a woman prisoner, evidently the wife of one of the
accused thieves who had died, reveals that she had approached the
group and demanded her husband's share by asking, "What am I to eat
with you?" She relates that the group eventually gave her the amount
alloted to each member, ten *deben* of silver and 2 *deben* of gold. "I
took the share of my husband," she continues, "and put it aside in my
store-room and I took one *deben* of silver thereof and bought shesh-
grain [*šзšзḫ*] with it."[220] A gardener named Peikharu testified that his
father had chanced upon priests who had stolen a fine sarcophagus.
They cited hunger as the reason for their theft and offered him a bribe
to keep quiet about it:

> They said to him, This inner coffin is ours. It belonged to some
> great person. We were hungry and we went and brought it away,
> but you be silent and we will give you a *daui*-garment.[221]

The severity of penalties for tomb robbery also suggests that only
individuals who were *in extremis* would resort to such actions. Suspects
were interrogated with the aid of severe beatings and twisting of the
arms and legs.[222] The ultimate fate of the accused is not spelled out in

---

217 Peet, *The Great Tomb-Robberies*, 143.

218 Peet, "Fresh Light on the Tomb Robberies at Thebes," 41; *The Great
Tomb-Robberies*, 158 n. 4. The term "bread" has taken a similar slang meaning in
more recent American usage.

219 Faulkner, *Concise Dictionary of Middle Egyptian* (Oxford: Griffith Institute,
1962) 50, 62; compare in Hebrew לֶחֶם as "profit, revenue," usually ill-gained:
"the bread of wickedness" Prov 4:17; cf. 20:17, 23:3; "bread of idleness," 31:27.

220 Peet, *The Great Tomb-Robberies*, 149.

221 Peet, *The Great Tomb-Robberies*, 151–52.

222 See Peet, *The Great-Tomb Robberies*, 20–21. The records of testimony
typically recount a series of tortures until the witness says, "Stop, I will tell."

the extant trial papyri, but there are indications that those who were found guilty were executed. One witness recounts a quarrel among suspects in which a man said to another: "You'll be put to death for this theft which you committed in the necropolis."[223] Another defendant in trials under Ramesses XI protested his innocence and exclaimed:

> I saw the punishment which was done to the thieves in the time of
> the vizier Khaemwese. Am I the man to go looking for death when
> I know what it means?[224]

It would appear that this man had witnessed the execution of suspects convicted in the trials in the 16th year of Ramesses IX. The scant evidence of how the death penalty was carried out suggests that it was by impaling. In the tomb robbery papyri a common oath before testifying is: "If I be found to have spoken untruth may I be placed upon the *tp ḫt* ['the top of the wood']." Papyrus Mayer A closes with a series of lists, one of which names seven men who had previously been put to death "on the stake" [*ḥr tp ḫt*].[225] Although many seem to have had no fear of conviction, surely the threat of these sanctions was serious enough to dissuade all but the most desperate. Grave robbery continued to escalate nonetheless. By the end of the Ramesside period the plundering had become so severe that the authorities removed the remaining undisturbed mummies from the necropolis and stashed most of them in a common cache at Deir-el-Bahari, where they were found in 1875.[226]

As grave robbery reached its heights under Ramesses IX–XI, there is evidence that priests began looting their own temples. Papyrus B.M. 10053 *verso* recounts numerous expeditions by thieves, all of whom were priests, to strip gold off the gilded portals of a temple, probably the Ramesseum.[227] Later in the text the thefts are said to go beyond the metals, which were perhaps by then exhausted, and to have

---

[223] Peet, *The Great Tomb-Robberies*, 146.

[224] Peet, *The Great Tomb-Robberies*, 26.

[225] Peet, *The Great Tomb-Robberies*, 27. On the penalty *rdy ḥr tp ḫt*, see W. Boochs, "Über den Strafzweck des Pfählens," *GM* 69 (1983) 7–10.

[226] The Deir-el-Bahari find was the source of most of the New Kingdom mummies which have survived to modern times. Accounts of the discovery are in G. Maspero, *La trouvaiile de Deir el-Bahari* (Cairo: Imprimerie Nouvelle du "Moniteur Egyptien," 1883); and *Les momies royales de Deir el-Bahari* (Cairo: Memoires ... mission archeologique au Caire I,2, 1887) 511–788.

[227] Peet, *The Great-Tomb Robberies*, 112–121.

attacked the actual wood of the structure of the temple.[228] As with the tomb robberies, greed is sure to have motivated many of these thefts, but again there are hints that the provision of food was the most urgent concern. In the text just mentioned a temple worker named Kar describes several visits made to take quantities of gold from the doorways. He then continues:

> We paid another visit to the door-jambs together with the priest Hori, son of Pakharu, the scribe of the temple, Sedi, and the priest Nesamun ... We took away 5 *kite* of gold and we bought barley with it in Thebes, and split it among ourselves.[229]

The tomb and temple robberies of the later Ramesside period show just how low the social situation had sunk. The combination of economic hardship among the residents of Thebes and official neglect, if not active abuse, sealed the doom of the pharaonic administration.

To summarize the preceding sections: the later Ramesside period in Egypt was characterized by economic disruption, caused in part by unfavorable international developments, aggravated domestically by widespread corruption in the royal grain distribution system. The consequence was economic desperation among those who depended on that system, evidenced especially by strikes in the necropolis and looting of tombs and temples. In these socio-economic circumstances the Instruction of Amenemope was composed. We turn now to the treatment of wealth and poverty in the text.

---

[228] Cf. Peet, "Fresh Light on the Tomb Robberies at Thebes," 52–53; and James, *Pharaoh's People*, 263–4.

[229] Pap. BM 10053 verso, translation of James, *Pharaoh's People*, 264; cf. Peet, *The Great Tomb Robberies*, 118.

IV
WEALTH AND POVERTY IN THE INSTRUCTION
OF AMENEMOPE

The theme of wealth and poverty, like the other traditional themes of Egyptian wisdom, undergoes a marked transformation in Amenemope. Previous studies have treated some aspects of this change. H. Brunner, for example, has observed that in comparison to the earlier Egyptian Instruction literature, Amenemope places unprecedented emphasis on concern for the poor and offers a new perception of wealth as ethically problematic.[1]

From a literary perspective these shifts reflect a reshaping of received tradition as well as the incorporation into the Instruction of traditional material from other genres. As I. Grumach has shown, the Instruction of Amenemope presents a carefully crafted, unified literary work despite the author's extensive use of earlier tradition.[2] To the extent that the individual identity of the author recedes behind the text's pseudonymous form, the work accords with the premium placed upon humility in the Instruction tradition. The received tradition in

---

[1] "Die religiöse Wertung der Armut im Alten Ägypten," 325–28, 332.

[2] I. Grumach, *Untersuchungen zur Lebenslehre des Amenope.* Cf. M. Fox's summation: "Amenope took older material from the wisdom tradition and other literary genres, including psalmody, and reworked it and expanded upon it to produce a new wisdom book that expressed his own character. The wise-man sees himself as a vehicle for transmission of the wisdom of the ancients, but not as a passive transmitter. He remolds wisdom as he passes it on" ("Two Decades of Research in Egyptian Wisdom Literature," *ZÄS* 107 [1980] 131).

Amenemope acquires so distinctive a shape, however, that the text may be viewed as the product of a single Ramesside personality.

Amenemope contains significant allusions to earlier Instruction texts, especially Ptahhotep and Any.[3] The author is also inspired, however, by the ideal autobiographical tradition and by the popular piety of the New Kingdom period. Many of the distinctive features of Amenemope—its intensely personal religiosity, for example, or the contrast between the types of the "truly silent" ($gr\ m3^\varsigma$) and the "heated one" ($\check{s}mm$)—derive frm these influences outside the Instruction genre. This interplay of genres and traditions has also effected changes in the Instruction's view of wealth and poverty.

From an historical point of view, Amenemope's reworking of the sapiential tradition on wealth and poverty reflects the influence of the social and economic conditions of the Ramesside period. Four aspects of Amenemope's treatment of the theme can be related to the social-historical background that we have reviewed in the previous sections: (1) The prohibition of corrupt practices and unjust gain becomes more prominent and more specific. (2) The doctrine of the "act-consequence relation," which associates prosperity with moral probity, is undermined. (3) The "$3\underline{h}$-saying," forerunner to the Hebrew טוב-proverb, is standardized as a literary form and is focused on the theme of wealth and poverty. (4) Affirmative concern for the poor is expressed with new urgency.

AGAINST CORRUPTION AND UNJUST GAIN

Honesty is an important value throughout the Egyptian Instruction, and generic warnings against greed are common:

> Guard against the vice of greed:
> A grievous sickness without cure,
> There is no treatment for it (Ptahhotep maxim 10; *AEL* 1.68.)
> A wretch is who desires the land [of his neighbor],
> A fool is who covets what others possess (Merikare
> 41; *AEL* 1.100.)

---

[3] Compare for example Amenemope 8.17–18 and Ptahhotep 161–62; Amenemope 6.15–7.6 and Any 8.6–10. For a discussion of intertextuality among other examples of the Instruction genre, see H. Brunner, "Zitate aus Lebenslehren," in E. Hornung and O. Keel, eds., *Studien zu altägyptischen Lebenslehren* (OBO 28; Freiburg: Universitätsverlag/ Göttingen: Vandenhoeck & Ruprecht, 1979) 105–172.

Amenemope, however, exceeds all previous teaching against dishonesty by denouncing in detail the methods of corrupt scribes.

The Egyptian grain redistribution system was administered by scribal functionaries of various ranks. Scribes were responsible, for example, for overseeing the weighing and measuring of each year's harvest. A typical grain harvest and storage operation in the New Kingdom is depicted in the reliefs of the eighteenth-dynasty tomb of Paheri.[4] Here, once the barley has been cut and threshed, a figure identified as "the scribe of counting grain, Djehutnufe," appears perched on a heap of barley. From this vantage point he counts the measured grain sacks being carried to the storehouse by the workers below. Another figure, perhaps a foreman, appears to make an informal tally of bushels on the side of a winnowing scoop.

Each estate in New Kingdom Egypt would have been supervised by officers like these who registered the crop. On the basis of the scribes' records, a portion of the harvest was levied as tax, another was alloted for seed for the next year, and finally an amount was left for the peasants who grew the grain.[5] The levied grain was in fact measured several times in the course of its transportation, storage, and eventual use: first on the threshing floor, then as it was loaded onto ships for transport to the royal stores, next at the loading of the storehouses, and finally once more as it was dispensed.[6] Each occasion presented dishonest clerks with an opportunity for graft.

Amenemope addresses scribal corruption in close detail because it was a serious and widespread problem. As we have seen, during the period when Amenemope was composed, the pharaonic grain distribution system was so corrupt that the entire economy was crippled. Many of the class of scribes to whom the Instruction of Amenemope is addressed would have been implicated in these abuses. The corrupt ship captain Khnumnakht, for example, who under Ramesses IV and V managed to convey only nine per cent of his

---

[4] Line drawings of the reliefs of the tomb of Paheri (originally published by J. J. Tylor and F. Ll. Griffith, *The Tomb of Paheri* [London: Kegan, Paul, Trench, Trübner, 1894]), are reproduced in T. G. James, *Pharaoh's People*, 108–129, figures 8–12. For the scribe Djehutnufe, see p. 127, fig. 11.

[5] Cf. I. Grumach, *Untersuchungen zur Lebenslehre des Amenope*, 177.

[6] See M. Stoof, "Untersuchungen zur Bevorratung und Lagerung von Getreide im alten Ägypten," *Ethnographisch-Archäologische Zeitschrift* 23 (1982) 453–464, with 10 illustrations.

stipulated grain shipments to the Elephantine temple could not have succeeded without the complicity of a network of dishonest scribes.[7] The author of Amenemope thus prohibits abuses which scribal students could be expected to witness. Because there were so many cheaters in the administration, Amenemope urges:

> If you see someone who cheats (*sh3*),
> keep your distance from him (18.5-6).

The word *sh3*, meaning fundamentally "to diminish," is a key term in Amenemope for referring to professional misconduct. It includes the falsification of grain measures, accounts and legal documents, as well as the mistreatment of people. The two central groups of chapters in Amenemope, 12-14 and 15-17, are organized around the detailed treatment of this key category, *sh3*.[8]

In the prologue Amenemope is credited with the title "overseer of grains who controls the measure" (*im-r nfr.t gsgs wḏ3.t*, 1.15). Thus in chapter 17 an extended passage is devoted to the prohibition of false measure. Nowhere else in the Instruction literature do we find so detailed a description of the methods by which an unscrupulous scribe might embezzle grain:

> Beware of disguising the measure (*wḏ3.t*),
> So as to falsify its fractions;
> Do not force it to overflow,
> Nor let its belly be empty.
> Measure according to its true size,
> Your hand clearing exactly.
> Do not make a bushel of twice its size,
> For then you are headed for the abyss.
> The bushel is the Eye of Re,
> It abhors him who trims;
> A measurer who indulges in cheating,
> His Eye seals (the verdict) against him
> (18.15-19.3).

---

[7] Cf. J. Wilson (*The Burden of Egypt*, 280): "The ship captain could not have engaged in such wholesale robbery without the knowledge and participation of a host of agents, all the way up from the farmers who delivered the grain to his boat in the Delta to the clerks who registered it at the Temple of Knuhm at the First Cataract. The sacks which disappeared were recorded as the 'total of the grain of the Temple of Khnum, Lord of Elephantine, on which this ship captain conspired with the clerks, administrators, and peasant-farmers of the Temple of Khnum, and they looted it and made free with it for their own purposes.'"

[8] I. Grumach, *Untersuchungen zur Lebenslehre des Amenope*, 92-93, cf. p. 109.

The verb ꜥšg, used in Amenemope 18.15 for "disguising" the measure, designates peculation of temple rations or other fraudulent procedures in 6.14, 7.17, 18.12. Here perhaps it should be taken in a concrete sense of "to overlay," describing a practice in which the inner surface of the measure was coated so as to obscure the graduated measurements inscribed there.[9]

Amenemope uses various terms to refer to the grain measure: dbḥ (17.19), ip.t (18.21, 23), and wḏꜣ.t (18.15). The latter term, wḏꜣ.t, literally "the sound, whole (one)," along with the expression "the bushel (ip.t) is the eye of Re" (18.23) alludes to the mythological identification of the fractions of the grain measure with the reunified parts of the eye of Horus, which had been destroyed in his conflict with Seth. The restored eye was called wḏꜣ.t.[10] Here in Amenemope, in accordance with the prominence Amun-Re had attained in the religious milieu of the late New Kingdom, the bushel is placed under the protection of Re. No falsification of the measure escapes notice, because the bushel is the embodiment of the all-seeing Eye of Re in the world. If a measurer violates the bushel, "His Eye seals (the verdict) against him" (19.3).

Amenemope 18.15–19.3 also plays on the sense which the word wḏꜣ acquires in the prologue. There the term in its typical sense "to prosper" describes the state of well-being promised to the one who heeds the Instruction:

The instructions for well-being (mtr.w n-wḏꜣ)
To make him prosper upon earth (r-s:wḏꜣ=f ḥr-tp-tꜣ)
(1.2, 8, cf. 4.1–2, 7.10).

The present passage shows, however, that like biblical Hebrew צְדָקָה and טוֹב, wḏꜣ in Amenemope can refer to moral soundness, or integrity, as well as to material prosperity.[11]

---

[9] Brunner translates: "Hüte dich, den Scheffel zu beschmieren" (Altägyptische Weisheit, 249; cf. p. 480 n. 352). Griffith reads: "Beware of covering up (?) the waze-measure" ("The Teaching of Amenophis the Son of Kanakht," 215.)

[10] A. Gardiner explains the origin of this conception of the grain measure: "The symbols employed in this, as shown in the accompanying cut, are derived from the ancient myth according to which the eye of the falcon-god Horus, often depicted in the monuments in the form , was torn into fragments by the wicked god Seth. Later, the ibis-god Thoth miraculously 'filled' or 'completed' (mḥ) the eye, joining together the parts, whereby the eye regained its title to be called the wḏꜣ.t, 'the sound eye'" (EG §266.1). Cf. I. Grumach, Untersuchungen zur Lebenslehre des Amenope, 121–22.

[11] Cf. Prov 8:18, 20 (צְדָקָה); Job 22:18, Ps 37:27 (טוֹב).

Unscrupulous scribes had the opportunity to defraud both parties to the grain measuring system, the royal administration and the growers. By "forcing the measure to overflow" (18.17), the measurer would take more than the registered amount; later it could be embezzled. On the other hand, by using the measure in such a way as to "let its belly be empty" (18.18), apparently placing a false bottom or inert filler in the bushel, a scribe would inflate the number of bushels at which a peasant's crop was registered. This would result in a disproportionately high levy and too large an amount alloted to seed. (The seed allotment belonged to pharaoh's store, and would not necessarily be returned in full to the farmer who contributed it). The extortion would have perpetuated itself from year to year, since an inflated record of a previous year's harvest would oblige the farmer to produce an unrealistically high crop for the next year.[12] Amenemope thus forbids injury to the grain growers or the collecting administration:

> Do not desire a measure of the fields,
> Nor neglect those of the treasury (17.20–21).
> Do not accept a farmer's dues
> And then assess him so as to injure him;
> Do not conspire with the measurer,
> So as to defraud the share of the Residence.
> Greater is the might (*b3w*) of the threshing floor
> Than an oath by the great throne (19.4–9).

Amenemope's mention of the "might *b3w* of the threshing floor" (19.8) invokes the Egyptian conception of a divine power which irresistibly compels the guilty to confess if charged with wrong (here perhaps the cobra-goddess of the harvest, Renenutet, identified with the threshing floor).[13] Oaths performed at the palace will not save scribes who have embezzled at the threshing floor from discovery and conviction.

Although Amenemope's prohibition of false measure is unique in the Instruction genre, there is ample reference to the crime in other Egyptian sources. In the Middle Kingdom "Protests of the Eloquent Peasant," for example, the peasant complains of graft:

---

[12] Cf. I. Grumach, *Untersuchungen zur Lebenslehre des Amenope*, 121.

[13] See H. Brunner, *Altägyptische Weisheit*, 479–81; and J. F. Borghouts, "Divine Intervention in Ancient Egypt and its Manifestation (*b3w*)," in R. J. Demarée and J. J. Janssen, eds, *Gleanings from Deir el-Medîna* (Leiden: Nederlands Instituut voor het Nabije Oosten, 1982) , 1–70.

The measurer of grain-heaps trims for himself,
He who fills for another shaves the other's share
(*AEL* 1.174).

Also from the Middle Kingdom have survived the papers of a small
farmer named Hekanakhte, who lived a few miles south of Thebes. As
Hekanakhte managed various plots from some distance, his records
reflect anxiety that in his absence he might be cheated out of grain. To
insure the accurate collection of dues from his holdings Hekanakhte
insisted on the use of his own measure for such transactions.
Hekanakhte writes to the overseer Hrunufe that he is sending two
agents, Nakhte and Sinebnut, to collect certain amounts of barley and
emmer:

> Now see! I have got them to bring the corn-measure (*ipt*) in which
> it is to be measured; it is decked with black hide.[14]

Another papyrus lists the accounts of grain owed to Hekanakhte by
various individuals. Certain sums are described as "being what is to be
measured in the big measure (*ipt ꜥ3*) which is in Nebeseyet."[15] If
measures were only approximately standardized in the early Middle
Kingdom period, Hekanakhte's preference for his own vessel is
understandable. His concern also makes clear, however, how ripe the
situation was for fraud. T. G. H. James remarks:

> An inaccurate measuring vessel could be used distinctly to the
> advantage of its owner; an over-large measure might be used when
> the harvest was checked for tax purposes, or when a debt was
> recovered or a payment received; a measure of less than proper
> size would, on the other hand, be useful for the payment of taxes,
> or of a debt to another.... Use your own measure, specify your
> own measure for transactions, and you will probably know where
> you stand. Use another man's measure, and you will probably
> suffer a loss.[16]

At Deir el-Medinah the measuring and dispensing of grain was a
common source of dispute. One text records a complaint from the

---

[14] Hekanakhte letter III, 5-6 in T. G. H. James, *The Hekanakhte Papers and
Other Early Middle Kingdom Documents* (New York: Metropolitan Museum of
Art, 1962) 46.

[15] Hekanakhte letter VI, 12-13 in James, *The Hekanakhte Papers and Other
Early Middle Kingdom Documents*, 63. An examination of the figures in this
account suggests that the "big measure" (*ipt ꜥ3*) is a double-*khar* measure (p. 64).

[16] James, *Pharaoh's People*, 126. For later cases of stipulating particular
measuring vessels, see the literature cited by James, *The Hekanakhte Papers and
Other Early Middle Kingdom Documents*, 49.

laborers that the local administrative scribe Paser, who delivered payments and orders to the work site, had provided an undersized *ipt*-measure, containing only 38 *hin* instead of the true volume of 40 *hin* (O. Leipzig 2=*Hier. Ostr.* 34.4).[17] The record of this incident shows that scribes might commit such abuses with impunity. Nothing is mentioned about a punishment for Paser, although the scribe's offense was apparently clear. The scribe seems to have had the vizier on his side against the complaining workers.[18]

In addition to false measures, Amenemope forbids false scales and weights:

> Do not move the scales nor alter the weights ...
> The Ape sits by the balance,
> His heart is in the plummet;
> Where is a god as great as Thoth,
> Who invented these things and made them?
> Do not make for yourself deficient weights,
> They are rich in grief through the might of god
> (*b3w n-ntr*) (17.18, 21, 18.1–5).

The prohibition of false scales and weights, which is familiar from the Hebrew Bible, is unknown in Egyptian Instruction outside of Amenemope.[19] A sentence from the "Protests of the Eloquent Peasant" refers to the inviolability of the scales:

> The hand balance—it tilts not;
> the stand balance—it leans not to one side (*AEL* 1.181).

The clearest background to this passage in Amenemope, however, is the description of the judgment in the afterlife in chapter 125 of the Book of the Dead. Here the god Thoth, in the form of a baboon, attends the weighing of the deceased's heart. As the heart is measured in a scale against the feather-light weight of *ma'at*, Thoth records and announces the verdict.[20] Amenemope's allusion to the

---

[17] C. J. Eyre, "Work and the Organisation of Work in the New Kingdom," 178; J. Janssen, *Commodity Prices from the Ramessid Period*, 549; J. Černý, *A Community of Workmen at Thebes in the Ramesside Period*, 204–205.

[18] J. J. Janssen, "The Mission of the Scribe Pesiur." *Gleanings from Deir el-Medîna* (eds. R. J. Demarée and J. J. Janssen; Leiden: Nederlands Instituut voor het Nabije Oosten, 1982) 141–42.

[19] For Hebrew texts, see Prov 11:1, 16:11, 20:10–23, Deut 25:13–16, Lev 19:35, Hos 12:8, Amos 8:5, Mic 6:10–11, Ez 45:10. Cf. J. Fichtner, *Die altorientalische Weisheit in ihrer Israelitisch-Jüdischen Ausprägung*, 26.

[20] For a description of the scene, see S. Morenz, *Egyptian Religion* (Ithaca, N.Y.: Cornell University Press, 1960) 126–27.

judgment of the dead is especially apt for the present context; the scene would be sure to send shivers down the spine of a scribe who had falsified weights. The use of scales in the afterlife judgment recalls the very sin here prohibited. Moreover the god Thoth who records the verdict, as the god of writing and reckoning, is the patron god of scribes. The offending scribe will find himself doubly convicted by this scene. The use of fraudulent weights also appears in the list of sins in the negative confession of chapter 125 of the Book of Dead:

> I have not added to the weight of the balance,
> I have not falsified the plummet of the scales (*AEL* 2.125).

The invocation here of the *b3w n-ntr*, "the might of the god" (18.5) once again suggests that the scribe who falsifies weights in life will not succeed in denying the offense in the judgment of the afterlife.

Besides the sins which might be committed by scribes in the measuring and weighing of grain, Amenemope addresses offenses in their activities as scribes *per se*, as "writers". The prologue identifies Amenemope as a scribe "who acts for the king in his listing of taxes" (2.1). Thus the Instruction prohibits fraudulent registration:

> Do not cheat a man < through > pen on scroll,
> The god abhors it (15.20-21).

> Do not assess a man who has nothing,
> And thus falsify your pen (16.3-4).

> Do not dip your pen to injure a man.
> The finger of the scribe is the beak of the Ibis,
> Beware of brushing it aside.
> The Ape dwells in the House of Khmun,
> His eye encircles the Two Lands;
> When he sees one who cheats with his finger,
> He carries his livelihood off in the flood.
> The scribe who cheats with his finger,
> His son will not be enrolled (17.6-14).

Thoth is invoked here in the familiar forms of the ibis and the ape. By identifying the finger of the scribe with the "beak of the Ibis," Amenemope illustrates the gravity of the scribe's responsibility. The god works through the hand of the scribe; if he should use his pen falsely, he "brushes aside" the instrument of the god.[21] Such conduct must have serious consequences for the scribe: his livelihood (*drpw=f*, "his offerings, grain rations" i.e. sustenance) will be carried away by

---

[21] I. Grumach, *Untersuchungen zur Lebenslehre des Amenope*, 112.

the god. The final lines of this passage acknowledge the hope of New Kingdom scribes that they would be succeeded in office by their sons. That hope will be frustrated, however, for fraudulent scribes.

In the prologue Amenemope is also identified as a scribe "who records the markers on the borders of the fields" and "who makes the land-register of Egypt" (1.19, 2.2). Accordingly Amenemope devotes a chapter to the preservation of land boundaries:

> Do not move the markers on the borders of fields,
> Nor shift the position of the measuring-cord.
> Do not be greedy for a cubit of land,
> Nor encroach on the boundaries of a widow.
> The trodden furrow worn down by time,
> He who disguises it in the fields,
> When he has snared it by false oaths,
> He will be caught by the might of the Moon.
> Recognize him who does this on earth:
> He is an oppressor of the weak,
> A foe bent on destroying your being,
> The taking of life is in his eye.
> His house is an enemy to the town,
> His storage bins will be destroyed;
> His wealth will be seized from his children's hands,
> His possessions will be given to another.
> Beware of destroying the borders of fields,
> Lest a terror carry you away;
> One pleases god with the might of the lord
> When one discerns the borders of the fields.
> Desire your being to be sound,
> Beware of the Lord of All;
> Do not erase another's furrow,
> It profits you to keep it sound (Chap 6=7.12–9.16).

The displacement of boundary markers was considered a grave offense throughout the ancient Near East. Since the arable land of ancient Egypt comprised only a narrow strip along the Nile, any encroachment, even that of a single furrow, could be a serious injury.[22] The Nauri decree of Seti I deals with the offense as follows:

> Now as to any magistrate, any superintendent of fields belonging to this estate, any keeper of plow-oxen, or any agent who shall violate the boundary of fields belonging to the Foundation so as to move their boundaries, punishment shall be done to him by cutting off his nose and his ears, he being put as a cultivator in the Foundation.[23]

---

[22] Cf. H. Brunner, *Altägyptische Weisheit*, 477 n. 131.

[23] Nauri Decree I.B.3.a-b, translated by W. F. Edgerton, "The Nauri Decree of Seti I," 223.

The list of potential offenders given in this decree shows that the falsifying of boundaries was a crime possible only for certain higher classes of officials. Often the moving of a boundary stone would not benefit the measurement official directly, but rather was to the advantage of the official's clients. Thus the economically weak and socially defenseless (e.g., the widow, Amenemope 7.15) deserved particular protection.[24] Likewise the scribe is instructed to stay independent from associates who might place him in their obligation with gifts:

Do not recall yourself to a man,
Nor strain to seek his hand.
If he says to you: "Here is a gift,"
"No have-not" will refuse it (16.16–19).[25]

The god Thoth, as lord of reckoning and measurements, also watches over the land-registry. Hence Thoth is invoked here as the "Moon" who sees all and apprehends the offender (7.19).[26] A word-play in this passage makes further allusion to Thoth: Amenemope 8.15 forbids "treading on the furrow" (*hbhb dnm*), while 7.16 refers to "the furrow, to tread upon it" (*dnm n-h3b*), which can also be interpreted as the "furrow of the Ibis (*hb[y]*, i.e. Thoth)".[27] This text plays as well on the meaning of the term *wd3*, "to be sound, well, intact". Here first the scribe is warned: "Desire your being (*h^c=k*, properly, "your body") to be sound" (*wd3*, 8.13); and then later, "Do not erase another's furrow, it profits you to keep it sound" (*wd3*, 8.15–16).

Lines 8.5–8 describe the unhappy end of the offender's property: "His wealth will be seized from his children's hands" (8.7). This refers to the fact that ancient Egyptian inheritance had to be verified by local authorities. The bad reputation of a testator could be grounds for nullifying a bequest.[28]

It was often the role of scribes to serve as judges in the resolution of disputes.[29] Amenemope thus devotes considerable attention to

---

[24] Cf. I. Grumach, *Untersuchungen zur Lebenslehre des Amenope*, 61.

[25] The scribe's vulnerabilty to corruption as a magistrate must also be in view here.

[26] For further references to Thoth as the moon, see J. Ruffle, "The Teaching of Amenemope and its Connexion with the Book of Proverbs," 159.

[27] I. Grumach, *Untersuchungen zur Lebenslehre des Amenope*, 61. This differs from the reading of Lichtheim, *AEL* 2.151, given above. Grumach translates: "Die Furche zum Treten, es verkürzt die Lebenszeit."

[28] H. Brunner, *Altägyptische Weisheit*, 477 n. 140.

[29] See, for example, A. Eggebrecht, "Die frühen Hochkulturen: Das Alte Ägypten," in *Geschichte der Arbeit: Vom Alten Ägypten bis zur Gegenwart*, 84.

the scribe's conduct in court. The following lines prohibit the falsification of court documents:

> Do not make for yourself false documents,
> They are a deadly provocation;
> They (mean) the great restraining oath,
> They (mean) a hearing by the herald.
> Don't falsify the oracles in the scrolls,
> And thus disturb the plans of god;
> Don't use for yourself the might of god
> As if there were no Fate and Destiny.
> Hand over property to its owners,
> Thus do you seek life for yourself (21.9–18).

The instruction to "hand over property to its owners" (21.17) indicates
that inheritance and other property disputes are envisioned. Such
disputes were often resolved by appeal to an oracle of Amun. The
response was recorded by the attendant scribe, who is thus enjoined not
to falsify the record of the oracle's response (21.13).[30]

Each of the passages examined so far treats particular abuses of
the scribal office. In addition to denouncing these corrupt practices,
Amenemope has much to say about greed in principle, as we will see in
later sections.

DISSOLUTION OF THE "ACT-CONSEQUENCE RELATION"

Amenemope's reversal of the "act-consequence relation" effects
a major turn in the social orientation of Egyptian Instruction. Common
to the heritage of all ancient Near Eastern Wisdom is the primitive
moral dogma that one who "does good" in life will "do well": just
conduct issues in social and material success. Following the influential
attempt of K. Koch to show that the chief moral sanction in the Hebrew
Bible is inherent justice rather than divine retribution, scholars have
referred to this doctrine as the "act-consequence relation" (*Tat-Ergehen
Zusammenhang*).[31] Koch's thesis regarding the Hebrew Bible is some-

---

[30] See G. Posener, "Aménémopé 21,13 et *bꜣj.t* au sens d'"oracle'," *ZÄS* 90
(1963) 99.

[31] See Koch, "Gibt es ein Vergeltungsdogma im Alten Testament?" *ZTK* 52
(1955) 1–42; reprinted in *Um das Prinzip der Vergeltung in Religion und Recht des
Alten Testaments* (ed. K. Koch; Wege der Forschung 125; Darmstadt:
Wissenschaftliche Buchgesellschaft, 1972); abridged English translation in
Theodicy in the Old Testament (ed. J. Crenshaw; Issues in Religion and Theology
4; Philadelphia: Fortress, 1983) 57–87.

what overdrawn—divine retribution is a vital principle in the Hebrew Scriptures.[32] But Koch's category of the "act-consequence relation" supplies nonetheless an appropriate designation for the complex of beliefs in ancient Near Eastern Wisdom that associates wealth and social security with moral probity.

By designating the conception here as "primitive," I intend no negative value judgment, but refer instead to the simplicity of the doctrine and its primary place in the evolution of cultures. Since non-urban societies typically display this type of social sanction in some form, the act-consequence relation can be assumed to belong to the pre-urban cultural heritage of the ancient Near Eastern sages.[33]

The operative force of the act-consequence relation may be conceived as an immanent principle (Koch's *schicksalwirkende Tatsphäre*) or as an external order of justice, in dynastic Egypt, *ma'at*.[34] One who lives in accord with *ma'at*, dealing honestly with others, can expect to enjoy social esteem and prosperity. The negative corollary also applies: one who violates the moral order of *ma'at* must suffer bad consequences.

The social function of this doctrine in the Egyptian Instruction is ambiguous. In the earlier contexts of clan or village, the act-consequence principle would have assured reciprocal social relations and would have discouraged anti-social behavior. Since writing and the beginning of statehood are coeval in early Egyptian history, we can only surmise the value of the term *ma'at* in pre-dynastic culture, but the word must have belonged to the earliest language and probably had

---

[32] See especially P. D. Miller, Jr., *Sin and Judgment in the Prophets*; SBLMS 27 (Chico, California: Scholars Press, 1982) 5-6, 121-39; and the criticism of Koch by M. Fox, *Qohelet and His Contradictions*, JSOTSup 71 (Sheffield: Almond Press, 1989) 125-26.

[33] For an interpretation of the doctrine in Hebrew wisdom in terms of ethnographic reciprocity theory, see C.-A. Keller, "Zum sogenannten Vergeltungsglauben im Proverbienbuch," in H. Donner et al., eds., *Beiträge zur alttestamentliche Theologie*, fs. W. Zimmerli (Göttingen: Vandenhoeck & Ruprecht, 1977) 223-238. Keller's treatment of the Hebrew texts is not entirely convincing, but the comparative ethnographic material he adduces, mostly from Melanesian cultures, illustrates that the act-consequence doctrine is the common property of non-urban societies.

[34] For an overview of the concept of *ma'at*, see H. H. Schmid, *Wesen und Geschichte der Weisheit*, 17-20; H. W. Helck and E. Otto (eds.), *Lexicon der Ägyptologie* (Wiesbaden: Harrassowitz, 1972), 3.1110-1111.

ethical import before it was associated with pharaonic institutions. It is significant that the earliest hieroglyph for the term *maʿat* appears to represent "straightness" or "evenness," suggesting a semantic development parallel to that of Hebrew יָשָׁר, from a concrete sense of "straight" or "true" (i.e., "square"), to a derived ethical sense of "(up)right" or "correct".[35] This development would have preceded the identification of maʿat with the primeval mound of creation, symbolized in pharaonic Egypt by the plain square pediment upon which rested the pharaoh's throne, and likewise the divine throne in Egyptian temples.[36]

Once it belongs to the ideology of the pharaonic state, however, the act-consequence doctrine legitimates the dominance of the elite members of a sharply stratified society. *Maʿat*, having been established at creation by the primordial god, is constantly renewed by the king. One participates in the moral order of *maʿat* by submitting to the king's rule:

> Do that which pertains to *maʿat* (*bw maʿat*) for the king,
> For what the king (or "god") loves is *maʿat*!
> Speak what pertains to *maʿat* to the king,
> For what the king loves is *maʿat*![37]

Theoretically the king's administration realizes *maʿat* in human society, and so it exemplifies the act-consequence relation as taught in the Instruction texts: those who conform to justice attain standing in officialdom. People who are prosperous and powerful must necessarily be virtuous: "A man of character is a man of wealth" (Ptahhotep l. 167). Ptahhotep teaches that only wealth acquired justly will endure:

> Great is *maʿat*, lasting in effect
> Unchallenged since the time of Osiris.
> One punishes the transgressor of laws,
> Though the greedy overlooks this;
> Baseness may seize riches,
> Yet crime never lands its wares;
> In the end it is *maʿat* that lasts (*AEL* 1.64).

---

[35] See Gardiner, *EG*, Aa11; and cf. S. Morenz, *Egyptian Religion*, 113.

[36] For the latter development, with reference also to the image in the Hebrew Bible, see H. Brunner, "Gerechtigkeit als Fundament des Thrones," *VT* 3 (1958) 426–428.

[37] From the inscription of the vizier Kagemni, R. Edel, "Inschriften des Alten Reiches," *Mitteilungen des Instituts für Orientforschung* 1 (1953) 213. The fragmentary conclusion to an Instruction written for Kagemni survives on the Papyrus Prisse (Lichtheim, AEL 1.59–60). It is likely that these lines in Kagemni's funerary inscription are quoted from the Instruction (cf. Morenz, *Egyptian Religion*, 112).

The literate scribal class to whom this teaching of the Old Kingdom period belongs, however, is a small circle, perhaps a fraction of 1 per cent of the population, almost exclusively connected to the royal court.[38] In validating the authority of those who rule, the act-consequence doctrine necessarily puts the poor in their place and keeps them there. Ptahhotep teaches that the poor should subject themselves willingly to the rich, because the wealthy deserve respect:

> If you are poor, serve a man of worth,
> That all your conduct may be well with the god.
> Do not recall if he once was poor,
> Don't be arrogant toward him
> For knowing his former state;
> Respect him for what has accrued to him,
> For wealth does not come by itself.
> It is their [the gods'] law for him whom they love,
> His gain, he gathered it himself;
> It is the god who makes him worthy
> And protects him while he sleeps (maxim 10, *AEL* 1.66).

In the Old Kingdom texts generally, we hear relatively little of poverty and more frequently of wealth.[39] In these contexts, it appears that one need not be ashamed of prosperity; on the contrary the biographical inscriptions of the period boast unreservedly of high titles, offices, and possessions. Wealth is a divine bestowal, to be accepted with pride and joy:

> When wealth has come, follow your heart,
> Wealth does no good if one is glum!
> (Ptahhotep maxim 11, *AEL* 1. 66).

In the Old Kingdom literary environment, as H. Brunner observes, *"der Zusammenhang zwischen Tun und Ergehen ist eng und scheint unproblematisch."*[40]

The connection between act and consequence becomes problematic, however, during those periods of Egyptian history when the pharaonic administration falters and consequently the social security of members of the official class deteriorates. The response of the literary class to the first such major episode, the First Intermediate

---

[38] Cf. H. H. Schmid, *Wesen und Geschichte der Weisheit*, 36–38. J. Baines estimates the literacy rates in Old Kingdom Egypt to have been between 0.33% and 1% of the total population ("Four Notes on Literacy," 67).

[39] Cf. H. Brunner, "Die religiöse Wertung der Armut im alten Ägypten," 322.

[40] Ibid.

period (dynasties 7–11, c. 2200–2050 BCE) is revealing. During the First Intermediate the Memphite kings had lost control of all Egypt. The primary beneficiaries of the kings' loss of ability to levy the country's resources were the provincial governors, while those who had been connected to the royal court suffered the greatest dislocations.[41]

In the "Prophecies of Neferty" and the "Admonitions of Ipuwer" (both of which hearken back to the First Intermediate period, although the texts were not written then) the elevation of the poor to higher status is presented as the disruption of *ma'at*. Neferty declares:

> I show you the land in turmoil ...
> The beggar will gain riches
> The great [will rob] to live.
> The poor will eat bread,
> The slaves will be exalted (*AEL* 2.143).

The advent of a king (presumably Amenemhet I), who would reestablish unified rule and restore *ma'at* is announced:

> Then a king will come from the South ...
> Then Order (*ma'at*) will return to its seat,
> While Chaos is driven away (*AEL* 2.144).

Similarly Ipuwer charges a king with abandoning *ma'at*:

> Authority, Knowledge, and Truth (*ma'at*) are with you—[yet] turmoil is what you let happen in the land [*AEL* 2.160].

Among the signs of the abandonment of *ma'at* are the following:

> Lo, poor men have become men of wealth,
> He who could not afford sandals owns riches ...
> Lo, the land turns like a potter's wheel,
> The robber owns riches, [the noble] is a thief ...
> Lo, every have-not is one who has ...
> See, he who had nothing is a man of wealth,
> The nobleman sings his praise.
> See, the poor of the land have become rich,
> The man of property is a pauper [*AEL* 2.151–57].

The social location of formulations like these is obvious. This material belongs to those whose elite position is validated by the traditional doctrine of *ma'at*. The facile employment of the act-consequence

---

[41] See B. J. Kemp, "Old Kingdom, Middle Kingdom, and Second Intermediate Period," *Ancient Egypt: A Social History*, 113.

doctrine is not possible during times of instability when the security of those at the top is threatened.

Another such period was the Ramesside era, when Amenemope was composed. As was shown in the previous sections, the instability of the Ramesside economy produced an unprecedented volatility of fortunes among those nearer the top of the socio-economic scale. The traditional doctrine of the act-consequence relation no longer upheld the claim of the official class to superiority and security.

Amenemope's setting, moreover, is different from that of the earlier Instruction literature. Social mobility among the scribal ranks is a greater possibility in the New Kingdom; at least entry into the lower levels of the bureaucracy is more open. Whereas the older Egyptian Instruction had descended from elite circles, Amenemope was written for mid- to lower-level members of the scribal bureaucracy, many of whose social origins were modest.

There are notes of the old act-consequence relation in Amenemope. As we have seen, the Instruction promises prosperity, $w\underline{d}3$, in the spirit of the older Instruction (1.2,8; 4.1,2; 7.10). Amenemope 17.5 appears to be an unaltered reassertion of the old doctrine: "Do the good and you will prosper."[42]

Amenemope, however, contains no advice to the poor that they accept their position as divinely ordained. Amenemope abandons the doctrine that prosperity necessarily follows just conduct. In the face of the social experience of the Ramesside period, the doctrine of the "act-consequence" relation has dissolved. In place of the immanent moral sanction of the act-consequence relations, Amenemope sets a theological principle. The divine will, for Amenemope, is arbitrary and unaccountable. The gods bless whom they wish with wealth.

A change in attitude is evident already in Amenemope 9.10ff:

Do not set your heart on wealth,
There is no ignoring Fate and Destiny.
Do not let your heart go straying,
Every man comes to his hour.
Do not strain to seek increase,
What you have, let it suffice you.[43]

---

[42] Cf. D. Römheld, *Wege der Weisheit: Die Lehren Amenemopes und Proverbien 22,17–24,22*, 165.

[43] The interpretation of the two divinities invoked here, *š3yt* and *rnnt*, as Fate and Destiny, is discussed in S. Morenz and D. Mueller, "Untersuchungen zur Rolle des Schicksals in der ägyptischen Religion," *ASAW*, phil.-hist. Kl. 52, 1 (1960) 20.

Here prosperity is not the result of one's conformity to *ma'at*, or divine justice; wealth is dispensed by arbitrary divine forces regardless of one's good or bad character.

Even more noteworthy is Amenemope 24.13-17:

> Man is clay and straw,
> The god is his builder.
> He tears down, he builds up daily.
> He makes a thousand poor by his will,
> He makes a thousand into chiefs,
> When he is in his hour of life.[44]

Line 16, "He makes a thousand poor by his will," is unthinkable by the standards of the older Egyptian wisdom literature. The phrase "by his will," *n mr=f*, denotes completely arbitrary action.[45] Here the act-consequence relation is severed entirely. The new perspective is also illustrated by Amenemope 21.5-6:

> *Ma'at* is a great gift of god,
> He gives it to whom he wishes.

THE "*3ḫ*-SAYING: RELATIVE PRAISE OF POVERTY

The Egyptian "*3ḫ* (better)"-saying is the formal and material prototype of the biblical טוב-proverb (e.g., Prov 12.9; 15.16; 16.8, etc.)[46] In the Instruction of Amenemope the Egyptian "better"-saying undergoes two important transformations. First, the grammatical form is regularized. Of the thirteen Middle Kingdom examples of the "better"-saying, nine begin with adjectival predicate plus the comparative construction (*wr*, "be great," four times; *nfr*, "be good, beautiful," three times; *3ḫ*, "be good, profitable," two times; *ksn*, "be difficult," once; and *dgi*, "be hidden," once), while four examples have verbal predicate (sometimes appended to an auxiliary *iw* or *wn*). In Amenemope, all but one of the nine examples are with adjectival predicate, six of these with *3ḫ*.

---

[44] This line is apparently a reference to the working of the sun god through various divinities, each of whom is given sway over the earth for one hour of the day (A. Volten, "Der Begriff der Maat," *Les sagesses du Proche-orient, Colloque de Strasbourg, 1962* [Paris: Presses universitaires de France, 1963] 88; Lichtheim *AEL* 2.163 n. 27.

[45] H. Brunner ("Der freie Wille Gottes," *SPOA* 109) comments, "With such a formulation ... the *ma'at* conception of older wisdom is abandoned."

[46] For the following, see G. Bryce, "'Better'-Proverbs: An Historical and Structural Study," *SBL Seminar Papers* 108 (1972) 2.343-54. Bryce traces the origin of the form to the Old Kingdom Instruction for Kagemni, which may be as

Secondly, in Amenemope the subject matter of the "better"-saying is concentrated on the theme of wealth and poverty. Older Instruction used the "better"-saying to address themes of good character, speech or silence, and the quality of the traditional writings. Amenemope preserves some of these, but five of the "better"-sayings in Amenemope are new, and all deal with the theme of wealth and poverty. One of these directly undermines the command of earlier Instruction to respect the rich: "More beloved of god is the honoring of the poor, than is the worship of the wealthy" (26.13-14).[47] Another supports Amenemope's admonitions against corruption: "Better is a bushel given you by the god, than five thousand through wrongdoing" (8.19-20). Most significant is Amenemope's use of the comparative form to place poverty in a position of relative praise.[48] In Amenemope we find, for the first time in the Egyptian tradition, sayings such as 9.5-8:

> Better is poverty in the hand of god,
> Than wealth in the storehouse.
> Better is bread with a happy heart,
> Than wealth with vexation.

A. Alt first analyzed the apparent doublet to this passage in 16.11-14:[49]

> Better is praise with the love of men
> Than wealth in the storehouse.
> Better is bread with a happy heart
> Than wealth with vexation.

Alt surmised that the first version, "Better is poverty in the hand of god," was Amenemope's own creation. I. Grumach claims to have found the source of the second version, "Better is praise with the love of men," in the Mentuhotep stele, which stresses the value of good reputation.[50] Amenemope thus has taken over the "better"-saying tra-

---

old as the third dynasty, c. 2600 BCE (p. 345).

[47] My translation, to preserve the comparative form of the sentence. Cf. Lichtheim (*AEL* 2.161): "God prefers him who honors the poor."

[48] Cf. Brunner, "Die religiöse Wertung der Armut," 327-28.

[49] "Zur literarischen Analyse der Weisheit des Amenemope," *Wisdom in Israel and the Ancient Near East*, fs. Rowley; 19-20 (VTSup 3; Leiden: E. J. Brill, 1955).

[50] *Untersuchungen zur Lebenslehre des Amenope*, 101. For an opposing view cf. A. Altenmueller, "Bemerkungen zu Kapitel 13 des Lehre des Amenemope (Am. 15,19-16,14)," *Fontes atque Pontes: Studien zu Geschichte, Kultur und Religion Ägyptens und des Alten Testaments*, fs. H. Brunner (ed. M. Görg;

dition and adapted it to address wealth and poverty in an unprecedented fashion. We will see that this application of the "better"-saying is very influential in the book of Proverbs, even outside 22:17–24:22.

AFFIRMATIVE CONCERN FOR THE POOR

Generosity to the poor is commended as a virtue in Egyptian literature beginning with the earliest period. The Old Kingdom autobiographical inscription of Harkhuf proclaims

> I gave bread to the hungry
> Clothing to the naked,
> I brought the boatless to land.[51]

Similarly the Instruction of Ptahhotep warns against mistreating the poor (ll. 74–77). Amenemope, however, raises a uniquely partisan voice on behalf of the poor. The first words of Amenemope's instruction proper (i.e., following the prologue) are: "Beware of robbing a poor person" (4.4). This priority of place reflects the centrality of the theme throughout the Instruction of Amenemope.

Because Egyptian scribes often performed judicial duties, the Instruction tradition had long emphasized impartiality, so that the contending parties in a suit might be satisfied fairly.[52] According to the New Kingdom "Installation of the Vizier":

> The abomination of the god
> is a show of partiality.[53]

Amenemope's express concern, however, is that a judge not favor the wealthy to the disadvantage of the poor. This is a new emphasis:

> Do not confound a person in the law court,
> In order to brush aside one who is right.
> Do not incline to the well-dressed person,
> And rebuff the one in rags.

Ägypten und Altes Testament 5; Wiesbaden: Harrassowitz, 1983) 6.

[51] The stela of Harkhuf is the best known of the Old Kingdom ideal autobiographies. For the translation of this passage see Lichtheim, *AEL* 1.24.

[52] On the judicial functions of the scribal office, see e.g., A. Eggebrecht, "Die frühen Hochkulturen: Das Alte Ägypten," 84; B. J. Kemp, "Imperialism and Empire in New Kingdom Egypt (c. 1575–1087 BC)," 17.

[53] From the tomb of Rekhmire at Thebes; see J. Wilson, *The Burden of Egypt*, 173; T. James, *Pharaoh's People*, 61; for the text, R. O. Faulkner, "The Installation of the Vizier," *JEA* 41 (1955) 23.

Do not accept the gift of a powerful,
And deprive the weak for their sake.
Ma'at is a great gift of the god ...
It saves the poor from their blows (21.1–8).[54]

Legal documents contemporary to Amenemope indicate that the standard penalty for forfeiture of debts was a flogging of 100 blows.[55] The final line of this passage apparently refers to the threat of such punishment. In the earlier Instruction literature the actual function of the conception of *ma'at* is often to protect propertied interests. Amenemope, however, emphasizing relief of the poor, here develops the significance of *ma'at* toward a broader, socially redemptive end.

Although Amenemope enjoins accuracy and honesty in fiscal administration (17.6–20; 18.15–19.9), the Instruction goes far beyond this in favor of the poor with the following charge:

If you find a large debt against a poor person,
Make it into three parts;
Forgive two, let one stand (16.5–7).

A likely antecedent to this teaching of Amenemope is found in the eleventh-dynasty stela of Mentuhotep:

When a list of tax-dues to the Treasury of commoners, widows, orphans is reported, reduce the amount of that dues to a fraction, to let breathe one who has fallen into wretchedness.[56]

This advocacy of the poor, even to the detriment of impartial arbitration, is otherwise foreign to the standard Instruction genre. In

---

[54] Translating the last line, *sw šd i3d m-n3y=f knkn* literally (cf. I. Grumach: "sie rettet den Elenden vor seinen Schlägen," *Untersuchungen zur Lebenslehre des Amenope*, 134); H. Brunner: "[sie] befreit den Bedrückten von den Schlägen" ("Die religiöse Wertung der Armut im Alten Ägypten," 333). On this passage, see also H. Brunner, "Die religiöse Antwort auf die Korruption in Ägypten," 72.

[55] S. Allam, "Justice in an Ancient Egyptian Village," *Everyday Life in Ancient Egypt* (Prism Archaeological Series 1; Cairo: Prism Publications, 1985) 80; cf. Allam, "L'apport des documents juridiques de Deir-el-Medineh," in *Le droit egyptien ancien* (Colloque organisee par l'Institut des Hautes Etudes de Belgique, 1974) 139–62. Compare also the penalties stipulated in the Nauri Decree of Seti I and the edict of Horemheb: W. Edgerton, "The Nauri Decree of Seti I: A Translation and Analysis of the Legal Portion," *JNES* 6 (1947) 219–230; K. Pflüger, "The Edict of King Haremhab," *JNES* 5 (1946) 260–276.

[56] H. Goedicke, "A Neglected Wisdom Text," *JEA* 48 (1962) 27. W. Schenkel dates the text to the twelfth dynasty ("Eine neue Weisheitslehre?" *JEA* 50 [1964] 6–7. For the connection with Amenemope 16.5–6, cf. Goedicke, p. 34, and I. Grumach, *Untersuchungen zur Lebenslehre des Amenope*, 101.

cultivating this attitude, Amenemope is influenced less by the antecedent scribal Instruction texts than by the popular piety of the Ramesside period, in which the appeal of the destitute was lifted to the god Amun: "Give breath, O Amun."[57]

It was Breasted who first described Ramesside religion as a development of "personal piety," and B. Gunn who characterized as "the religion of the poor" in ancient Egypt the deep dependence of the lowly upon god as expressed in the votive stelae of the workers of Deir el-Medinah.[58] It is now recognized that the personal piety of these unofficial cults has its origins well before the Ramesside age.[59] Likewise these religious strains are found outside Thebes and are no longer attested solely by the workers' community at Deir el-Medinah.[60] The Theban milieu of the Ramesside era, however, out of which the Instruction of Amenemope emerged, remains the most abundantly illustrated source of this type of Egyptian piety. Here to an unparalleled extent we find the high god conceived as protector of the poor. Following are some typical invocations of Amun in this context:[61]

> You [Amun] are the protector of the poor (OBO 28, #21).
> [Amun], who comes to the cry of the poor
> when they are sad, who gives breath to the one
> who knows no more (ÄHG A 4–5).
> You beloved god, who hears the cry,
> who extends a hand to the poor (OBO 28, #38).
> You are the father of the motherless,

---

[57] P. Anastasi IV, 15 "Supplication to Amun in a year of need;" in R. Caminos, *Late Egyptian Miscellanies*, 171.

[58] J. H. Breasted, *Development of Religion and Thought in Ancient Egypt* (New York: Harper, 1912); cf. R. J. Williams, "Piety and Ethics in the Ramessid Age," *JSSEA* 8 (1978) 131–37; B. Gunn, "The Religion of the Poor in Ancient Egypt," *JEA* 3 (1916) 81–94.

[59] See for example G. Posener, "La piété personelle avant l'âge amarnien," *RdE* 27 (1975) 195–210. Prayer ostraca published here by Posener date back at least to the time of Amenhotep II. Cf. J. Assmann, "Weisheit, Loyalismus, und Frömmigkeit," in *Studien zu altägyptischen Lebenslehren* (OBO 28; eds. E. Hornung and O. Keel; Göttingen: Vandenhoeck & Ruprecht, 1979) 15 n. 9.

[60] A. I. Sadek, *Popular Religion in Egypt during the New Kingdom* (HÄB 27; Hildesheim: Gerstenberg, 1987), shows similar evidence of popular religion at Pi-Ramesses, Memphis, Giza, Abusir, and in numerous parts of Thebes outside the Deir el-Medinah complex.

[61] The following citations are my translation of the German of J. Assmann, *Ägyptische Hymnen und Gebete* (Zurich and Munich: Artemis, 1975) and "Weisheit, Loyalismus, und Frömmigkeit," OBO 28; 11–72.

the husband of the widow (ÄHG 147.12-13).
Amun, it is you who intervenes for the poor,
when they are in distress (OBO 28, #54).
[Amun], father of the poor, who lies in bonds,
You who raise up the suffering, when they call
(ÄHG 99.49-53).[62]

In Amenemope, the role of Thoth, patron divinity of scribes, as vindicator of the dispossessed poor (e.g., 7.12-19) is very close to that of Amun, champion of the poor in Ramesside religion. Just as Amenemope begins the Instruction proper with a warning against mistreating the poor, the Instruction closes by urging special consideration for the impoverished:

Do not prevent people from crossing the river,
If you stride freely in the ferry ...
Take the fare from one who is wealthy,
And let pass one who is poor (26.16-17; 27.4-5).

The following statement of Amenemope evokes the spirit of Ramesside piety and stands in sharp contrast to the earlier Instruction tradition:

More beloved of god is the honoring of the poor
Than is the worship of the wealthy (26.13-14).

Concern for the protection of the socially and economically weak appears in the literatures of the whole ancient Near East.[63] Nowhere in the ancient Near Eastern background, however, do we find a motif so close to the divine "preferential option for the poor" emphasized in contemporary biblical theology, as in the explicit intervention of the chief Ramesside god Amun on the behalf of the poor and oppressed. Since the initial discovery of the Instruction of Amenemope interpreters have admired its ethical outlook and compared it to that of the Hebrew Bible. We shall see in Part Two of this study that much of the affirmative social ethic of the Hebrew Proverbs is the result of the influence of Amenemope upon the biblical book.

---

[62] See also G. Posener, "Amon juge du pauvre," *Beiträge zur Ägyptischen Bauforschung und Altertumskunde*, 12, fs. H. Ricke (Wiesbaden: Harrassowitz, 1971) 59-63.

[63] For a convenient survey, see F. C. Fensham, "Widow, Orphan, and the Poor in Ancient Near Eastern Legal and Wisdom Literature," *SAIW* 161-174.

V

SUMMARY OF RESULTS

The Instruction of Amenemope was written in Thebes during the late Ramesside era, c. 1100 BCE, one of the most amply documented periods in the history of dynastic Egypt. The text was composed for scribal instruction, but the social position of the text's audience was not so privileged as is often assumed. While literacy remained the property of relatively few compared to the total Egyptian population, scribal ranks swelled to meet the imperial needs of the New Kingdom. Scribal office was not an exclusively hereditary possession; thus there was considerable social mobility between the non-literate and literate classes. New Kingdom scribes are best described as an administrative sub-elite whose situation was not as favored as some scribal propaganda (e.g., the Satire of the Trades) claimed.

The disintegration of the New Kingdom empire dominates the social-historical context of the later Ramesside period. Major economic disruptions are indicated by repeated crises in staple grain supplies at the capital city of Thebes. Administrative corruption was a principal contributing factor to the economic difficulties. Royal dependents in the Theban complex were driven to organized protest to receive their rations, and tomb and temple robberies became rife as a result of economic deprivation.

These circumstances shaped Amenemope's approach to the ethical problem of wealth and poverty. Unlike earlier examples of the Instruction genre, Amenemope addresses a lower class of officialdom. While the earlier Instruction condemns unjust gain in principle,

Amenemope goes into unprecedented detail to denounce graft and other corrupt practices of petty scribes. Against the volatile social and economic background of the collapsing Ramesside regime, Amenemope dissolves the doctrine of the "act-consequence relation". This sapiential tenet, which had served ideologically to justify the position of the upper Egyptian classes, is replaced in Amenemope with a theological assertion of the gods' prerogative to bless whom they will.

Amenemope's audience was arguably closer to the poor than the recipients of the Instruction of the Old and Middle Kingdom periods. Thus in the "ȝḫ-saying," prototype of the biblical "טוֹב-saying," poverty is conceived as praiseworthy, at least when compared to other social ills. Yet this is not the superior attitude of an author for whom poverty is a mere abstraction. Amenemope's defense of the poor against oppressors reflects the popular piety of the Ramesside period in which the chief god Amun was invoked as the protector of the poor. As we turn to the Hebrew Proverbs, we will see how profoundly Amenemope's advocacy of the poor has influenced biblical wisdom. Amenemope's teachings about wealth and poverty, moreover, provided a corrective to a strain of Hebrew sayings about the rich and poor which were open to abuse, as they could be invoked by the rich to "blame the victims" of social inequity.

PART TWO:
THE HEBREW PROVERBS

VI
DATING THE COMPOSITION AND
REDACTION OF THE BOOK OF PROVERBS

The book of Proverbs is singularly difficult to date.[1] Unlike the Instruction of Amenemope, the Hebrew Book of Proverbs is the result of a centuries-long process of formation, much of it incremental and impossible to reconstruct. The number of doublets in the Book of Proverbs reflects the accumulation of traditional material by various collector-editors whose outlook may best be summed up by the adage of Ben Sira:

> One who is intelligent and hears a wise saying
> Praises it and adds to it (21:15a).[2]

---

[1] As C. Camp has observed, there is a broad consensus that the Book of Proverbs was completed during the post-exilic period, but the basis for this agreement is seldom set forth in the current literature (*Wisdom and the Feminine in the Book of Proverbs*; Bible and Literature Series 11 [Sheffield: JSOT Press, 1985] 233). It will be clear in the following that—apart from the linguistic material—I have taken Camp's thorough treatment of the question (pp. 233–238) as my point of departure. I do not agree with Camp's more recent change of position in which she opts for a Hellenistic date for the final redaction of the book ("What's So Strange About the Strange Woman?" *The Bible and the Politics of Exegesis: Essays in Honor of Norman K. Gottwald on His Sixty-Fifth Birthday* [eds. D. Jobling et

Apart from the Psalms, no other literature in the Hebrew Bible has lent itself so readily to growth by accretion.[3]

The book of Proverbs itself attributes the content of various sections of the book to different sources: Solomon (1:1, 10:1), the חֲכָמִים (22:17, cf. BHS and the commentaries; 24:23), the men of Hezekiah (25:1), Agur (30:1), and Lemuel (31:1). These superscriptions, along with differences in form and content among the sections have led to the recognition of sub-collections among the Proverbs, some of which may have originated independently. Thus we can identify as distinct units: 1:1–9:18; 10:1–15:33; 16:1–22:16; 22:17–24:22; 24:23–34; 25:1–27:27; 28:1–29:27; 30:1–14, 15–33; 31:1–9, 10–31. Among these sub-collections appear traces of smaller units which may also have originated as independent compositions. For example, Prov 29:22–27 comprises a limited alphabetic sequence, with lines marked by the letters א–ב (v. 22a–b), ג (v. 23), ה (v. 24), ה (v. 25), ר (v. 26), ת–ת (v. 27a–b). The term תּוֹעֲבַת at the head of each hemistich in v. 27 begins and ends with ת, providing an unmistakable four-fold end-marker. This repetition of the character ת at the end of the sequence presently marks the conclusion of the "Hezekian" collection (25:1–29:27), but it seems originally to have concluded a smaller unit.[4]

This evidence of a complex history vexes any attempt to date the book as a whole. Most critical interpreters distinguish with confidence

---

al.; Cleveland: Pilgrim, 1991] 303).

[2] Doublets are identified as single lines or couplets appearing in similar or identical forms in different contexts; compare e.g., 11:15 and 17:18; 18:8 and 26:22; 10:1 and 15:20; 10:2 and 11:4; 11:14b and 24:6b; 15:18a and 29:22a; 24:23b and 28:21a. For a catalog of doublets in the book of Proverbs see C. H. Toy, *A Critical and Exegetical Commentary on the Book of Proverbs* (ICC; New York: Charles Scribner's Sons, 1899) vii–viii.

[3] Cf. W. O. E. Oesterley, *The Book of Proverbs* (London: Methuen & Co., 1929) xx; R. B. Y. Scott, *Proverbs-Ecclesiastes*, 2nd ed. (AB 18; Garden City, New York: Doubleday, 1965) 17.

[4] Cf. F. Delitzsch, *Biblical Commentary on the Proverbs of Solomon* (Edinburgh: T. & T. Clark, 1874–75) 257–59. The number of recognizable sub-units in the book of Proverbs can be multiplied. G. E. Bryce has proposed that Prov 25:2–27 is a literary unit patterned after the Egyptian Instruction of Sehetepibre ("Another Wisdom-'Book' in Proverbs," *JBL* 91 (1972) 145–57; cf. Bryce, *A Legacy of Wisdom*, 135–62. R. C. van Leeuwen, following Bryce's lead, has attempted to construe six coherent "proverb poems" as sub-units in Prov 25–27 (*Context and Meaning in Proverbs 25–27* [SBLDS 96; Atlanta: Scholars Press, 1988]). The poem against drunkenness in 23:29–35 clearly originated as an independent unit; see W. G. E. Watson, *Classical Hebrew Poetry: A Guide to Its*

between sub-collections which appear to be chiefly pre-exilic (10:1–15:33; 16:1–22:16; 22:17–24:22; 24:23–34; 25;1–27:27; 28:1–29:27) and those of apparent post-exilic origin (1:1–9:18; 30:1–14, 15–33; 31:1–9, 10–31).[5] The criteria for these distinctions are not as secure as is usually assumed, however. The formal distinction between the shorter, thus presumably earlier, units of sentence literature and the allegedly late literary style of extended periods like those found in chapters 1–9 was disproved decades ago through comparison with the ANE Instruction literature.[6] Most thematic criteria are equally unreliable, but the assumption persists that early and late collections are readily distinguishable on a thematic basis.

N. Gottwald, for example, has scholarly consensus on his side when he asserts that most of the sentence literature collections are pre-exilic "since they allude regularly to kingship and an operative state structure".[7] But a royal court setting for many of the king-sayings in Proverbs is very unlikely. F. Golka has recently shown that many of the Hebrew proverbs about kings compare more closely to folk sayings among contemporary traditional societies where a king is experienced as a remote and awe-inspiring figure.[8] Many of the proverbial king-sayings are likely to have originated as village wisdom, not royal court teaching. The conclusion of W. L. Humphreys concerning the courtier motif in the sentence literature of Proverbs is also pertinent:

> Of the 538 sayings in Proverbs 10–29, only about 30 have the courtier as the primary addressee. There may have been material in the royal Israelite court that developed the motif more fully, but little of this has survived in Proverbs. Thus, while a court establishment for the training of courtiers may have played a role in the development of a limited segment of this material, the restricted use of the motif suggests that other areas of life be considered as well in the developmental history of Proverbs, and the the role of the royal court has been greatly exaggerated.[9]

Techniques; JSOTSup 26 (Sheffield: JSOT, 1984) 20–30.

  [5] Thus, e.g., N. Gottwald, *The Hebrew Bible: A Socio-Literary Introduction*, 571.

  [6] See especially C. Bauer-Kayatz, *Studien zu Proverbien 1–9: Eine form- und motivgeschichtliche Untersuchung unter Einbeziehung Ägyptischen Vergleichsmaterials* (WMANT 22; Neukirchen-Vluyn: Neukirchener, 1966); W. McKane, *Proverbs: A New Approach* (OTL; Philadelphia: Westminster, 1970) 1–10.

  [7] *The Hebrew Bible*, p. 571; cf., for example, H.-J. Hermisson, *Studien zur israelitischen Spruchweisheit*, 71.

  [8] "Die Königs- und Hofsprüche und der Ursprung der israelitischen Weisheit," *VT* 36 (1986) 13–36.

Some of the traditional Hebrew king-sayings never circulated at the royal court, and may have been first written down during the post-exilic period. Others, whatever their origin, appear to have undergone adaptation during the Persian era, acquiring greater significance after the demise of the Judean monarchy (e.g., Prov 16:14). In no case does the presence of king-sayings require the conclusion that the sub-collections containing them were finished compositions of the pre-exilic period.[10]

The most extensive attempt to determine the date and social background of the presumed pre-exilic collections is that of U. Skladny, *Die ältesten Spruchsammlungen in Israel*.[11] Skladny places three collections early in the monarchic period: Prov 10-15, 28-29, and 16:1-22:16. A fourth collection, Prov 25-27, he dates late in the monarchy (the appearance of Ezekiel serving as a *terminus ad quem*).[12] Skladny's analysis, despite its heuristic value, has not been widely accepted, however.[13] His relative chronological judgments are based on form-critical assumptions that are no longer tenable. For example, Prov 25-27 is taken to be relatively late because the admonition form, prominent in these chapters, is assumed to be a secondary development from the declarative wisdom sentence.[14] Nor are Skladny's thematic assessments sustainable. Agricultural references (esp. 27:23-27) lead Skladny to term Prov 25-27 a "*Bauernspiegel*," but much of the language of this collection clearly belongs to a literary elite rather than to uneducated farmers.[15]

Rather than pursuing the variegated pre-history of the sub-collections in Proverbs, my concern is to determine when the book of Proverbs reached its final form as a unified composition.[16] I will

---

[9] "The Motif of the Wise Courtier in the Book of Proverbs," in J. G. Gammie et al., eds., *Israelite Wisdom: Theological and Literary Essays in Honor of Samuel Terrien* (New York: Union Theological Seminary, 1978) 187.

[10] On the "royal" proverbs see also R. N. Whybray, *Wealth and Poverty in the Book of Proverbs*, 45-59.

[11] (Göttingen: Vandenhoeck & Ruprecht, 1961).

[12] *Die ältesten Spruchsammlungen in Israel*, 76-81.

[13] See for example H.-J. Hermisson, *Studien zur israelitischen Spruchweisheit* (Neukirchen-Vluyn: Neukirchener, 1968) 17; R. N. Whybray, *Wealth and Poverty in the Book of Proverbs*, 62.

[14] Cf. W. McKane, *Proverbs: A New Approach*, 13.

[15] Skladny, *Die ältesten Spruchsammlungen in Israel*, 56-57; cf. especially R. C. Van Leeuwen, *Context and Meaning in Proverbs 25-27*, 73, 131-43.

[16] On Prov 1-31 as a unified "work," see especially C. Camp, *Wisdom and the*

confirm the general view that the book of Proverbs is a post-exilic production, but I will also challenge the assumption that the present book contains largely undisturbed pre-exilic collections of wisdom sentences. It will emerge, rather, that the Proverbs have undergone a unitary editing, transforming the diverse materials of the book into a recognizable product of the Restoration community.

Prov 25:1, with its reference to the editorial activity of the "men of Hezekiah," gives a *terminus a quo* of c. 700 BCE for the creation of the book.[17] A *terminus ad quem* is provided by Ben Sira, who around 190 BCE presupposes the Hebrew Book of Proverbs. Ben Sira relies thematically upon the Proverbs (especially in developing the figure of personified Wisdom), and appears to have access to the present text of the Hebrew Proverbs. In celebrating Solomon, for example, as the author of "song" and "proverb" (שִׁיר and מָשָׁל, cf. 1 Kgs 5:12), "riddle" and "hard saying" (חִידָה and מְלִיצָה, Sir 47:17), Ben Sira alludes to the list of these types of sayings in Prov 1:6.[18] The time

---

Feminine in the Book of Proverbs, 179–208.

[17] It is significant that the book in its own terms claims to have been still in formation as late as Hezekiah's reign. But while the note in Prov 25:1 is generally regarded as historically reliable (e.g., O. Plöger, *Sprüche Salomos (Proverbia)* [BKAT 17; Neukirchen-Vluyn: Neukirchener, 1984] 293; McKane, *Proverbs: A New Approach*, 14; Scott, *Proverbs-Ecclesiastes*, 155; B. Gemser, *Sprüche Salomos*, 2nd ed. [HAT 16; Tübingen: Mohr, 1962] 4; H. Ringgren, *Sprüche/Prediger* [Das Alte Testament Deutsch 16/1; Göttingen: Vandenhoeck & Ruprecht, 1962] 8), it cannot be taken at face value. Neither the identity of these editors (royal scribes, wisdom teachers?), nor the meaning of the verb הֶעְתִּיקוּ ("transmitted," "transcribed," "preserved"?), is clear. For recent discussion see M. Fishbane, *Biblical Interpretation in Ancient Israel* (Oxford: Clarendon, 1985), 32–33; M. Weinfeld, *Deuteronomy and the Deuteronomic School* (Oxford: Clarendon, 1972), 161–2. Although chapters 25–29 must contain some sentences from the monarchic period, neither the content nor the arrangement of the collection can be ascribed entirely to the time of Hezekiah. The superscription in 25:1 is significant as an acknowledgement that the compositional process continued for centuries after the Solomonic era, but one can most easily imagine editors invoking the authority of Hezekiah's court some centuries after his reign, especially since Hezekiah would stand half-way in time between Solomon and the post-exilic age of the final editors of Proverbs. Note also that Deuteronomistic editors (2 Kgs 18:3–6) viewed Hezekiah virtually as Solomon *redivivus*.

[18] Cf. O. Eissfeldt, *The Old Testament: An Introduction* (New York: Harper & Row, 1965), 473. For Ben Sira's use of Proverbs, see the bibliography in B. Lang, *Die weisheitliche Lehrrede: Eine Untersuchung von Sprüche 1–7* (Stuttgart: Katholisches Bibelwerk, 1972) 50 n. 10, especially J. G. Snaith, "Biblical Quotations in the Hebrew of Ecclesiasticus," *JThS* 18 (1967) 1–12.

range extending from Hezekiah to Ben Sira can be narrowed by examining three types of evidence: (1) linguistic, (2) structural, and (3) thematic.

LINGUISTIC EVIDENCE

Aphoristic forms of expression tend to be linguistically conservative.[19] It is not surprising therefore that the Hebrew Proverbs, as the repository of centuries of accretive development, contain some archaic language. For example, alongside frequent references to חָכְמָה, "wisdom," appears the ostensibly plural form חָכְמוֹת (1:20; 9:1; 14:1; 24:7) preserving PNWS singular *ḥukmatu, originally perhaps the name of a feminine divinity.[20] Such linguistic traces of the ancient roots of Hebrew wisdom can complicate an attempt to determine whether the language of the book reflects a late period of composition. The situation is again comparable to that of the Psalms, which contain extremely ancient elements, yet reflect linguistic developments continuing well into the Second Temple period. Moreover, the description of Late Biblical Hebrew continues to be disputed.[21] The typological criteria

---

[19] Thus, for example, contemporary English speakers cite biblical proverbs with archaic English usage: "Pride goeth before a fall" (11:2a), etc.

[20] For חָכְמוֹת (< *ḥokmat) as a Canaanite singular, see W. A. van der Weiden, *Le livre des Proverbes: Notes philologiques* (Rome: Biblical Institute Press, 1970) 85–86. B. Lang has developed the thesis, originating with Albright, that the figure of personified Wisdom in Proverbs is the survival of an ancient divinity: *Wisdom and the Book of Proverbs: An Israelite Goddess Redefined* (New York: Pilgrim, 1986). Additional vestiges in Proverbs of pre-Israelite language and literary form are suggested by C. I. K. Story, "The Book of Proverbs and Northwest-Semitic Literature," *JBL* 64 (1945) 319–337; and W. F. Albright, "Some Canaanite-Phoenician Sources of Hebrew Wisdom," *Wisdom in Israel and in the Ancient Near East*, fs. Rowley; 1–15 (eds. M. Noth and D. W. Thomas; VTSup 3; Leiden: E. J. Brill, 1955). "Proverbs," says Albright, "teems with isolated Canaanitisms," (p. 9).

[21] On Late Biblical Hebrew see the surveys of N. M. Waldman, *The Recent Study of Hebrew: A Survey of the Literature with Selected Bibliography* (Cinncinati: Hebrew Union College/Winona Lake, Indiana: Eisenbrauns, 1989) 80–82; B. K. Waltke and M. O'Connor, *An Introduction to Biblical Hebrew Syntax* (Winona Lake, Indiana: Eisenbrauns, 1990) 12–15; and especially R. Polzin, *Late Biblical Hebrew: Toward an Historical Typology of Biblical Hebrew Prose*; (HSM 12; Missoula, Montana: Scholars Press, 1976); G. A. Rendsburg, "Late Biblical Hebrew and the Date of 'P'," *JANES* 12 (1980) 65–80; A. E. Hill, "Dating the Book of Malachi: A Linguistic Reexamination," *And the Word of the Lord Shall Go Forth: Essays in Honor of David Noel Freedman in Celebration of his Sixtieth Birthday* (eds. C. L. Meyers and M. O'Connor; Winona Lake:

developed by R. Polzin for identifying LBH relate chiefly to prose syntax and hence cannot be applied to Proverbs.

It is precarious to date biblical books on the basis of their vocabulary alone, but the lexical inventory of the Proverbs can at least contribute to evidence for dating the book. Several vocabulary items suggest a late biblical semantic milieu, indicating a time of final composition after the end of the Judean monarchy. The term פְּנִינִים, "corals," (or perhaps, "pearls"; Prov 3:15; 8:11; 20:15; 31:10), is of no clear Semitic derivation, but is found among the late Greek lexicographers Herodianus, Hesychius, and Choeroboscus, as well as in Pliny and Cicero.[22] Outside Proverbs the term occurs once in Job (28:18), once in Lamentations (4:7), and three times in Ben Sira (7:19; 30:15; 31:6). The verb כתר in the H-stem, "to be crowned" (Prov 14:18), is a denominative from the noun כֶּתֶר, "head ornament," which occurs elsewhere only in Esther (1:11; 2:17; 6:8). The use of the verb אלף in the G-stem as "to become acquainted with, learn," occurs in biblical Hebrew only in Prov 22:25 (cf. D-stem, "to teach," Job 15:5; 33:33; 35:11) but is common to later Jewish Aramaic and Syriac.[23] Prov 8:4 contains the apparently late alternative plural form אִישִׁים, "men" (cf. Isa 53:3, Ps 141:4, and Phoenician ʾšm. Additional words which are common only to Proverbs and other exilic or post-exilic texts are בטה, G participle, "one who speaks rashly" (Prov 12:18, Sir 5:13); חוג, "circle, orbit" (Prov 8:27; Isa 40:22; Job 22:14; Sir 43:12); חֶתֶף, "robber" (Prov 23:28; cf. Sir 32/35:21; 50:4); מַצָּה, "strife" (Prov 13:10; 17:19; Isa 58:4; Sir 31:26); קבע, "to rob(?)" (Prov 22:23; Mal 3:8–9).

None of these words singly constitutes conclusive evidence, but as a group they suggest a pattern of later Hebrew diction. Significantly, these terms are not confined to Prov 1–9, 30–31 (usually regarded as the latest sections of the book), but are distributed throughout the various sub-sections. This militates against the view that most of the

---

Eisenbrauns, 1983) 77–89; J. M. O'Brien, *Priest and Levite in Malachi* (SBLDS 121; Atlanta: Scholars Press, 1990) 125–131.

[22] The term appears in Greek as πίνη, πίνα, or πίννα, and the Latin equivalent *pina, pinna*; see H. G. Liddell, R. Scott, eds., *A Greek-English Lexicon*, rev. H. S. Jones (Oxford: Clarendon, 1968) 1405; P. G. W. Glare, ed., *Oxford Latin Dictionary* (Oxford: Clarendon, 1982) 1380; cf. *HALAT* 3.891.

[23] M. D. Coogan suggests that the verb is denominated from the name for the first letter of the Hebrew alphabet: "*ʾlp, 'To be an Abecedarian'," *JAOS* 110 (1990) 322.

sentence literature in chapters 10-29 was set in its present form during the monarchic period.[24]

This impression is confirmed by evidence of Aramaic influence upon the language of Proverbs, which points to the Persian period as the time when the bulk of material in the book assumed its present form. The cluster of Aramaisms in the "Words of Lemuel" (31:1-9; בַּר, 3 times in v. 2; מְלָכִין, v. 3) has suggested to some scholars that this collection originated as an extra-Israelite composition.[25] But Aramaic influence is found throughout the book of Proverbs.[26] For example, frequent in Proverbs is the feminine abstract substantive with the termination -*ût*: רְפָאוּת, "healing" (3:8); עִקְּשׁוּת, "crookedness" (4:24, 6:12); לְזוּת, "deviation" (4:24); הַכְלִילוּת, "dullness" (23:29); אַכְזְרִיּוּת, "cruelty" (27:4); עַצְלוּת, "sluggishness" (31:27). The -*ût* termination is found in earlier Hebrew, but becomes common only at a later stage under the influence of Aramaic.[27] Clear examples of Aramaic diction are found in חֶסֶד, "reproach" (14:34; cf. 25:10; Sir 14:2); נחת "to descend" (17:10); רעע, "to break" (18:24); קבל (D), "to receive," (19:20); קֹשְׁט, "truth" (22:21; cf. קְשֹׁט, Dan 2:47; 4:34).[28]

---

[24] Contrast B. Lang, who argues that late vocabulary is not present in Proverbs (*Die weisheitliche Lehrrede*, 58-60).

[25] Gemser suggests that it may be an example of Edomite wisdom (*Sprüche Salomos*, 107).

[26] It is no longer possible to assume that Aramaisms in a biblical book necessarily indicate a late date. The pattern of Aramaic influence in Proverbs, however, is consistent with that in other recognized late books such as Esther and Ben Sira. On the significance of Aramaisms for dating biblical texts, see G. R. Driver, "Hebrew Poetic Diction," *Congress Volume: Copenhagen*, 26-39 (VTSup 1; Leiden: E. J. Brill, 1953); J. Barr, review of M. Wagner, *Die lexicalischen und grammatikalischen Aramaismen im alttestamentalichen Hebräisch*, JSS 14 (1969) 252-56; A. Hurvitz, "The Chronological Significance of 'Aramaisms' in Biblical Hebrew," *IEJ* 18 (1968) 234-40; C. Rabin, "Hebrew," *Current Trends in Linguistics 6. Linguistics in South West Asia and North Africa* (ed. T. A. Sebeok; The Hague: Mouton, 1970) 304-46; R. Polzin, *Late Biblical Hebrew*, 10-12; N. Waldman, *The Recent Study of Hebrew*, 59-60.

[27] This development is exemplified by the attestation of the term מַלְכוּת, "kingdom," only sporadically in pre-exilic texts but multiplying in later sources such as Esther, Daniel, Ezra-Nehemiah, and 1-2 Chronicles. See M. Wagner, *Die lexicalischen und grammatikalischen Aramaismen im alttestamentlichen Hebräisch* (BZAW 96; Berlin: Toepelmann, 1966) p. 131, and nos. 12, 94, 104, 178f, 211, 226, 285, 304, the bulk of which are post-exilic references. Cf. GKC O86k; H. Bauer and P. Leander, *Historische Grammatik der hebräischen Sprache* (Halle: Niemeyer, 1922) O61oi; P. Joüon, *Grammaire de l'hébreu biblique* (Rome: Pontifical Biblical Institute, 1923) O88Mj.

[28] Cf. O. Eissfeldt, *The Old Testament: An Introduction*, 474. For קְבֵל, "to

Also pertinent, but less conclusive in my opinion, is M. Wagner's treatment of the following as examples of lexical Aramaism: אכף, "to urge, press on" (Prov 16:26; Wagner, no. 13), cf. Sir 46:5,16; אתה, "to come" (Prov 1:27; Wagner, no. 31); בהל, "to hurry" (Prov 28:22; Wagner, no. 36); בֵּית, in the sense of "between" (Prov 8:2; Wagner, no. 41); חזה, "to see" (Prov 22:29, 24:32, 29:20; Wagner, no. 93); מלל, "to say" (Prov 6:13; Wagner, no. 171); מִלָּה, "word" (Prov 23:9; Wagner, no. 172); קִנְיָן, "possession" (Prov 4:7; Wagner, no. 266); שַׂכִּין, "knife" (Prov 23:2; Wagner, no. 296); שתק, "to cease" (Prov 26:20; Wagner, no. 319).[29] The distribution of these indications of Aramaic influence among the various sub-collections likewise points to the Persian period as the linguistic environment for the formation of the book as a whole.

This milieu, however, can be posited no later than the Persian period, in view of the almost complete absence of Greek influence upon the language of Proverbs. The word אֵטוּן, "fine linen" (Prov 7:16) had earlier been regarded as a Greek loan word from ὀθόνη,[30] but the shift from Greek θ to Hebrew ט is unlikely. Hebrew אֵטוּן is now recognized to be a loan word in Semitic from Egyptian ydmy. In Greek the word is already in use by the time of Homer. It is likely to have reached Greek through Northwest Semitic rather than vice versa.[31] The term certainly does not reflect Hellenistic influence upon the vocabulary of Proverbs.

A. Wolters has made a convincing argument that the G-participle צוֹפִיָּה in Prov 31:27 is a deliberate wordplay on the Greek term σοφία.[32] This does not, however, compel the conclusion that the book of Proverbs was still in formation after the conquest of Alexander the Great.[33] Already during the two centuries before 332 BCE Palestine had

---

receive," cf. Esther 4:4; 9:23, 27; Ezra 8:30; Sir 15:2; 41:1; 50:12; Job 2:10; 1 Chr 12:19; 21:11; 2 Chr 29:16; 29:22. This term belonged to the earlier Hebrew vocabulary, but appears to have fallen out of use in favor of לקח and then revived in later Hebrew under the influence of Aramaic (M. Wagner, *Die lexicalischen und grammatikalischen Aramaismen*, #251; cf. *HALAT* 3.993).

[29] M. Wagner, *Die lexicalischen und grammatikalischen Aramaismen*, 17–120.

[30] D. G. Wildeboer, *Die Sprüche* (KHAT 15; Tübingen: Mohr, 1897) 23; Oesterley, *The Book of Proverbs*, 53; G. Fohrer, *Introduction to the Old Testament* (Philadelphia: Fortress, 1970) 319.

[31] T. O. Lambdin, "Egyptian Loan Words in the Old Testament," *JAOS* 73 (1953) 147; *HALAT* 1.36.

[32] "*Ṣôpiyyâ* (Prov 31:27) as Hymnic Participle and Play on *sophia*," *JBL* 104 (1985) 577–87. Wolters's proposal seems to be gaining a wide acceptance. See e.g., G. Rendsburg, "Bilingual Wordplay in the Bible," *VT* 38 (1988) 354.

[33] So R. C. Van Leeuwen, *Context and Meaning in Prov 25–27*, 143; and C.

seen a heavy influx of Greek culture. Greek trade with the Palestinian coast had, in fact, been a formidable cultural influence since the late Bronze Age. By the late seventh century there were Greek settlements on the coast, fostering Greek trading connections with even the small towns of central Palestine. Conscripted Greek soldiers were an important element in the Persian army from the sixth-century beginnings of the Achaemenid Empire, and in the fifth century the Persians started using increasing numbers of Greek mercenaries. Along with these soldiers came more Greek merchants, goods (especially pottery), and after the sixth century, coins.[34] The earliest Greek coin to be found in Palestine, unearthed in Giv'at-Ram, a suburb of Jerusalem, was minted in Athens by Pisistratus, c. 550 BCE.[35]

Although the Samaritan papyri discovered at Wadi Daliyeh have not yet been fully published, they are acknowledged to attest to the penetration of Hellenistic culture deep into northern Palestine before Alexander's arrival.[36] Cross observes from the seals of the Wadi Daliyeh deposit: "One is particularly struck with the vivacity of Attic Greek influences in the glyptic art of Samaria in the era before the coming of Alexander."[37] O. Sellers summarizes the evidence of the material culture at Beth Zur, just south of Jerusalem:

Camp, "What's So Strange About the Strange Woman?", 303; but Wolters himself allows that an earlier date, before Alexander, is possible "Ṣôpîyyâ (Prov 31:27) as Hymnic Participle and Play on *sophia*," 586 n. 44.

[34] For details, see M. Smith, *Palestinian Parties and Politics that Shaped the Old Testament*, 2nd edition (London: SCM, 1987) 42–54. Also very useful is D. Auscher, "Les relations entre la Grèce et la Palestine avant la conquête d'Alexandre," *VT* 17 (1967) 8–30. For the extent of imported Greek pottery see E. Stern, *Material Culture of the Land of the Bible in the Persian Period, 538–332 BCE* (Warminster: Aris & Phillips, 1982) 137–42, 283–86; and most recently, R. Wenning, "Attische Keramik in Palästina. Ein Zwischenbericht," *Transeuphratène* 2 (1990) 157–168. Also of value is J. Elayi, *Pénétration grecque en Phénicie sous l'Empire perse* (Nancy: Presses Universitaires de Nancy, 1988), reviewed by J. Sapin, *Transeuphratène* 1 (1989) 194–198.

[35] J. Meshorer, "An Attic Coin from Jerusalem," *'Atiqot* 3 (1961) 185.

[36] See, e.g., M. E. Stone, *Scriptures, Sects, and Visions: A Profile of Judaism from Ezra to the Jewish Revolts* (Philadelphia: Fortress, 1980) 27–28.

[37] F. M. Cross, Jr., "The Discovery of the Samaria Papyri," *BA* 26 (1963) 110–21; "Papyri of the Fourth Century BC from Dâliyeh," *New Directions in Biblical Archaeology*, 45–69 (ed. D. N. Freedman and J. C. Greenfield; Garden City, N.Y.: Doubleday, 1969); "The Papyri and Their Historical Implications," *Discoveries in the Wâdī ed-Dâliyeh*, 17–29 (ed. P. W. Lapp and N. L. Lapp; AASOR 41; Cambridge, Mass.: American Schools of Oriental Research, 1974); "Samaria Papyrus I: An Aramaic Slave Conveyance of 335 BCE," *EI* 18 (1985) 7*–17*; "A Report on the Samaria Papyri," *Congress Volume: Jerusalem*, 17–26

Culturally, from the early part of the fifth century on, Palestine was dominated by Greece. The few objects showing Persian influence are almost negligible. There is no change in pottery forms or other objects at the coming of Alexander. That conqueror did not introduce Greek culture into Palestine ... he found ... it there.[38]

Emblematic of the advance of the Greek language in Palestine before 332 BCE is the spread of Greek names.[39] Phoenician nobility of the late Persian period were likely to have a Greek form of their names (for example Strato, King of Sidon at the time of Artaxerxes II Mnemon, 404–358 BCE).[40] Similarly Sanballaṭ III, the last governor of Samaria under Persian authority, gave his daughter the Greek name Nikaso.[41]

If Proverbs contained numerous Greek loan words (an unlikely proposition since even Qohelet has none), or if the book showed clear thematic interaction with Greek ideas, we might be compelled to regard the book as still under formation in the Hellenistic era (post-Alexander). But the Hebrew-Greek wordplay in Prov 31:27 is only a veiled polemical tag, suggesting a clever author who has had some contact with the Greek language but who has not been particularly influenced by Greek thought.[42] The author knows enough about

---

(VTSup 40; Leiden: E. J. Brill, 1988.

[38] O. Sellers, *The Citadel of Beth Zur: A Preliminary Report of the First Excavation Conducted by the Presbyterian Theological Seminary, Chicago, and the American School of Oriental Research, Jerusalem, in 1931 at Khirbat et Tubeiqa* (Philadelphia: Westminster, 1933) 41; quoted by M. Smith, *Palestinian Parties and Politics that Shaped the Old Testament*, 46.

[39] See M. Hengel, *Judaism and Hellenism: Studies in their Encounter in Palestine during the Early Hellenistic Period* (Philadelphia: Fortress, 1974) 1.61; 2.44

[40] Hengel identifies three Phoenician princes named Strato: (1) the King of Sidon mentioned above, (2) a prince of Aradus, (3) a king of Tyre, the last two contemporary to Alexander the Great. "Presumably the Phoenician name was ʿAbdʿaštart and Strato was the Greek form" (Hengel, *Judaism and Hellenism*, 2.44 n. 26).

[41] Josephus, *Antiquities* 11.303. On this Hengel refers to G. E. Wright, "The First Campaign at Tell Balâṭah (Shechem)," *BASOR* 144 (1956) 15. For the circumstances of Sanballaṭ III and his daughter Nikaso, see F. M. Cross, Jr., "Aspects of Samaritan and Jewish History in Late Persian and Hellenistic Times," *HTR* 59 (1966) 201–11.

[42] Cf. Wolters: The allusion to Greek sophia can be viewed "as a cleverly veiled barb in a religious polemic," concentrating the intent of the poem to present "a very practical and down-to-earth ideal of God-fearing wisdom which stands in vivid contrast to the intellectual ideal of wisdom favored by Hellenism" ("*Ṣôpiyyâ*

Hellenic wisdom to engage in name-calling, but clearly does not operate, even as a resister, in a Hellenized intellectual environment. It is also telling that by the Hellenistic era proper, the significance of the wordplay seems to have been lost upon Greek speakers. The LXX translators give no indication of having understood either the Hebrew term or the Hebrew-Greek pun.[43] This picture comports with the other linguistic evidence we have surveyed in this section. Thus the language of Proverbs suggests that the composition of the book was essentially finished during the Persian era.

STRUCTURAL FEATURES

A further indication of late composition, as well as of unitary editing of the Proverbs, is the numerical system which governs the structure of the book. P. Behnke first observed in 1896 that the sub-collection of Prov 10:1–22:16, bearing the superscription מִשְׁלֵי שְׁלֹמֹה, "Proverbs of Solomon" (10:1), contains 375 single-line proverbs, a figure which is equivalent to the sum of the numerical values of the consonants of the name שלמה: ש=300, ל=30, מ=40, ה=5. Behnke also suggested a correspondence between the name Hezekiah in 25:1 (reading חזקיהו for MT חזקיה) and his count of 136 sayings in the Hezekian collection of chapters 25–29: ח=8, ז=7, ק=100, י=10, ה=5, ו=6.[44]

P. Skehan refined this analysis.[45] He noted that there are actually 140 verse lines (as opposed to sayings) in the Hezekian collection, and this number agrees with the value of the name Hezekiah if it is spelled יחזקיה: י=10, ח=8, ז=7, ק=100, י=10, ה=5. The latter reading of the name is reasonable, since it appears this way at Hos 1:1 and Mic

---

(Prov 31:27) as Hymnic Participle and Play on *sophia*") 586.

[43] Wolters, "*Ṣôpîyyâ* (Prov 31:27) as Hymnic Participle and Play on *sophia*," 587.

[44] P. Behnke, "Spr. 10,1.25,1," *ZAW* 16 (1896) 122.

[45] For the following see P. Skehan, *Studies in Ancient Israelite Poetry and Wisdom* (CBQMS 1; Washington, D.C.: Catholic Biblical Association, 1971) 43–45. This summarizes the results of a series of studies reprinted here in revised form, pp. 9–45: "The Seven Columns of Wisdom's House in Proverbs 1–9," *CBQ* 9 (1947) 190–98; "A Single Editor for the Whole Book of Proverbs," *CBQ* 10 (1948) 115–30; "Wisdom's House," *CBQ* 29 (1967) 468–86.

1:1. The loss of the initial י in the MT at Prov 25:1 is easily explained by haplography to the final י of the preceding word: אנשי]י[חזקיה.[46] Skehan takes the reference to the "Words of the Wise" in Prov 22:17 as a title for all the material in Prov 22:17–31:31 that is not referred either to Hezekiah (25:1–29:27), Agur (30:1–6), Lemuel (31:2–9), or the אֵשֶׁת חַיִל (31:10–31). The numerical value of the term חֲכָמִים is 118 (ח=8, כ=20, מ=40, י=10 , מ=40), and there are 118 lines in the sections of Proverbs which Skehan places under this rubric: 22:17–24:32; 30:7–14. The arrangement is crowned by the fact that the superscription to the book contains names whose sum numerical equivalent is 930: Proverbs of Solomon (שלמה, 375), son of David (דוד, 14), king of Israel (ישראל, 541). This is remarkably close to the 934 lines of the present MT, given the inevitability of some textual corruption.[47]

This intricate network of interlocking numerical equivalences is, as R. Murphy has put it, "too striking to be coincidental".[48] It must reflect a deliberately designed numerical control for the content of each section, and thus indicates intentional editing for the book as a whole. The numerical system strongly suggests significant editorial activity at a late date, because alphabetic-numerical reckoning is not a feature of other biblical texts.[49] The rabbinic interpretive method known as

---

[46] Skehan suggests that we would expect an editor of Proverbs in the Persian period to agree with the superscripts to Hosea and Micah in the spelling of the name, and refers also to a Persian period coin found at Beth-Zur bearing the name with *yod*-prefix (*Studies in Ancient Israelite Poetry and Wisdom*, 44 n. 25).

[47] Skehan arrives at a count of 930 lines for the present text by excluding 1:16 (=Isa 59:7), 8:11 ("a gloss based on 3:15, out of grammatical harmony with the present context," p. 14), and 24:33–34 (cf. 6:10–11; *Studies in Israelite Poetry and Wisdom*, 44). The titles in 1:1, 10:1, 22:17, 24:23, 25:1, 30:1, 31:1 also are not counted. Skehan surmises they might have been distinguished by red ink, noting that Qumran scribes practiced rubrication (p. 30). This is also supported by the precedent of Egyptian scribal practices (cf. above, p. 1, on the Amenemope papyrus BM 10.474) and by evidence of rubrication in the Deir ʿAlla inscription and at Kuntillet ʿAjrud.

[48] *Wisdom Literature: Job, Proverbs, Ruth, Canticles, Ecclesiastes, and Esther* (FOTL 13; Grand Rapids: Eerdmans, 1981) 50.

[49] An exception might be Qohelet, where similar patterns have been suggested by A. Wright: "The Riddle of the Sphinx Revisited: Numerical Patterns in the Book of Qoheleth," *CBQ* 30 (1968) 313–34; "Additional Numerical Patterns in Qoheleth," *CBQ* 45 (1983) 32–43. Not all of Wright's proposals are convincing (cf. M. Fox, *Qoheleth and His Contradictions*, [JSOTSup 71; Sheffield: Almond, 1989] 156), but one is persuasive: The numerical value of the *inclusio* הבל הבלים הכל הבל (1:2; 12:8) is 216, and there are in fact 216 verses in 1:1–12:8 (Wright,

gematria, whose roots we perhaps discern here, is a post-biblical development.[50] Extra-biblical use of the Hebrew alphabet for numerical figures is first found on coins of the Maccabean period.[51]

Skehan himself posits an editor in the late sixth or early fifth century.[52] This view depends in part on the theory of a second architectonic scheme in Proverbs in which the major sections of the book are proportioned to the dimensions of Solomon's Temple as described in 1 Kgs 6. Thus Skehan asserts:

> The Book of Proverbs is the house of Wisdom. That is to say, its author-compiler-designer (for he was all three) wrote the Hebrew text of his composition in such a way that its layout in the columns of his scroll visibly showed forth the design of a house, which he himself identified (Prov 9:1) as Wisdom's House.[53]

Skehan then reconstructs the Proverbs scroll, arguing that the tri-partite divisions of Proverbs (1–9, 10–22:16, and 22:17–31:31) correspond proportionally to the front porch, nave, and inner sanctum, respectively, of Solomon's Temple. The seven pillars mentioned in Prov 9:1 appear in the scroll as seven "front porch" columns of text (chs. 2–7), each of twenty-two lines (the acrostic pattern setting their length).

Skehan's architectural plan for Proverbs is admittedly more speculative than the argument for numerical controls in the book and its parts. Several rearrangements of text are necessary to arrive at Skehan's result.[54] But it is, as C. Camp has remarked, "rather amazing" how the pieces of Skehan's reconstruction fit together

---

"Numerical Patterns in Qoheleth," 43).

[50] On the gematria, cf. R. Kasher, "The Interpretation of Scripture in Rabbinic Literature," *Mikra: Text, Translation, Reading and Interpretation of the Hebrew Bible in Ancient Judaism and Early Christianity* (ed. M. Mulder; Philadelphia: Fortress/Assen-Maastricht: Van Gorcum, 1988) 571. For the possibility of numeric encoding at Ezek 4:5, 9 (MT, Aquila, and Symmachus), see M. Fishbane, *Biblical Interpretation in Ancient Israel*, 464 n. 13.

[51] Aramaic-Greek royal coins employing the system date to the 20th & 25th years of Alexander Janneus (83 and 78 BCE; J. Naveh, "Dated Coins of Alexander Janneus," *IEJ* 18 [1968] 20–26; A. Kindler, "Addendum to the Dated Coins of Alexander Janneus," *IEJ* 18 [1968] 188–91.

[52] "Wisdom's House," in *Studies in Ancient Israelite Wisdom and Poetry*, 28.

[53] "Wisdom's House," 27.

[54] Some of these, however, have also been proposed by other commentators; e.g., moving 5:21–23 to the end of ch. 4. Cf. R. B. Y. Scott, *Proverbs-Ecclesiastes*, 49–52.

proportionately in the end.[55] Skehan's theory gains plausibility when we recall that another early post-exilic author envisioned a scroll sized according to Solomon's Temple: Zechariah's vision of a flying scroll (Zech 5:1-2), twenty by ten cubits in size, is too large for an actual scroll, but conforms precisely to the dimensions given in 1 Kgs 6 for the front porch of the temple, as well as the area occupied by the cherubim in the inner sanctum.[56] A likely time for the original Proverbs scroll to have been structured to represent the dimensions of Solomon's Temple is early in the post-exilic period, before the completion of the Second Temple.[57] Knowing the tradition of Solomon's Temple and perhaps familiar with its ruins, this editor constructed a literary replacement, the house of Wisdom.

The LXX Proverbs give additional evidence of the age of the MT Proverb's structure. The order of the LXX Proverbs is quite different from that of the Hebrew, but a comparison of the two makes clear that the MT structure has priority.[58] The order of the sections in the two versions is presented in Table 3 below. The LXX book is somewhat longer than the Hebrew due to expansive translation and the intrusion of supplementary lines.[59] Despite these accretive tendencies, however, the LXX preserves each of the sub-collections of the MT in recognizable form, and no new sub-collections are found in the LXX. The placement of sections I-III and IX is unchanged in the LXX, but sections IV-VIII are ordered differently. The LXX thus preserves the function of the poem on the אֵשֶׁת חַיִל (31:10-31) as part of an *inclusio* referring from the end of the book back to the role of Woman Wisdom in chapters 1-9.[60] Since the *inclusio* is a Hebraic poetic feature, this is a first clue that the LXX order derives from a prior structure belonging to the Hebrew tradition.

---

[55] *Wisdom and the Feminine in the Book of Proverbs*, 320 n. 7.

[56] See C. L. and E. M. Meyers, *Haggai, Zechariah 1-8* (AB 25B; Garden City, N.Y.: Doubleday, 1987) 279-83; D. L. Petersen, *Haggai and Zechariah: A Commentary* (OTL; Philadelphia: Westminster, 1984) 247.

[57] Cf. C. Camp, *Wisdom and the Feminine in the Book of Proverbs*, 238.

[58] On the arrangement of the sections in the LXX Proverbs, cf. P. J. Nel, "Israelite Wisdom in the Persian Period: The Motivation of its Ethos," *OTWSA* 25 (1982) 131-32. Nel's aim is to establish that chapters 1-9 were in a fixed form before the second century.

[59] See W. McKane, *Proverbs: A New Approach*, 33-47; G. Gerleman, "The Septuagint Proverbs as a Hellenistic Document," *OTS* 8 (1950) 15-27; *Studies in the Septuagint, III, Proverbs*; Lunds Universitets Arsskrift, N.F., Avd. I, Bd. 52, Nr. 3 (1956).

[60] On Prov 1-9, 31:10-31 as a stylistic and thematic *inclusio* see especially C.

TABLE 3. COMPARATIVE ORDER OF THE MT AND LXX VERSIONS OF PROVERBS

Masoretic Text	Septuagint
(I) 1:1–9:18 (Introductory Instruction)	(I) 1:1–9:18
(II) 10:1–22:16 (Proverbs of Solomon)	(II) 10:1–22:16
(III) 22:17–24:22 (Words of the Wise)	(III) 22:17–24:22 + 11 lines
(IV) 24:23–34 (Also Words of the Wise)	(VI) 30:1–14
(V) 25:1–29:27 (Hezekian Collection)	(IV) 24:23–34
(VI) 30:1–14 (Words of Agur)	(VII) 30:15–33
(VII) 30:15–33 (Numerical Sayings)	(VIII) 31:1–9
(VIII) 31:1–9 (Words of Lemuel)	(V) 25:1–29:27
(IX) 31:10–31 (אֵשֶׁת חַיִל)	(IX) 31:10–31

H. Gese is one of the few interpreters who has attempted to discern a reason for the LXX ordering of the middle sections.[61] Gese's interpretation of the LXX sequence is not entirely accurate (sections IV and VI–VIII are not arranged according to the number of proverbs they comprise), but Gese is correct in concluding that the LXX arrangement presupposes a knowledge of the basic structure of the Hebrew book.[62]

The LXX sequence is not an arbitrary rearrangement of the MT order. Rather, the LXX order results from an editorial attempt to strengthen the pseudepigraphical attribution of the entire book to Solomon. Of the section titles in the Hebrew text (1:1, 10:1, 22:17, 24:23, 25:1, 30:1, 31:1), only two, attributing the material to Solomon, are preserved by the LXX (1:1, 25:1). The Greek translation suppresses the MT's attribution of two sub-collections to non-Solomonic figures: Agur and Lemuel are not named at LXX 30:31 and 31:1. Similarly, the admission of the Hebrew text that some sayings belong to "the Wise" (22:17, 24:23) is replaced in the LXX by the first person voice of the pseudepigraphical author (Solomon). Compare the Hebrew and Greek versions of Prov 24:23:

Camp, *Wisdom and the Feminine in the Book of Proverbs*, 186–91.

[61] "Wisdom Literature in the Persian Period," *The Cambridge History of Judaism*, Vol 1, *Introduction; The Persian Period* (eds. W. D. Davies and L. Finkelstein; Cambridge: Cambridge University Press, 1984) 200–201.

[62] Gese's view of the date of the Hebrew composition also deserves note: "Even if the material collected in Proverbs 10 onwards originated predominately in the pre-exilic period, whereas the composition of chapters 1–9 could easily date from the earliest Hellenistic period, the essential shaping of this work must nevertheless have occurred in the Persian period" ("Wisdom Literature in the Persian Period," 189).

MT:

גַּם־אֵלֶּה לַחֲכָמִים

These also are by the Wise.

LXX:

Ταῦτα δὲ λέγω ὑμῖν τοῖς σοφοῖς ἐπιγινώσκειν·

I say these things to you that you may understand wise matters.[63]

In the MT, the sayings of Agur and Lemuel are placed at the end of book, probably because of the foreign authors involved.[64] In contrast, in the LXX these collections are interlaced among the other smaller collections, situated between the major collections of Solomonic proverbs (chs. 10-24, 25-29). Thus (despite their presentation in Rahlfs's *Septuaginta*) the words of Agur and Lemuel in the LXX belong to a seamless grouping of proverbs attributed to Solomon which extends from 1:1 to 31:9 (LXX 1:1-24:22; 30:1-14; 24:23-34; 30:15-33; 31:1-9). The entire book then is presented as two Solomonic sections, the first called proverbs (παροιμίαι Σαλωμῶντος, 1:1), the second identified as teachings (παιδεῖαι Σαλωμῶντος, 25:1) written down in the court of Hezekiah. Consistent with the intensified interest in pseudepigraphical tradition during the later Hellenistic period, the LXX editor thus makes the Solomonic attribution of the Proverbs more thoroughgoing than in the Hebrew tradition.[65] This accounts for the difference between the MT and LXX order and makes clear the priority of the MT sequence. The LXX rearranges an intricately constructed Hebrew structure which predates the later Greek recension. If Skehan's reconstruction of the original scroll of Prov 1-31 is valid, there has been some development of the text's structure within the Hebrew tradition (compare, for example, the place of 31:10-31 in Skehan's reconstructed original scroll and in the MT) but it seems safe to view the MT as a Persian period literary structure while the LXX represents a Hellenistic model.

---

[63] Or, "I say these things to you, O wise ones, that you may understand." In either case the LXX has clearly taken a Hebrew attribution of sayings to anonymous sages and converted it to a saying of Solomon. Likewise in Prov 22:17, despite the reference to the λόγοις σοφῶν, the emphasis is again on the first person speech (of Solomon): ἄκουε ἐμὸν λόγον, "hear my speech."

[64] Cf. H. Gese, "Wisdom Literature in the Persian Period," 201.

[65] Since priority in translating was given to the Torah and Prophets, the LXX Proverbs translation was probably not completed before the second century BCE. For a recent review of the literature, see R. Giese, "Wisdom and Wealth in the Septuagint of Proverbs" (Ph.D. diss., University of Wisconsin, Madison, 1990)

THEMATIC EVIDENCE

The present section will investigate the key theme of the relation of Law and Wisdom for evidence of the place of Proverbs in the historical development of the biblical literature. C. Camp's 1985 study argues that the "failure of the book of Proverbs to reflect explicitly on Torah," and in particular the lack of effort to connect the concept of Wisdom with Torah, shows that Proverbs reached its essential form prior to the return of Ezra with an authoritative book of Law which subsequently permeated the theology of the community.[66] I agree that the place of Torah in Proverbs points to a relatively early post-exilic setting, but the question of the relation of Law and Wisdom in Proverbs deserves further attention.

In the first place, Ezra's transmission of the Law cannot be used as an historical reference point. Assuming that Ezra actually was an historical figure, the date of his activity in Jerusalem continues to be an unsolvable problem.[67] Moreover, recent studies have made clear that the biblical portrait of Ezra is shaped by the author's intent to present a religious counterpart to the civil leadership of Nehemiah.[68] There is some evidence that the central Persian authorities promoted an empire-wide program of codification of local law.[69] This would tend to corroborate, at least in principle, something like Ezra's mission. The Ezra of the biblical narrative, however, is a highly developed literary character whose purpose is to teach Torah. Thus he is presented in the

---

12–28.

[66] *Wisdom and the Feminine in the Book of Proverbs*, 234.

[67] G. Garbini has revived the proposal of C. C. Torrey (*Ezra Studies*; 1910; reprint [New York: Ktav, 1970]), that Ezra never existed, but is the product of later literary activity (*History and Ideology in Ancient Israel* (New York: Crossroad, 1988) 151–69. This possibility deserves more consideration than it has generally received. For a review of the attempts to determine the chronological order of Ezra and Nehemiah see J. A. Soggin, *Introduction to the Old Testament*, 3rd ed., 492–95; G. Widengren, "The Persian Period," *Israelite and Judean History* (ed. J. Hayes and J. M. Miller; OTL; Philadelphia: Westminster, 1977) 503–509.

[68] See T. C. Eskenazi, *In An Age of Prose: A Literary Approach to Ezra-Nehemiah* (SBLMS 36; Atlanta: Scholars Press, 1988) 136–154.

[69] J. Blenkinsopp, "The Mission of Udjahorresnet and Those of Ezra and Nehemiah," *JBL* 106 (1987) 409–21; *Ezra-Nehemiah: A Commentary*; Old Testament Library (Philadelphia: Westminster, 1988) 157.

idealized role of lawgiver both as a second Moses and as the founder of synagogue worship.[70] R. Rendtorff has argued persuasively that the Aramaic term דָּת, which stands for "law" in Ezra 7:14, 25 denotes royal decrees and cannot be equated with the תּוֹרָה of Neh 8. This secondary identification is made only at the literary level by the author of Ezra 7:6.[71]

Thus the Restoration community's recognition of Torah as the supreme unifying authority was not mechanically instigated by Ezra's delivery of a Torah-book. The biblical account of Ezra's mission and covenant ceremony represents schematically what was historically a much more protracted social development. A truer picture of the earlier, and thus inchoate, status of Torah on its way to becoming the ideological center of the community emerges from the book of Proverbs.

C. Camp remarks in reference to Prov 1–9:

> The Proverbs poems are clearly concerned to offer a theological legitimation of Wisdom. Why then was there no effort made to connect this tradition with the Torah...?[72]

There is, however, a significant degree of Law-Wisdom assimilation in both sections of Proverbs, chs. 1–9 and 10–31. In Prov 1–9 the term תּוֹרָה can denote sapiential instruction in the family setting. This might be taken to be far away from the world of Torah piety. For example, Prov 1:8:

> Hear, my child, your father's instruction (מוּסָר), and reject not your mother's teaching (תּוֹרָה) (cf. 4:1–4).

Deuteronomy, however, emphasizes teaching the Law in the family (4:9) and in the home (6:7,9; 11:19) so the two pictures are closer than they might at first appear.

Deuteronomy ch. 4 identifies Yhwh's "statutes and ordinances"

---

[70] The Torah reading of Nehemiah 8 contains key elements of the synagogue liturgy; e.g., ceremonial bringing of the Torah scroll, mounting the raised platform, the blessing and communal Amen, Aramaic paraphrase of the text (v. 8?). For more detail cf. K. Galling, "Erwägungen zur antiken Synagoge," *ZDPV* 72 (1956) 163–78; U. Kellermann, *Nehemiah: Quellen, Überlieferung und Geschichte* (BZAW 102; Berlin: Töpelmann, 1967) 29–30.

[71] R. Rendtorff, "Esra und das 'Gesetz'," *ZAW* 56 (1984) 165–84. See also Rendtorff, *The Old Testament: An Introduction* (Philadelphia: Fortress, 1986) 68.

[72] *Wisdom and the Feminine in the Book of Proverbs*, 234.

(חֻקִּים, מִשְׁפָּטִים, v. 1), "this whole Law" (כֹּל הַתּוֹרָה הַזֹּאת, v.8) as
Israel's "wisdom and discernment" (בִּינָה, חָכְמָה, v. 6) in the eyes of
the nations. Then in Prov 1-9, theological wisdom assumes the features
of the תּוֹרָה of Deuteronomic piety.[73] In Prov 3:1-3, for example, the
command to remember the teacher's תּוֹרָה and מִצְוֹת (v. 1) is completed
by the exhortation:

> Do not let loyalty and faithfulness forsake you;
> bind them around your neck, write them on the
> tablet of your heart (v. 3; cf. 7:1-3).

McKane comments:

> The demand not to forsake loyalty and steadfastness is followed by
> phraseology redolent of law and covenant (cf. Exod 13:9, 16; Deut
> 6:8; 11:18; Jer 31:3, cf. 17:1). For the most part, the
> resemblances in vocabulary between other biblical books and
> Proverbs 1-9 which Robert adduces are too general to serve any
> useful purpose, but this instance is of a different kind, and it is an
> unmistakable literary reminiscence (cf. *RB* xliii, p. 51). It may
> even represent a contrived, free conflation of passages from law
> and prophecy, and the application of imperatives connected with
> covenant and commandments ('bind', 'write') to the demand for
> loyalty and steadfastness.[74]

Prov 6:20-23 has long been recognized as an adaptation of Deut
6:7-8 (cf. 11:18-19):[75]

> My child, keep your father's commandment,
> and do not forsake your mother's teaching.
> Bind them upon your heart always;
> tie them around your neck.

---

[73] Cf. H. Gese, "Wisdom Literature in the Persian Period," 210.

[74] *Proverbs: A New Approach*, 291. McKane acknowledges here that the
command to "write them on the tablet of your heart" might be a later expansion,
since it makes the line long and is absent from LXX[B]. The study of A. Robert
referred to here is "Les attaches littéraires Bibliques de Prov. I-IX," *RB* 43 (1934)
42-68, 172-204, 374-84; 44 (1935) 344-65, 502-25.

[75] F. Delitzsch, *Biblical Commentary on the Proverbs of Solomon*, 1.149; A.
Robert, "Les attaches littéraires Bibliques de Prov I-IX," *RB* 43 (1932) 44; G.
Buchanan, "Midrashim Prétannaites, à propos de Prov. I-IX," *RB* 72 (1965) 232;
W. McKane, *Proverbs: A New Approach*, 326-27; M. Fishbane, *Biblical
Interpretation in Ancient Israel*, 288 n. 20; on Prov 6:20-35 in relation to Deut
5:6-6, cf. M. Fishbane, "Torah and Tradition," *Theology and Tradition in the Old
Testament* (ed. D. Knight; Philadelphia: Fortress, 1977) 284.

When you walk, they will lead you;
when you lie down, they will watch over you; and when you
awake, they will talk with you.
For the commandment is a lamp (נֵר)
and the teaching a light (אוֹר)
and the reproofs of discipline are the way of life.

Verse 23 evokes the language of Ps 119:105 in praise of the Law:

Your word is a lamp (נֵר) to my feet
and a light (אוֹר) to my path.[76]

Thus, while Prov 1–9 contains no explicit identification of Law and
Wisdom, the two are associated by the application of the language of
Torah piety to wisdom teaching. The merging of Law and Wisdom,
fundamentally a post-exilic development,[77] is already underway in Prov
1–9.

Nor is this development the sole property of Prov 1–9 in
distinction to chs. 10–29. Along with instances where the terms תּוֹרָה
and מִצְוָה seem to have the mundane sense of "teaching," "directive"
(e.g., 13:14; 10:8), the sentence literature contains passages where this
vocabulary is reinterpreted in the context of legal piety. For example,
Prov 19:16:

Those who keep the commandment (מִצְוָה) will live;
Those who are heedless of his ways will die.

The singular form of מִצְוָה without the definite article suggests that it is
used here in the later technical sense.[78] The reference to "his ways,"
(v. 16b, דְּרָכָיו, usually emended to דְּבַר or דְּרָכָם) applies to Yhwh,
reflecting the reapplication of an older instruction sentence to the new
context of post-exilic piety.[79]

In Prov 28:4, the verbs עֹזֵב and שֹׁמֵר suggest that their object,
תּוֹרָה, should be taken in the sense of "Law":

Those who forsake תּוֹרָה praise the wicked,
but those who keep תּוֹרָה struggle against them.[80]

---

[76] McKane, *Proverbs: A New Approach*, 327; G. Vermes, "The Torah is a
Light," *VT* 8 (1958) 436–37.

[77] E. Würthwein, "Der Sinn des Gesetzes im Alten Testament," *ZThK* 55
(1958) 269–70.

[78] W. O. Oesterley, *The Book of Proverbs*, 158.

[79] Cf. W. McKane, *Proverbs: A New Appoach*, 523.

[80] Toy, *Critical and Exegetical Commentary on the Book of Proverbs*, 496;

It is evident that תּוֹרָה includes not just the instruction of the wise, but Yhwh's revealed Law, especially when תּוֹרָה is linked with prayer (תְּפִלָּה):

> When one will not listen to תּוֹרָה,
> even one's prayers are an abomination (28:9).[81]

By pairing Prophecy (חָזוֹן) with Law (תּוֹרָה) in Prov 29:18, the sage incorporates both as the basis of wisdom teaching:

> Where there is no prophecy the people cast off restraint;
> but blessed are those who keep Torah.[82]

Later, in the Hellenistic environment of Ben Sira, the identification of Wisdom and Law becomes explicit (24:8-23), and a thoroughly melded sapiential-Torah piety suffuses the book (cf. Sir 17:11; 19:20; 39:1).[83] But as R. E. Clements observes,

> it appears that such assimilation of wisdom to Torah was already in
> the process of taking place before the pressures of hellenisation
> brought new incentives to Judaism.[84]

Proverbs is a clear witness to this thematic development of the post-exilic, pre-Hellenistic era. The incipient assimilation of Law and Wisdom in the sentence literature as well as chs. 1-9 indicates once more that the whole book, not just the introductory Instruction, has been shaped by post-exilic developments.

To summarize the conclusions of this section: the language of Proverbs is the repository of centuries of accretive development; thus

---

Oesterley, *The Book of Proverbs*, 249; McKane, *Proverbs: A New Approach*, 623.

[81] McKane, *Proverbs: A New Approach*, 623.

[82] For חָזוֹן as a technical term for prophecy, cf. 1 Sam 3:1; Dan 9:24. A few commentators take תּוֹרָה here as the teacher's instruction (e.g., Gemser, Ringgren), but the developed sense of "Law" is preferred by most (cf. Wildeboer, Oesterley, McKane, Plöger, Barucq, Scott).

[83] On the development in Ben Sira, see E. J. Schnabel, *Law and Wisdom from Ben Sira to Paul: A Tradition Historical Enquiry into the Relation of Law, Wisdom, and Ethics* (WUNT 2. Reihe 16; Tübingen: Mohr, 1985), ch. 1 "Ben Sira's Identification of Wisdom and Law," 8-92.

[84] "Wisdom," *It is Written: Scripture Citing Scripture: Essays in Honour of Barnabas Lindars, SSF* (eds. D. A. Carson and H. G. Williamson, Cambridge: Cambridge University Press, 1988) 76.

there are doubtless many pre-exilic sentences in the book. A number of late Hebrew terms and Aramaisms, however, along with the lack of significant Greek influence suggests that the book reached essentially its present form in the Persian period. This is confirmed by structural evidence. The system of numerical controls for the content of the sections of the book suggests unitary editing at a late date, as do the apparent traces of an architectonic scheme based on the traditional dimensions of Solomon's temple. Comparison with the LXX structure shows that the LXX presupposes the MT order. Despite the continued fluidity of the structure of the book, it seems likely that the Hebrew order was fixed basically as we know it before the Hellenistic era. A survey of the theme of Law and Wisdom in Proverbs points to the same time of composition.

The book of Proverbs therefore was finally formed in Judah during the time after the rise of Cyrus the Great but before that of Alexander, probably earlier rather than later in the period. A more precise dating is not possible, but since the social organization of post-exilic Judah was so different from that of the pre-exilic state, we can meaningfully reconstruct the social-historical context of Proverbs by drawing on evidence from the time of Ezra and Nehemiah. Before doing so, we must clarify the literary relation of Proverbs to Amenemope and other antecedent texts.

VII

THE RELATIONSHIP OF PROVERBS TO AMENEMOPE AND OTHER LITERARY ANTECEDENTS

Given the numerous close parallels—often verbatim agreement—between the book of Proverbs and the Instruction of Amenemope, some literary relationship must be posited. The chief literary and thematic parallels between Amenemope and Proverbs are listed in Table 4 below.[1] Attention has focused on the sub-collection of Prov 22:17–24:22, the "Words of the Wise,"[2] where affinities with the Instruction of Amenemope are concentrated. As Table 4 shows, however, there are close parallels between other sections of Proverbs and Amenemope, so the relation between the two texts may be complex. Hypothetically it is possible (1) that Proverbs is dependent upon Amenemope, (2) that Amenemope is dependent upon Proverbs, or (3) that Proverbs and

---

[1] The table makes no claim to completeness and lists only the passages on which the greatest majority of scholars agree. Cf. the tabulations of D. C. Simpson, "The Hebrew Book of Proverbs and the Teaching of Amenophis," *JEA* 12 (1926) 232–39; and W. Helck, "Proverbia 22,17 ff. und die Lehre des Amenemope," *AfO* 22 (1968) 26–27.

[2] Although there is no title to this section in the MT, the form of 22:17 in the LXX suggests that the superscription "Words of the Wise," דִּבְרֵי חֲכָמִים, has been incorporated into the Hebrew of the first verse. Most commentators restore the phrase as a title and read 22:17a: "Incline your ear and hear my words". See e.g., R. E. Murphy, *Wisdom Literature: Job, Proverbs, Ruth, Canticles, Ecclesiastes, and Esther*, 74.

Amenemope derive from a common source, either Egyptian or Semitic. Each of these possibilities has been intensively explored in the scholarly discussion, but the theory of Amenemope's priority remains most likely.

TABLE 4. LITERARY PARALLELS BETWEEN PROVERBS AND AMENEMOPE

Prov 15:16, 17:1	Amenemope 9.5-8, 16.11-14	"Better" Proverbs
Prov 16:11	Amenemope 18.2, 23	False Measures
Prov 17:5	Amenemope 24.9	Mocking the Poor
Prov 20:9	Amenemope 19.18	False Innocence
Prov 20:19	Amenemope 22.11	Foolish Talker
Prov 22:17-18	Amenemope 3.9	Give Heed
Prov 22:19-20	Amenemope 27.7	Thirty Sayings
Prov 22:21	Amenemope 1.5-6	Words of Truth
Prov 22:22	Amenemope 4.4	Do Not Rob the Poor
Prov 22:24	Amenemope 11.13	Heated Person
Prov 22:25	Amenemope 13.8	Dangerous Friend
Prov 22:28	Amenemope 7.12	Boundary Stone
Prov 22:29	Amenemope 27.16	Skilled Worker
Prov 23:1-3	Amenemope 23.13	Dining
Prov 23:4	Amenemope 9.14	Seeking Wealth
Prov 23:5	Amenemope 10.4	Wealth Vanishes
Prov 23:6-7	Amenemope 11.1-2	Stingy Person
Prov 23:8	Amenemope 11.17	Disgorgement
Prov 23:9	Amenemope 22.11	Speak to a Fool
Prov 23:10	Amenemope 7.12	Boundary Stone
Prov 27:1	Amenemope 19.11, 22.5-6, 23.8-9	What the Morrow Brings

Budge was the first to notice similarities between Proverbs and Amenemope. He suggested "Asiatic" (Hebraic) influence on the Egyptian text.[3] W. O. E. Oesterley followed with an extended argument for the originality of the Hebrew material.[4] His view, however, derived principally from the perception that Amenemope is morally and religiously superior to the rest of the Egyptian tradition, indicating, he argued, Hebraic inspiration of Amenemope. Such an *a priori* assumption of the moral superiority of the Hebrew material is obviously no valid basis for determining the relation of the texts.

Oesterley's proposal attracted some followers,[5] but generally faded until it was revived in more elaborate form in 1957 by E.

---

[3] *The Teaching of Amen-em-Apt*, 103.
[4] "The 'Teaching of Amen-em-ope' and the Old Testament," *ZAW* 45 (1927) 9-24; *The Wisdom of Egypt and the Old Testament in the Light of the Newly Discovered 'Teaching of Amen-em-ope'*. (London: SPCK, 1927).

Drioton.[6] Drioton developed the theory of an Israelite colony in Egypt during the Persian period, from which Hebrew wisdom traditions were transmitted to the Egyptians. This theory collapsed with the publication of the Turin and Stockholm fragments, which proved that Amenemope had been in use in Egypt as a school text four centuries before Drioton's translation was supposed to have been made. Drioton's linguistic arguments for Semitic influence in Amenemope were also refuted.[7]

Y. Grinz has argued that the author of Amenemope possessed a collection of "Hebrew-Canaanite proverbs," the wisdom of the pre-Exodus Israelite tribes in Egypt, which was also transmitted to later Israelites.[8] But Amenemope's principal source material is clearly the older Egyptian tradition itself, and Grinz fails to identify any "Semiticisms" in Amenemope that are not simply part of the late Egyptian language.[9]

The theory of a common Egyptian source for Prov 22:17–24:22

---

[5] R. O. Kevin, *The Wisdom of Amen-em-apt and its Possible Dependence upon the Hebrew Book of Proverbs*, JAOS 14 (1930) 115–57; J. McGlinchey, *The Teaching of Amen-em-ope and the Book of Proverbs* (D.S.T. diss., Catholic University of America, 1938). For a detailed critique of Kevin's study see J. Ruffle, "The Teaching of Amenemope and its Connexion with the Book of Proverbs" (M.A. thesis, University of Liverpool, 1964) 432–436.

[6] "Sur la sagesse d'Aménémopé," *Mélanges bibliques rédigés en l'honneur de André Robert* (Travaux de l'Institut catholique de Paris 4; Paris: Bloud and Gay, 1957) 254–280; "Un livre hébreu sur couverture égyptienne," *La Table ronde* (October 1960) 81–91; "Le livre des Proverbes et la sagesse d'Aménémopé," *Sacra Pagina: Miscellanea Biblica Congressus internationalis Catholici de Re Biblica*, 1.229–41 (eds. J. Coppens, A. Descamps, E. Massaux; Bibliotheca ephemeridum theologicarum Lovaniensium 12–13. Gembloux: J. Duculot, 1959); "Une colonie israélite en Moyenne Egypte à la fin du VIIe siecle av. J.-C." *A la rencontre de Dieu: Mémorial Albert Gelin* (Bibliothèque de la faculté catholique de théologie de Lyon 8. Le Puy: Xavier Mappus, 1961) 181–91.

[7] R. J. Williams, "The Alleged Semitic Original of the *Wisdom of Amenemope*," JEA 47 (1961) 100–106; B. Couroyer, "Amenemopé I,9; III,13: Egypte ou Israel?," RB 68 (1961) 394–400; "L'origine egyptienne de la Sagesse d'Amenemope," RB 70 (1963) 208–224; Ruffle, "The Teaching of Amenemope," 436–441.

[8] *From the Ancient Egyptian Literature* (Jerusalem: 1975 [Hebrew]); see the review discussion of M. Fox, "Two Decades of Research in Egyptian Wisdom Literature," ZÄS 107 (1980) 130. An English translation of Grinz's work appears as an appendix to D. Snell, *Twice-Told Proverbs and the Composition of the Book of Proverbs* (Winona Lake, Indiana: Eisenbrauns, forthcoming).

[9] Fox, ibid.

and Amenemope was developed by I. Grumach in her 1970 Basel Egyptological dissertation on Amenemope.[10] Grumach starts with Alt's analysis of doublets in Amenemope as evidence of a composite text.[11] She uses Proverbs to illumine the Egyptian text, reconstructing from the biblical material an "Alte Lehre," whose order and substance, she argues, is preserved in the Hebrew version of Prov 22:17–24:22.

Grumach's detailed exegesis of Amenemope is valuable. She shows that Amenemope drew on a range of Egyptian sources, including Ptahhotep, Mentuhotep, Any, and especially the Ramesside Prayer to Thoth.[12] Grumach's reconstructed Alte Lehre, however, remains entirely hypothetical and unattested. There is no reason to assume that Proverbs preserves the original order of the maxims common to the two texts.[13]

The most likely theory is that Prov 22:17–24:22 is influenced by the Egyptian text of Amenemope essentially as we have it.[14] It is an overstatement, however, to deem the Hebrew a virtual translation from Egyptian, as some scholars have done.[15] Only with extreme caution should the Hebrew text of Prov 22:17–24:22 be emended to agree with Amenemope. This has often been done[16]—in fact several of Erman's and Gressmann's emendations, proposed on the basis of Amenemope,

---

[10] *Untersuchungen zur Lebenslehre des Amenope,* 4–6.

[11] "Zur literarischen Analyse der Weisheit des Amenemope." For a critique of Alt's analysis, see H. Brunner, "Der Freie Wille Gottes in der ägyptischen Weisheit," *SPOA,* 109 n. 1.

[12] A scribal instruction text, Papyrus Sallier I (8.2–7), translated in Lichtheim, *AEL* 2.114. This is apparently the source of Amenemope's contrast between the "truly silent one" and the "heated person," a figure which is adapted in the biblical Proverbs (29:22; 15:18).

[13] Cf. the criticism of K. A. Kitchen, review of I. Grumach, *Untersuchungen zur Lebenslehre des Amenope, Or* 43 (1974) 127–8.

[14] Proposed by A. Erman, "Eine ägyptische Quelle der 'Sprüche Salomos'," *SPAW* 15 (1924) 86–93; and followed by the majority of biblical scholars since then.

[15] E.g., A. Erman, "Eine ägyptische Quelle der 'Sprüche Salomos'," 86; cf. H. Grimme, "Weiteres zu Amen-em-ope," *OLZ* 28 [1925] col. 58; W. Richter, *Recht und Ethos: Versuch einer Ortung des weisheitlichen Mahnspruches* [SANT 15; Munich: Kösel, 1966] 36–37).

[16] H. Grimme ("Weiteres zu Amen-em-ope und Proverbien" [*OLZ* 28 (1925) 58]) expresses the typical opinion: "The dependence of the above named Hebrew Proverbs (22:17–23:11) upon Amen-em-ope is so great that with the help of the Egyptian *Vorlage* a number of textual errors in the biblical text can be corrected." P. Humbert (*Recherches sur les sources Egyptiennes de la littérature sapientiale d'Israel* [Neuchatel: Secrétariat de l'universitairé, 1929] 18–25) drastically revises the biblical text of 22:17–24:22 to make it agree with Amenemope.

still appear in the textual apparatus to BHS.[17] Such use of Amenemope for text-critical purposes can be misleading, because at points where the correspondence between Amenemope and Proverbs is close, the differences between the Egyptian and Hebrew are sometimes significant.

Moreover, the sub-collection of Prov 22:17-24:22, where Amenemope's influence is the strongest, has close affinities with a wide range of other antecedent texts. Because the parallels between Amenemope and Prov 22:17-24:22 are so impressive, scholars have focused too narrowly on Amenemope as a source for this section. As I will now demonstrate, the sub-collection of Prov 22:17-24:22 has affinities with wisdom traditions from a large number of identifiable sources, Egyptian, Aramaic, and Akkadian.

Prov 22:20, "Have I not written for you thirty sayings?" derives from Amenemope 27:6, "Look to these thirty chapters."[18] Amenemope thus provides the structural model for a collection of thirty sayings in 22:27-24:22.[19] But the material correspondence between Amenemope

---

[17] Erman, "Eine ägyptische Quelle der 'Sprüche Salomos'," 86–91; Gressmann, "Die neugefundene Lehre des Amen-em-ope und die vorexilische Spruchdichtung Israels," *ZAW* n.s. 1 (1924) 272–81.

[18] The MT of Prov 22:20, Kethib, שָׁלְשׁוֹם, "formerly;" Qere, שָׁלִישִׁ[י]ם, "noble things;" is usually emended on the basis of Amenemope to שְׁלוֹשִׁים, "thirty." The emendation was first proposed by Erman ("Eine ägyptische Quelle der 'Sprüche Salomos'," 89). G. Bryce (*A Legacy of Wisdom: The Egyptian Contribution to the Wisdom of Israel* [Lewisburg: Bucknell University Press, 1979] 18, 36–37, 81–87, 95–96, 114–15) recapitulates the entire critical discussion on this verse.

[19] There is no agreement precisely how to reckon thirty units in the present form of 22:17-24:22. C. Steuernagel in his commentary, published just before Amenemope came to light, counted twenty-nine (*Sprüche* [Eds. E. Kautzsch and A. Bertholet; Die heilige Schrift des alten Testaments⁴; Tübingen: J. C. B. Mohr, 1923] 2.308). Since then scholars have made a variety of adjustments in order to arrive at the number thirty. Cf. H. Gressman, "Die neugefundene Lehre des Amen-em-ope und die vorexilische Spruchdichtung Israels," 285; P. Humbert, *Recherches sur les sources égyptiennes*, 28; W. M. W. Roth, *Numerical Sayings in the Old Testament*, VTSup 13 (Leiden: Brill, 1965) 88–89; R. B. Y. Scott, *Proverbs, Ecclesiastes*, 137–46; W. McKane, *Proverbs: A New Approach*, 374–406; Gemser, *Sprüche Salomos*, 69; P. Skehan, "A Single Editor for the Whole Book of Proverbs," *CBQ* 10 (1948) 120–125; but cf. Skehan, *Studies in Ancient Israelite Poetry and Wisdom*, 41. Apparently an earlier edition of Prov 22:17-24:22 originally circulated independently under the title "Words of the Wise," containing thirty sayings in accord with its introduction. This number was disturbed when the sub-collection was incorporated into the design of the larger book of Proverbs. In accomodating the sub-collection to the later redactional scheme with its larger system of numerical controls, the final editor has disturbed both the thirty unit control on 22:17-24:22 as well as the original reference to the

and Proverbs extends only from the prologue through the first ten sayings, 22:17–23:11.[20] The next saying, 23:13–14 (introduced by 23:12) is common to Ahiqar (81–82):

> Do not withhold discipline from your children;
> if you beat them with a rod, they will not die.
> If you beat them with the rod
> you will save their lives from Sheol.[21]

Even within the section which is materially based on Amenemope (Prov 22:17–23:11), one saying, 22:26–27, treats the theme of debt surety, unknown in Egyptian Instruction but present in the Aramaic and Akkadian wisdom tradition.[22]

A prime example of the reliance in the "Words of the Wise" upon other sources besides Amenemope is the poem against drunkenness in Prov 23:29–35. This text is a direct descendant of the Egyptian

---

number thirty, שְׁלֹשִׁים, in 22:20. The Kethib and Qere readings are attempts to make sense of the original reference to thirty.

[20] This was first pointed out in the earlier debate by E. Sellin, "Die Neugefundene 'Lehre des Amen-em-ope' in ihrer Bedeutung für die jüdische Literatur- und Religionsgeschichte," *DLZ* 26 (1924) col. 1874.

[21] Parental discipline is a frequent topic in ancient Near Eastern wisdom, but the similarities between Prov 23:13–14 and Ahiqar 81–82 are so close (cf. לֹא יָמוּת, Prov 23:13 and לֹא תמות, Ahiq 82; תציל, Prov 23:14 and [תהנצלנ]הי, Ahiq 81), that a common tradition must be assumed. Whether the biblical author knew the text of Ahiqar as we have it cannot be determined. See J. Lindenberger, *The Aramaic Proverbs of Ahiqar* (Baltimore: Johns Hopkins, 1983) 49–52. The likelihood of an Akkadian original of the proverbs of Ahiqar now seems questionable. Lindenberger favors a north Syrian origin, pp. 16–20.

[22] Ahiqar 111: "I have carried sand and hauled salt, but there is nothing more burdensome than [de]b[t]." For the restoration of זפתא, "debt" following the Syr parallel to Ahiqar, see Lindenberger, *Aramaic Proverbs of Ahiqar*, 98; McKane, *Proverbs: A New Approach*, 165. Ahiqar 130–31: "Do not take a heavy loan from an evil man. And if you take a loan, give yourself no peace until (you have re)pa(id) it. A loan is pleasant as ... but paying it back is a houseful." Lindenberger, *Aramaic Proverbs of Ahiqar*, 123. Cf. also saying no. 42. A closer extra-biblical parallel to Prov 22:26f is probably the (unfortunately corrupt) Akkadian Instruction of Suruppak, obv. 12–13.:

> qa-ta-te la te-p[u-uš ...]
> ù at-ta qa-t[a-te ...]
> Do not be a security ...
> Then you [will be] a security ...

(W. G. Lambert, *Babylonian Wisdom Literature* [Oxford: Clarendon, 1960], 95.)

tradition, although it has no antecedent in Amenemope.[23] The late
Egyptian school texts frequently rebuke scribal students for excessive
drinking and play. Often these texts are quite amusing—the dissolute
scribe is ridiculed in outlandish terms. Hebrew wisdom usually takes a
different attitude toward drinking. Typically the Biblical sages
commend the moderate enjoyment of wine (Qoh 2:24; Sir 31:25-30),
or give a grim reminder that the drunkard will end in destitution (Prov
21:17; 23:20-21; Sir 31:25-30). Only in the poem against drinking in
Prov 23:29-35 is the lampooning spirit of the Egyptian scribal
miscellanies imitated.[24]

The poem in Prov 23:29-35 comprises two stanzas.[25] Stanza one,
vv. 29-30, begins with an eight-line series of rhetorical questions, each
beginning with the preposition -לְ:

לְמִי אוֹי
לְמִי אֲבוֹי

Who has woe?
Who has sorrow?

These are followed by the answer (v. 30):

Those who linger late over wine,
those who keep trying mixed wines.

This series of questions followed by answer forms a self-standing unit.
The new unit, vv. 31-35 begins with an imperative (v. 31a):

אַל־תֵּרֶא יַיִן,

Do not look at wine.

The strophic structure of the second unit comprises fourteen lines,
suggesting that the author has expanded an original eight-line poem

---

[23] I have developed the analysis that follows in a paper, "The Case of the
Drunken Scribe: Proverbs 23:31-35 and Ancient Egyptian Scribal Instruction,"
presented to the Israelite and Early Christian Wisdom Section, Annual Meeting of
the Society of Biblical Literature, Chicago, November 21, 1988.

[24] Cf. D. Cox (*Proverbs* [Old Testament Message 17; Wilmington: Glazier,
1982] 194-95) who emphasizes the humor of the passage, and W. G. E. Watson
(*Classical Hebrew Poetry: A Guide to Its Techniques* [JSOTSup 26; Sheffield:
JSOT, 1984] 20-30) who conveys a satirical tone in his translation and analysis.
Watson's title for the poem: "Prov 23,29-35—Hangovers are Horrible" (p. 20).

[25] The strophic analysis and translation here follows Watson, *Classical Hebrew
Poetry*, 20-23.

(vv. 29–30) with fourteen more (vv. 31–35) to render an acrostic sized compostion, twenty two lines.[26]

The extended admonition against drinking in stanza two, vv. 31–35, is patterned after a section of the New Kingdom Egyptian Instruction of Any (4.6–11). Prov 23:31-35 and Any 4.6–11 each contain the following sequence: (1) Prohibition of drink; (2) Description of the unpleasant results that follow excessive drinking, *viz.*: (a) Perverse speech and mental confusion, (b) Prostration, (c) Abuse by companions. The lines to be compared in the two texts are as follows:[27]

1. Prohibition of Drink.

imi=k hd=k m swr ḥnkt

Don't overindulge in drinking from the beer jug (Any 4.6).

אַל־תֵּרֶא יַיִן כִּי יִתְאַדָּם כִּי־יִתֵּן בַּכּוֹס עֵינוֹ

Don't look at wine when it is red, when it sparkles in the cup (Prov 23:31a-c).

2. Description of the Unpleasant Results of Excessive Drinking.
a. Perverse Speech and Mental Confusion.

bn smi snw pr m r=k nn rḫ=k dd sw

lest bad utterances come out of your mouth, and you don't know what you are saying (Any 4.7).

עֵינֶיךָ יִרְאוּ זָרוֹת וְלִבְּךָ יְדַבֵּר תַּהְפֻּכוֹת:

Your eyes will see strange things and your mind will utter perversities (Prov 23:33).

b. Prostration.

tw=k h3y ... gm.tw=k sḏr ḥr iwtn iw=k mi ʿdd-sri

You fall down ... (10) one finds you lying on the ground, like a little child. (Any 4.7,10).

וְהָיִיתָ כְּשֹׁכֵב בְּלֶב־יָם וּכְשֹׁכֵב בְּרֹאשׁ חִבֵּל:

---

[26] Cf. Watson, *Classical Hebrew Poetry*, 22.

[27] The text of Any follows the hieroglyphic transcription of E. Suys, *La Sagesse d'Ani* (Analecta Orientalia 11; Rome: Pontifical Institute, 1935). The translation here is adapted from that of Suys and M. Lichtheim, *AEL* 2.137.

You will be like one who lies down on the high seas, like one who lies down at the top of the rigging (Prov 23:34).

c. *Abuse by Companions.*

ʿt=k ȝw nn ky dit ḏrt=k
nȝy.w=k iry.w swr st ʿḥʿ.w ḏd.w ḥri pȝ swr=f

You hurt your body, but no one holds out a hand to you. Your drinking companions stand up saying, "Away with this sot!" (Any 4.8–9).

הִכּוּנִי בַל־חָלִיתִי הֲלָמוּנִי בַּל־יָדָעְתִּי

"They beat me, but I felt no pain! They struck me, but I didn't realize it!" (Prov 23:35).

The common motifs in these two texts and the common order in which they are presented suggests that Any 4.6–11 is the primary literary source for the second stanza of the biblical poem against drinking.

Additional examples of reliance in the "Words of the Wise" upon sources besides Amenemope can be adduced. Prov 23:1–3, for example, is usually compared to Amenemope 23.13–16:

Do not eat in the presence of an official...
Look at the bowl that is before you.[28]

Despite the similarity of theme and the likelihood that Amenemope has influenced the Hebrew author, there is, as Ringgren has noted, no precise correspondence between Proverbs and Amenemope here.[29] A closer verbal correspondence exists between Proverbs and Ptahhotep:[30]

When you sit down to eat with a ruler,
observe carefully what is before you (Prov 23:1).

If you are one among guests
At the table of one greater than you,
Take what he gives as it is set before you;
Look at what is before you (Ptahhotep 119-22).

While Amenemope 23:13 contains a vetitive clause, "eat not bread," Ptahhotep 119 and Prov 23:1 each contains the sequence of a

---

[28] E.g., H. Grimme, "Weiteres zu Amen-em-ope und Proverbien," 57; D. C. Simpson, "The Book of Proverbs and the Teaching of Amenemophis," 237.

[29] *Sprüche/Prediger*, 92; cf. Gressmann, "Die neugefundene Lehre des Amen-em-ope und die vorexilische Spruchdichtung Israels," 276.

[30] Text: Z. Zába, *Les maximes de Ptahhotep* (Prague: Académie tchéco-slovaque des sciences, 1956) 25; translation: Lichtheim, *AEL* I.65.

conditional clause with an affirmative command followed by relative object. Ptahhotep 122, "look at what is before you," $gmḥ=k$ r ntt $m-bзḥ=k$, is equivalent to Prov 23:1, בִּין תָּבִין אֶת־אֲשֶׁר לְפָנֶיךָ.

Prov 23:6-8 is regarded as parallel to Amenemope 14.5-8, 17-18. The vivid motif of sickness and vomiting suggests the affinity of these texts, but the themes of the two passages are quite different. Amenemope enjoins:

> Do not covet a poor person's goods,
> nor hunger for their bread (14.5).

Prov 23:6, in contrast, counsels against eating with a miser:

> Do not eat the bread of the stingy,[31]
> do not desire their delicacies.

Notwithstanding the possible influence of Amenemope, the primary source of this counsel is found in the Old Kingdom Egyptian Instruction addressed to Kagemni:

> When you sit with a glutton,
> Eat when his greed has passed,
> When you drink with a drunkard,
> Take when his heart is content (I.8-10).[32]

In the company of an ungenerous host, this text advises, one should partake only after it is clear that the offer is not grudging. Similarly, Prov 23:7b cautions:

> "Eat and drink," they say to you,
> but they do not mean it.

The texts which have been adduced demonstrate that the sub-collection of Prov 22:17-24:22 has close affinities with a number of literary antecedents other than Amenemope. Amenemope is, however, the principal source for sayings about wealth and poverty in Prov 22:17-24:22, and is also the antecedent to the טוֹב-sayings of Prov 15:16, 17:1, which introduce the relative praise of poverty into the Hebrew collection. Thus the parallels between Amenemope and Proverbs will be the focus of our attention below as we examine the

---

[31] That רַע עַיִן designates an ungenerous person is established by Prov 22:9, where the טוֹב עַיִן is one who gives freely to the poor. Cf. 28:22 and McKane, *Proverbs: A New Approach*, 626.

[32] Text: G. Jequier, *Papyrus Prisse et ses variantes* (Paris: Libraire Paul Guethner, 1911). Translation: Lichtheim, *AEL* I.59f.

influence of the international tradition upon sayings about wealth and poverty in the Hebrew Proverbs.

VIII
THE SOCIAL-HISTORICAL BACKGROUND TO PROVERBS

SCRIBAL EDUCATION AS THE SETTING OF THE HEBREW PROVERBS

The relationship between Amenemope and Proverbs is only the most outstanding example of the deep influence of the Egyptian tradition upon Hebrew wisdom.[1] A Hebrew "wisdom school" has been posited as the channel for this influence. Typically it is maintained that the Judean monarchy from its inception must have had a training school for scribes, officers, and diplomats, where international wisdom materials were used in instruction.[2] It is argued that the Proverbs, or at

---

[1] In addition to G. E. Bryce, *A Legacy of Wisdom: The Egyptian Contribution to the Wisdom of Israel*, see also P. Humbert *Recherches sur les sources égyptiennes de la littérature sapientiale d'Israel*; R. Weill, "Les transmissions littéraires d'Egypte à Israel," *Revue d'Egyptologie, Cahier complémentaire* 1 (1950) 43–61; S. Morenz, "Ägyptologische Beiträge zur Erforschung der Weisheitsliteratur Israels," *SPOA* (Paris: Presses Universitaires de France, 1963) 63–71; S. Morenz, "Ägypten und die Bibel," *RGG* 1 cols. 117–21; E. Wurthwein, "Egyptian Wisdom and the Old Testament," *SAIW* 113–33; C. Bauer-Kayatz, *Studien zu Proverbien 1–9*; R. J. Williams, "Egypt and Israel," *The Legacy of Egypt* (ed. J. R. Harris; Oxford: Clarendon Press, 1971) 257–90.

[2] See H.-J. Hermisson, *Studien zur israelitischen Spruchweisheit*, 97–136; J. P. J. Olivier, "Schools and Wisdom Literature," *JNWSL* 4 (1975) 49–60; A. Lemaire, *Les écoles et la formation de la Bible dans l'ancien Israél* (OBO 39; Göttingen: Vandenhoeck & Ruprecht, 1981), esp. 46–54; and A. Lemaire, "Sagesse et écoles," *VT* 34 (1984) 270–81.

least earlier portions of the eventual book, represent the adaptation of Egyptian and Mesopotamian teaching material into Hebrew for school use.[3]

Scribal education is the most likely context in which Egyptian Instruction could have entered the Hebrew tradition, but as in the case of the Egyptian New Kingdom, the designation of this setting as a "wisdom school" is misleading. There are good reasons to doubt that schools as such existed in ancient Israel.[4] The Hebrew Bible contains no mention of schools—the first reference to such an institution is in Ben Sira 51:23 (בֵּית הַמִּדְרָשׁ).[5] Of the scant biblical evidence commonly cited to support the existence of schools in ancient Israel, little actually indicates literate instruction, and none confirms the assumption that there were schools.[6]

The epigraphic evidence for literacy schooling in monarchic Israel is equally inconclusive.[7] A. Lemaire interprets inscriptions (mostly abecedaries on ostraca and other fragmentary samples of script) found at Izbet Sarta, Gezer, Lachish, Khirbet el-Qom, Arad, Aroer, Kadesh-Barnea, and Kuntillet ʿAjrûd as school exercises.[8] These

---

[3] R. N. Whybray, for example, argues in his earlier work that Proverbs chs. 1–9 "consist of an original lesson-book designed for use in scribal schools and closely modelled on Egyptian prototypes" (*Wisdom in Proverbs: The Concept of Wisdom in Proverbs 1–9* [SBT 45; London: SCM, 1965] 7).

[4] See especially F. W. Golka, "Die israelitische Weisheitsschule oder 'Des Kaisers neue Kleider'," *VT* 33 (1983) 257–70; "Die Königs- und Hofsprüche und der Ursprung der israelitische Weisheit," *VT* 36 (1986) 13–36. J. Crenshaw's review of the issues emphasizes the extent to which education probably took place in a family setting ("Education in Ancient Israel," *JBL* 104 [1985] 601–15).

[5] For the background to this expression, see H. M. Gevaryahu, "Privathaüser als Versammlungsstätten von Meister und Jüngern," *ASTI* 12 (1983) 5–12. The post-exilic בֵּית הַמִּדְרָשׁ has its roots in private familial or apprenticeship educational settings; it is not descended from a royal court school.

[6] A. Lemaire examines the eleven passages most frequently adduced as evidence of schools (1 Sam 1–3; 2 Sam 20:24–25; 1 Kgs 12:8–10; 2 Kgs 6; 2 Kgs 10:1,5,6; 2 Kgs 12:3; Isa 8:16; Isa 28:7–13; Isa 50:4–6; 1 Chron 27:32; 2 Chron 17:7–9) and concludes that the biblical evidence is "quite vague and insufficient to prove the existence of schools" (*Les écoles et la formation de la Bible dans l'ancien Israël*, 34–41). Cf. F. Golka, "Die israelitische Weisheitsschule," 258–61; J. Crenshaw, "Education in Ancient Israel," 602–4.

[7] A useful survey of the epigraphic evidence is given by A. R. Millard, "An Assessment of the Evidence for Writing in Ancient Israel," *Biblical Archaeology Today: Proceedings of the International Congress on Biblical Archaeology, April 1984*, Avraham Biran, Chairman, Organizing Committee (Jerusalem: Israel Exploration Society, 1985) 301–312.

[8] *Les écoles et la formation de la Bible dans l'ancien Israël*, 7–33.

isolated inscriptions, however, reveal nothing about the organization of education in monarchic Israel. They show only that someone practiced their writing—we can determine neither how nor where they were taught, their age, nor whether they were professional scribes. Evidence of individuals with rudimentary literacy skills does not, as Lemaire maintains, establish the existence of scribal schools at the sites where the artifacts were found.[9] Nor has archaeology disclosed any buildings from the monarchic period that can be interpreted as schools.[10]

Given the silence of biblical and archaeological records on the existence of institutional schools in ancient Israel, it seems most likely that training in writing occurred, as in the Egyptian New Kingdom, through a system of apprenticeship where members of each professional group trained their successors. There are indications that important scribal offices in ancient Israel were hereditary. Solomon's royal secretaries Elihoreph and Ahijah, for example, were the sons of David's secretary (called "Shisha" in 1 Kgs 4:3).[11] The family of Shaphan dominated the bureaucracy and controlled the office of royal secretary from Josiah to the exile (2 Kgs 22:3-14; Jer 26:24; 29:3; 36:9-21; 40:9). For the post-exilic period the Chronicler attests to familial guilds of scribes at Jabez (1 Chr 2:55).[12] Hence we can assume that in Israel, as in New Kingdom Egypt, the special skills and traditions proper to the scribal profession were transmitted from one generation to the next through an apprenticeship system.[13]

---

[9] Cf. Crenshaw, "Education in Ancient Israel," 605-606.

[10] On the ambiguity of the archaeological evidence, see Lemaire, "Sagesse et écoles," 277-78. Lemaire believes a school structure can be identified at Kuntillet ʿAjrûd (*Les écoles et la formation de la Bible dans l'ancien Israél* 30, 52). The room which he interprets as a classroom, however, is regarded by the excavators as a cultic storeroom (Z. Meshel, "Kuntillet ʿAjrûd, 1975-1976," *IEJ* 27 (1977) 52-53; and "Kuntillet ʿAjrûd, A Religious Center from the Time of the Judean Monarchy on the Sinai Border," *Israel Museum* [Jerusalem: 1978; Hebrew] catalogue no. 175); cf. N. Shupak, "The 'Sitz im Leben' of the Book of Proverbs in the Light of a Comparison of Biblical and Egyptian Wisdom Literature," *RB* 94 (1987) 103.

[11] This Shisha is to be identified with the שִׁיָא (Kethib) or שָׁוָא (Qere) of 2 Sam 20:25 and the שַׁוְשָׁא of 1 Chr 18:16. The proper name of David's secretary appears actually to have been Seraiah; for the origin of the variants see below.

[12] Cf. R. N. Whybray, *The Intellectual Tradition in the Old Testament* (BZAW 135; Berlin: de Gruyter, 1974) 38; A. Demsky, "Education in the Biblical Period," *Encyclopaedia Judaica* (Jerusalem: Keter, 1971) 6, col. 392; Golka, "Die israelitische Weisheitsschule," 263.

[13] On the likelihood of apprenticeship education in ancient Israel, cf. R. N. Whybray, *The Intellectual Tradition in the Old Testament*, 38-39; P. Nel, "The Concept 'Father' in the Wisdom Literature of the Ancient Near East," *JNWSL* 5

Scribal training is likely to have been less highly developed in Israel than in Egypt. The Hebrew script was easier to learn than the Egyptian (and Mesopotamian) writing systems.[14] W. Albright maintained that the Hebrew alphabet could be learned in one or two days by the brightest students, one or two weeks by the slowest.[15] B. Lang's less sanguine estimate of one to two years for mastery of the writing system may be closer to the mark.[16] Still, the simplicity of the 22-letter alphabet, compared to the hundreds of signs necessary for hieroglyphic and cuneiform writing, must have made basic writing skills easier to acquire. Elementary literacy training could easily have been accomplished in a private setting—no schools were necessary for this. Such rudimentary training would have been adequate for local scribes, such as those whose products may have been found, for example, at Izbet Sarta and Kuntilat ʿAjrud. Even at higher levels, the Jerusalem scribal bureaucracy would not have compared in size and complexity to the administrative network of the late Egyptian empire. The Judean court administered a smaller domain than that of the Egyptian New Kingdom.

(1977) 60–61; and F. Golka, "Die israelitische Weisheitsschule," 265. There is no need to assume that scribal offices were controlled exclusively by hereditary principles. New recruits might be admitted to the profession regardless of their parentage, under a "Magister-Famulus" system in which the supervisor acted *in loco parentis* to the apprentice. Hence the use of familial language for instruction, especially the reference to the teacher as father and the student as son (Prov 1:8; 2:1; 3:1; 4:1; 5:1; 6:1; 7:1), even when there was no blood kinship. This is comparable to the usage in Egypt from the Old Kingdom on which was examined in part one of this study.

[14] On the relative ease of learning the Hebrew script as opposed to the Egyptian writing system, cf. H. Brunner, "Die Methode des Anfängerunterrichts im alten Ägypten und ihre Bedeutung," in *Erziehung zur Menschlichkeit: Die Bildung im Umbruch der Zeit*; fs. E. Spranger (Tübingen: Max Niemeyer, 1957) 210.

[15] *City Invincible: A Symposium on Urbanization and Cultural Development in the Ancient Near East*; ed. C. H. Kraeling and R. M. Adams (Chicago: University of Chicago Press, 1960) 120; cf. A. R. Millard, "The Practice of Writing in Ancient Israel," *BA* 35 (1972) 102–103; M. Smith, "On the Differences Between the Culture of Israel and the Major Cultures of the Ancient Near East," *JNES* 5 (1973) 394; J. Crenshaw, "Education in Ancient Israel," 606.

[16] "Schule und Unterricht im alten Israel," *La Sagesse de l'Ancien Testament* (BETL 51; ed. M. Gilbert; Gembloux: Editions Duculot, 1979) 190. Most present-day teachers of Hebrew would confirm Albright's estimate from their own experience, but they generally teach adults who are already literate. A better comparison would be to primary grade school children who must learn the mechanics and meaning of writing at the same time.

Judean royal scribes, however, would have required special training for foreign correspondence, trade, and diplomacy. This would have included Akkadian and Egyptian in addition to regional dialects, especially Aramaic and Phoenician.[17] Thus, foreign literatures were probably cultivated in the select circles of the Jerusalem court, and perhaps also in a few other major cities such as Lachish and Gezer. In particular, the Instruction literature of Egypt and Mesopotamia seems to have been adapted for training Hebrew scribes in an apprenticeship system.

There are two avenues through which the Egyptian texts might have reached Hebrew scribes at an early date. A first possibility is the mediation of Egyptian literature *via* Canaanite culture; the second is that Hebrew scribes in the early monarchic court had direct access to Egyptian Instruction texts. We will consider each of these in turn.

Pre-Israelite Canaan

The extension of Egyptian imperial control into Syro-Palestine in the Late Bronze Age had considerable cultural impact.[18] Although Akkadian was the *lingua franca* of the age, the Amarna correspondence demonstrates that Egyptian-speaking scribes were active in Canaanite urban centers.[19] W. Helck shows that a significant number of Egyptian officers (e.g., diplomats, physicians) were in foreign service throughout the Empire during the New Kingdom period.[20] The narrative of Wen-Amun mentions Egyptian officers who were sent to Byblos and

---

[17] For evidence, see A. Demsky and M. Bar Ilan, "Writing in Ancient Israel and Early Judaism," *Mikra: Text, Translation, Reading and Interpretation of the Hebrew Bible in Ancient Judaism and Early Christianity* (ed. M. J. Mulder; Philadelphia: Fortress/Assen-Maastricht: Van Gorcum, 1988) 14; E. Ullendorff, "The Knowledge of Languages in the Old Testament," *BJRL* 44 (1962) 455–65.

[18] See W. Helck, *Die Beziehungen Ägyptens zu Vorderasien im 3. und 2. Jahrtausend v. Chr.*, 608–14; R. Giveon, *The Impact of Egypt on Canaan: Iconographical and Related Studies* (OBO 20; Göttingen: Vandenhoeck & Ruprecht, 1978); J. M. Weinstein, "The Egyptian Empire in Palestine: A Reassessment." *BASOR* 241 (1981) 1–28; S. Israelit-Groll, "The Egyptian Administrative System in Syria and Palestine in the 18th Dynasty," *Fontes atque Pontes: Studien zu Geschichte, Kultur und Religion Ägyptens und des Alten Testaments, Festgabe H. Brunner*, 334–42 (ed. M. Görg, Ägypten und Altes Testament 5; Wiesbaden: O. Harrassowitz, 1983).

[19] W. F. Albright, "The Egyptian Correspondence of Abimilki, Prince of Tyre," *JEA* 23 (1937) 190–203.

[20] *Die Beziehungen Ägyptens zu Vorderasien im 3. und 2. Jahrtausend v. Chr.*, 466–68.

resided there for 17 years before they died.[21] The New Kingdom Egyptian Instruction of Any refers to the teaching of Egyptian language to foreigners, including Syro-Palestinians:

> One teaches the Nubian to speak Egyptian,
> The Syrian and other strangers too.[22]

It is therefore plausible that Egyptian wisdom traditions could have been cultivated in the Canaanite cities and subsequently inherited by the literati of the Jerusalem court, either in Egyptian language or translated already into Semitic. I. Grumach surmises that the hypothetical *Alte Lehre* upon which the Instruction of Amenemope is based was composed in the 14th century BCE, around the time of the Edict of Haremhab, and mediated through Canaanite culture to the Hebrew Proverbs. Grumach compares this to the process by which the Amarna Hymn to the Aten is presumed to have entered the stock of Canaanite hymnody before assuming its Israelite form in Psalm 104.[23] Although I am skeptical of the existence of the *Alte Lehre*, Grumach's picture of cultural relations and literary influence from Egypt to Canaan in the Late Bronze Age is plausible. M. V. Fox discusses the possibility of a similar process to account for the influence of Egyptian love poetry upon the Song of Songs.[24] There is ample evidence of the familiarity of scribes at Ugarit with Akkadian and Hurrian didactic literature.[25] One would expect that, in the two centuries after the destruction of Ugarit, the educated class of other principal Canaanite urban centers would have had similar familiarity with the Egyptian didactic texts, and that the tradition could then have been inherited by the Israelite successors to the Canaanite city-states.

---

[21] Wen-Amun 2,51–52; Lichtheim, *AEL* 2.228.

[22] Epilogue to the Instruction of Any: Lichtheim, *AEL*, 2.144.

[23] *Untersuchungen zur Lebenslehre des Amenope*, 6; cf. Hermisson, *Studien zur israelitischen Spruchweisheit*, 115–16.

[24] *The Song of Songs and the Ancient Egyptian Love Songs* (Madison: University of Wisconsin Press, 1985) xxiv, 190–93.

[25] A complete review of the materials is provided by L. R. Mack-Fisher, "A Survey and Reading Guide to the Didactic Literature of Ugarit: Prolegomenon to a Study on the Sage," 67–80; and "The Scribe (and Sage) in the Royal Court at Ugarit," 109–115; *The Sage in Israel and the Ancient Near East* (ed. J. G. Gammie and L. G. Perdue; Winona Lake, Indiana: Eisenbrauns, 1990). See also in *Ras Shamra Parallels* 2 (ed. L. R. Fisher; Analecta Orientalia 50; Rome: Pontifical Biblical Institute, 1975) the following studies: D. E. Smith, "Wisdom Genres in RS 22.439," 215–47; J. Khanjian, "Wisdom," 371–400.

The United Monarchy

The second possibility, that Hebrew scribes under the United Monarchy had direct access to Egyptian Instruction texts, is even more likely. Close diplomatic relations were established between the United Monarchy and the Egyptian 21st dynasty (1069-945 BCE). This is reflected by the diplomatic marriage between Solomon and the daughter of Pharaoh (Siamun, 978-959 BCE), which is attested by five independent passages in 1 Kings (3:1; 7:8; 9:16,24; 11:1).[26] The administration of the united monarchy was modelled after the late Egyptian bureaucracy, with the highest offices under David and Solomon imitating Egyptian prototypes. The bearer of the Hebrew title סֹפֵר הַמֶּלֶךְ, "royal secretary," performed the duties of the New Kingdom Egyptian sš šʿt (n) nśw n pr-ʿꜣ, "royal letter-writer of Pharaoh"; the title and office of מַזְכִּיר, "royal herald," is patterned after Egyptian wḥmw, "herald"; and the Hebrew אֲשֶׁר עַל הַבַּיִת, "house minister," corresponds to the Egyptian mr pr wr, "high steward".[27] It

---

[26] A. Malamat, *Das davidische und salomonische Königsreich und seine Beziehungen zu Ägypten und Syrien* (Österreichische Akademie der Wissenschaften Philosophisch-historische Klasse Sitzungsberichte 407; Vienna: Verlag der Österreichschen Akademie der Wissenschaften, 1983) 21; cf. A. R. Green, "Solomon and Siamon: A Synchronism between Dynastic Israel and the Twenty-First Dynasty of Egypt," *JBL* 97 (1978) 353-67. For other accounts of relations between the United Monarchy and the Egyptian Tanite dynasties, see the earlier studies of Malamat: "The Kingdom of David and Solomon in its Contact with Egypt and Aram Naharaim," *BA* 21 (1958) 96-102; "Aspects of the Foreign Policies of David and Solomon," *JNES* 22 (1963) 1-17; "A Political Look at the Kingdom of David and Solomon and its Relations with Egypt," *Studies in the Period of David and Solomon and Other Essays: Papers Read at the International Symposium for Biblical Studies, Tokyo, 5-7 December, 1979* (ed. T. Ishida; Winona Lake, Indiana: Eisenbrauns, 1982) 189-204; and also D. B. Redford, "Studies in Relations Between Palestine and Egypt During the First Millennium B. C. I. The Taxation System of Solomon," *Studies on the Ancient Palestinian World* (ed. J. W. Wevers and D. B. Redford; Toronto: University of Toronto, 1972) 141-56; Alberto R. Green, "Israelite Influence at Shishak's Court?" *BASOR* 233 (1979) 59-62.

[27] Cf. R. de Vaux, "Titres et fonctionnaires égyptiens à la cour de David et de Salomon," *RB* 48 (1939) 394-405; J. Begrich, "Sofer und Mazkir. Ein Beitrag zur inneren Geschichte des davidisch-salomonischen Grossreiches und des Königsreiches Juda," *ZAW* 58 (1940-41) 1-29; T. Mettinger, *Solomonic State Officials: A Study of the Civil Government Officials of the Israelite Monarchy* (CB OT Series 5; Lund: Gleerup, 1971) 25-110.

is also likely that the Hebrew רֵעַ הַמֶּלֶךְ, "friend of the king," is related to the Egyptian title *rḫ nśwt*, "king's acquaintance".[28] The new administration in Jerusalem may have employed Egyptian personnel. This would be in keeping with the general pattern of Egyptians in service at other foreign courts during the period. There are textual indications that David may have appointed a native Egyptian as his personal secretary. The variant designations of David's secretary Seraiah (שִׁישָׁא, 1Kgs 4:3; שִׁיא (Kethib) and שְׁוָא (Qere), 2 Sam 20:25; שַׁוְשָׁא, 1 Chr 18:16) are best explained as corruptions of the Egyptian title *sš šʿt*, "correspondence secretary".[29] T. Mettinger sees a number of indications that Seraiah himself may have been Egyptian: (1) he apparently bore the Egyptian title, *sš šʿt*; (2) his Hebrew name can be understood as a Yahwist adaptation of Egyptian names such as *sr*, *srw*, *sry*; (3) he appears to have given one of his sons, Eliho[re]p, a name with the Egyptian theophoric element *ḥp* = Apis.[30]

During the tenth century BCE, as contacts between Egypt and Israel multiplied, the Instruction of Amenemope found increasing circulation in Egypt. As we saw in chapter II, although Amenemope was written under the later Ramesside rulers, the chronological distribution of fragments of Amenemope suggests that the text came into widespread use during the 21st and 22nd dynasties. Thus the Instruction of Amenemope became a standard text in Egyptian scribal education during the period roughly of Solomon's alliance with Siamun (978–959 BCE) and the later interventions of Shoshenq I (945–924 BCE) into Israelite and Judean affairs (1 Kgs 11:40; 14:25–26). This was probably the period during which the text was transmitted to Judean scribal circles. In Jerusalem Amenemope would have entered the Hebrew Instruction tradition which finally would be incorporated into the Hebrew Proverbs. At this early stage, the social location of the Egyptian and Hebrew tradents would have been comparable.

---

[28] Mettinger, *Solomonic State Officials*, 63–69; cf. de Vaux, "Titres et fonctionnaires égyptiens," 403–405.

[29] A. Cody, "Le titre égyptien et le nom propre du scribe de David," *RB* 72 (1965) 381–393; T. Mettinger, *Solomonic State Officials*, 27–29.

[30] R. de Vaux compares this to the names בנחף and יתנחף from Elephantine ("Titres et fonctionnaires égyptiens," 399). The original name אליחף, witnessed by the LXX readings ελιαφ and ελιαβ, has been altered to a pejorative אליחרף in the MT, similar to the alteration of the theophoric element of Baʿal names to בשת (e.g. 2 Sam 3:14–15; 1 Chr 8:33; *Solomonic State Officials*, 29–30).

The Divided Monarchy

Assuming that Egyptian materials, including the Instruction of Amenemope, had entered the Hebrew tradition by the end of the tenth century, what was the social location and function of these traditions after the division of the kingdoms? How were literacy, scribalism, and education related to one another between 922 and 587 BCE? Our approach to these questions is facilitated by the recent work of D. W. Jamieson-Drake, *Scribes and Schools in Monarchic Judah: A Socio-Archeological Approach.*[31] Jamieson-Drake seeks to place the conventional biblical and epigraphic evidence for scribes and schools into a broader socio-archeological framework, charting the organization of the Judean state through the period of the divided monarchy. He defines scribes as "professional administrators," shifting the focus from their literacy to the question of the utilization of their skills toward larger socio-political purposes.[32] The archaeological analysis conducted by Jamieson-Drake is based on a comprehensive survey of settlement patterns, public works, and luxury items for Judean sites from the twelfth through the sixth centuries BCE.

The survey of these factors points to limited regional administrative control of Judah before the eighth century. From this point on, however, settlement patterns and public works converge with the distribution of luxury items to indicate a rapidly developing system of administration, tied to Jerusalem in every facet. Evidence for writing is limited to sites directly dependent, administratively or militarily, upon the capital. Jamieson-Drake concludes:

> It could hardly be a coincidence that every site outside Jerusalem containing direct evidence of writing was to some degree administratively dependent upon Jerusalem. The conclusion to which this evidence points is that professional administrators were trained in Jerusalem, and only
> in Jerusalem.[33]

Even local, nonprofessional examples of writing, Jamieson-Drake finds, are restricted to sites with dependence upon Jerusalem. Outside the professional administrative class, there was at no time during the monarchic period widespread literacy among the Judean population.

---

[31] (Social World of Biblical Antiquity Series 9; Sheffield: JSOT, 1991).

[32] *Scribes and Schools in Monarchic Judah*, 8.

[33] *Scribes and Schools in Monarchic Judah*, 148.

If Jamieson-Drake's analysis is correct, then we can assume that up until the time of the Exile, the international Instruction materials which were eventually incorporated into Proverbs remained the property of a closely defined professional class.[34] The key transformation of the social location and function of the Hebrew Instruction material occurred in the shift from the monarchic to the post-exilic period. This entailed the virtual elimination of the professional scribal class that had been connected to the Judean royal administration. The broader social and economic circumstances were radically changed as well. We may now examine these circumstances more closely.

ACHAEMENID JUDAH AS THE SETTING OF PROVERBS[35]

Throughout the biblical period, the Judean economy was based fundamentally on agriculture, despite the indispensable role of crafts and commerce in the urban centers.[36] In late pre-exilic Judah land was held, on the one hand, by the state (including extensive royal properties and perhaps also some temple lands), and, on the other hand, by agnatic collectives (extended families), both lay and priestly.[37]

---

[34] Cf. especially the following studies in *Congress Volume: Jerusalem 1986* (VTSup 40; Leiden: E. J. Brill, 1988): M. Haran, "On the Diffusion of Literacy and Schools in Ancient Israel," 81–95; E. Lipiński, "Royal and State Scribes in Ancient Jerusalem," 157–64; E. Puech, "Les écoles dans l'Israel préexilique: données épigraphiques," 189–203.

[35] The present section draws on work prepared in collaboration with Prof. Ben C. Ollenburger in connection with a work-in-process on "Third Isaiah and the Post-exilic Temple Economy."

[36] Note especially Ezek 27:12–25, a description of Tyre's commercial empire. According to this text, Tarshish brought precious metals to Tyre, the Ionians traded in bronze vessels, Rhodes payed with ivory and ebony, and Edom traded in precious stones and manufactured goods (embroidery and linen); but Judah and Israel dealt only in "wheat, olives and early figs, honey, oil, and balm" (v 17). As H. Kreissig says, "the cities of Judah, even Jerusalem, were agricultural cities" (*Die sozialökonomische Situation in Juda zur Achämenidenzeit* [Schriften zur Geschichte und Kultur des Alten Orients 7; Berlin: Akademie-Verlag, 1973] 64). For post-exilic Judah, S. Talmon maintains "the existence of a substantial rural class with agricultural interests," not the "landless urbanized citizenry as Weber surmised" ("The Emergence of Jewish Sectarianism in the Early Second Temple Period," *Ancient Israelite Religion: Essays in Honor of Frank Moore Cross* [eds. P. D. Miller, Jr., Paul D. Hanson, and S. Dean McBride; Philadelphia: Fortress, 1987] 597).

[37] J. Weinberg, "Die Agrarverhältnisse in der Bürger-Tempel-Gemeinde der Achämenidenzeit," *Wirtschaft und Gesellschaft im Alten Vorderasien* (ed. J.

This arrangement was disrupted by the Babylonian conquest and deportations. Estimates of the total number of deportees differ, and probably always will, due to the conflicting biblical reports (cf. 2 Kgs 24:12, 14–16; 25:11, 18–20; Jer 24:1; 39:9; 52:10, 15, 25–30).[38] However, it is generally agreed that only a relatively small proportion of the total population was removed. Estimates of the ratio of those exiled to those remaining in the land range from 1:8 (Kreissig) to 1:10 (Weinberg).[39]

Archaeological data from exilic Palestine, collected by E. Stern, confirm this picture, showing a marked continuity of material culture between the pre-exilic and exilic periods. Stern reports that from seventy to eighty per cent of all the pottery found in Babylonian Judah conforms to indigenous pre-exilic types.[40] Although the major urban centers were destroyed along with most of southern Judah, many smaller towns and villages continued to be inhabited during the exilic period, especially in the northern part of Judah. Of the sites which were destroyed, many were resettled almost immediately at a cruder

---

Harmatta and G. Komoróczy; Budapest: Akademiai Kiadö, 1976) 473–86, esp. p. 479. For the evidence of pre-exilic temple land holdings, see pp. 476–77. In both sectors much of the labor was done by tenant farmers who possessed no land of their own.

[38] K. Galling estimates that the total of deportees, including women and children, could not have been more than 20,000 (*Studien zur Geschichte Israels im persischen Zeitalter* [Tübingen: Mohr, 1964] 51–52). J. Weinberg's estimate is roughly equivalent ("Demographische Notizen zur Geschichte der nachexilischen Gemeinde in Juda," *KLIO* 54 [1972] 47); S. Talmon suggests a total of 30,000 to 40,000 deportees ("The Emergence of Jewish Sectarianism in the Early Second Temple Period," 595); Kreissig's estimate is somewhat lower: 15,600 (*Die sozialökonomische Situation in Juda zur Achämenidenzeit*, 22). E. Janssen basically accepts tha report of Jer 52:28–30 and assumes a total of 4,600 deportees (*Juda in der Exilszeit* [FRLANT, 69; Göttingen: Vandenhhoeck & Rupprecht, 1956] 35). See W. Schottroff, "Zur Sozialgeschichte Israels in der Perserzeit," *VF* 27 (1982) 49; P. Ackroyd, *Exile and Restoration: A Study of Hebrew Thought of the Sixth Century B. C.* (OTL; Philadelphia: Westminster, 1968) 22–23 n. 24.

[39] Kreissig, *Die sozialökonomische Situation in Juda zur Achämenidenzeit*, 23; Weinberg, "Demographische Notizen zur Geschichte der nachexilischen Gemeinde in Juda," 47.

[40] E. Stern, *Material Culture of the Land of the Bible in the Persian Period, 538–332 BC* (Warminster: Aris and Phillips, 1982) 229; cf. J. Weinberg, "Demographische Notizen zur Geschichte der nachexilischen Gemeinde in Juda," 47 n. 15.

level of technical sophistication.[41]

Even if the deportees were small in number, they were none-theless by Babylonian design the major land-holders of Judah; they included the king and his court, the Jerusalem nobility, and the upper classes of the surrounding settlements as well (2 Kgs 24:12ff., Jer 29:1-2).[42] "None remained except the poorest people of the land" (2 Kgs 24:14). There are indications that the Babylonian regime endowed these "poor peasants, considered incapable of making trouble," with ownership of lands in the countryside where they lived and had formerly worked as tenants.[43] Some may have remained clients, working royal properties under Babylonian supervision (2 Kgs 25:12; Jer 52:16; cf. 40:7),[44] but others seem to have assumed actual possession of the estates which they had formerly worked as sharecroppers (Jer 39:10; Ezek 33:23-29; 11:15).

A cult of some sort must also have survived in exilic Judah, although its precise nature is not known. P. R. Ackroyd surmises that "an improvised or temporary altar" may have been reconstructed on the ruins of the Jerusalem temple during the exile.[45] That must remain uncertain, but according to Jer 41:4-8, eighty people came from Shechem, Shiloh and Samaria bringing offerings and incense to the "house of Yahweh," apparently indicating some form of cultic observance in the Jerusalem temple during the exile. Lam 1:4 might be

---

[41] For example, Gibeon, Geba, Bethel, and Mizpah, were not severely disrupted (J. Weinberg, "Demographische Notizen zur Geschichte der nachexilischen Gemeinde in Juda," 47-48). On the resettlement of other sites see S. Weinberg, "Post-Exilic Palestine: An Archaeological Report," *Proceedings of the Israel Academy of Sciences and Humanities* 4 (1970) 84.

[42] Cf. J. Weinberg, "Die Agrarverhältnisse in der Bürger-Tempel-Gemeinde der Achämenidenzeit," 479.

[43] The quotation is from J. Bright, *A History of Israel* (Philadelphia: Westminster, 3d. edition, 1981) 331. E. Janssen discusses the takeover of land by those left behind during the exile (*Juda in der Exilszeit*, 49-54). Cf. K.-M. Beyse, *Serubbabel und die Königserwartungen der Propheten Haggai und Sacharja* (Stuttgart: Calwer, 1972) 15-16.

[44] J. Weinberg ("Die Agrarverhältnisse in der Bürger-Tempel-Gemeinde der Achämenidenzeit," 408) adduces epigraphic evidence from ʿEn-Gedi to argue that the Judean royal perfume works there continued in operation as a possession of the Babylonian king after 587.

[45] *Exile and Restoration*, 29. On the survival of the cult in Jerusalem during the exile see also F. I. Andersen, "Who Built the Second Temple?" *Australian Biblical Review* 6 (1958) 8; and the additional bibliography cited there.

taken as evidence that priests were waiting for these pilgrims. To the extent that the cult existed during this period, its economic significance was probably minimal.

Meanwhile the exiles, of course, maintained that YHWH had accompanied them to Babylon (e.g., Ezek 1:1–28; 11:16), and when some of them returned under Persian sponsorship to restore the official cult (Ezra 1:1–4), they naturally reasserted their right to the land against those who now occupied it. Such claims to the land are already visible in Ezekiel's polemic against those who stayed in Palestine during the exile (chs. 8; 11:14–21; 33:23–29).[46] Ezekiel quotes those remaining in Judah as saying that "the land has been given to us as a possession" (11:15), in response to which Ezekiel asserts polemically that the land of Israel (אַדְמַת יִשְׂרָאֵל) will be given back to the exiles (11:17; cf. 33:23–29). Thus as members of the golah-community began to return and reestablish themselves, conflict over the land was inevitable.[47]

Even when they succeeded in regaining control of their land, however, the returned exiles faced difficult conditions. The labor supply had been disrupted, the condition of the land was not good, and the growing seasons were bad (cf. Hag 1:10–11; 2:16–19).[48] In fact the drought was probably more catastrophic for the returned exiles than for the Judean peasants who had never left the land. The returned exiles, having grown up or lived in the Tigris-Euphrates valley, where they were sustained by irrigation agriculture, are not likely to have been adept at the traditional strategies of storage and exchange used by Judean farmers to cope with unreliable rainfall in the semi-arid climate of the hill country.[49] These unfavorable conditions are sure to have aggravated tensions over control of the land.

---

[46] W. Zimmerli, "The 'Land' in the Pre-Exilic and Early Post-Exilic Prophets," *Understanding the Word: Essays in Honor of Bernhard W. Anderson* (ed. J. T. Butler, E. W. Conrad, B. C. Ollenburger JSOTSup 37. Sheffield: JSOT, 1985) 247–62, esp. 257.

[47] Weinberg, "Die Agrarverhältnisse in der Bürger-Tempel-Gemeinde der Achämenidenzeit," 479–81.

[48] See Kreissig's assessment of the economic conditions in Judah during the early years of the post-exilic period, *Die sozialökonomische Situation in Juda zur Achämenidenzeit*, 39–56, 101–104.

[49] See C. L. Meyers and E. M. Meyers, *Haggai, Zechariah 1–8*, 28; and D. H. K. Amiran, "Land Use in Israel," *Land Use in Semi-Arid Mediterranean Climates* (Paris: Unesco, 1964) 101–12.

The efforts of the returned exiles to regain control of the land were buttressed by Persian endorsement of their control over the Jerusalem temple (Ezra 1:1-4, 6:1-12, 7:12-26). Ezek 11:15-17 already portrays both the non-deported Judeans and the exiles acknowledging that legal right to the land accrues to those with access to the cult (cf. Lev 25:23).[50] Now as the post-exilic Judean community began to take shape under Persian sponsorship, those who established membership in the temple community likewise secured their land rights.[51] Gradually, perhaps under Darius I, as wide-ranging reorganization was effected throughout the Persian Empire,[52] the returned exiles managed to consolidate their position. They established in Judah what J. Weinberg has called a *Bürger-Tempel-Gemeinde*, or "civic-temple community," a religio-political unit fictively constituted as an agnatic lineage of property-holding men and their families.[53] Membership in the temple community was determined by ostensible descent within a paternal estate (בֵּת אָבוֹת; Ezra 1:5; 2:59 = Neh 7:61; 2:68; 4:2-3; 8:1; 10:16; Neh 7:70-71; 11:13; 12:12, 22, 23).[54] Real property (אֲחֻזָּה,

---

[50] M. Smith, *Palestinian Parties and Politics that Shaped the Old Testament*, 75, 81-82; cf. J. Blenkinsopp, *Ezra-Nehemiah*, 60.

[51] Besides the studies of J. Weinberg cited in this section, see J. Blenkinsopp, *Ezra-Nehemiah*, 69, 83. For comparative evidence from Persian period Babylonia, where hereditary citizenship, cultic participation, and land tenure were linked, see M. Dandamayev, "Babylonia in the Persian Age," *The Cambridge History of Judaism*, vol I, *Introduction; The Persian Period* (eds. W. D. Davies and L. Finkelstein; Cambridge: Cambridge University Press, 1984) 330-31.

[52] For details, see J. M. Cook, *The Persian Empire* (London: J. M. Dent & Sons, 1983) 67-90; A. T. Olmstead, *History of the Persian Empire* (Chicago: University of Chicago Press, 1948) 119-134.

[53] J. P. Weinberg, "Demographische Notizen zur Geschichte der nachexilischen Gemeinde in Juda," *KLIO* 54 (1972) 45-58; "Das *Bēit ʾĀbōt* im 6.-4. Jh. v.u.Z.," *VT* 23 (1973) 400-14; "Der *ʿam hāʾāreṣ* des 6.-4. Jh. v.u.Z.," *KLIO* 56 (1974) 325-35; "Die Agrarverhältnisse in der Bürger-Tempel-Gemeinde der Achämenidenzeit;" in J. Harmatta and G. Komoróczy, eds., *Wirtschaft und Gesellschaft im Alten Vorderasien* (Budapest: Akademiai Kiadö, 1976) 473-86; "Zentral- und Partikulargewalt im achämenidischen Reich," *KLIO* 59 (1976) 24-43. Weinberg's theory is summarized by D. L. Petersen, *Haggai and Zechariah 1-8: A Commentary* (Philadelphia: Westminster, 1984) 30-31; and D. L. Smith, *The Religion of the Landless: The Social Context of the Babylonian Exile* (Bloomington, Indiana: Meyer-Stone, 1989) 106-108. Important criticisms of the *Bürger-Tempel-Gemeinde* model are given by J. Blenkinsopp, "Temple and Society in Achemenid Judah," *Second Temple Studies: 1. Persian Period* (ed. P. R. Davies; JSOTSup 177; Sheffield: JSOT Press, 1991) 22-53.

[54] J. Weinberg, "Das *Bēit ʾĀbōt* im 6.-4. Jh. v.u.Z."

נַחֲלָה Neh 11:3, 20) was distributed according to the divisions of this lineage.[55] Thus in the *Bürger-Tempel-Gemeinde* participation in the temple cult, land tenure, and citizenship were linked under the leadership of the heads of the paternal estates (רָאשֵׁי הָאָבוֹת), who presumably were among the larger property holders of the community.[56] According to Weinberg, this form of polity, which made participation in political and economic affairs dependent upon membership in the cult, was widespread under the Achaemenid empire, in Syria and Phoenicia, Asia Minor, Armenia, and Mesopotamia as well as Palestine.[57]

In Weinberg's view the civic-temple community emerged due to a number of economic factors common to much of the Near East under Persian rule. A general rise in economic productivity, development of monetary means of exchange, intensification of trade, and active urbanization all combined to promote the development of economic sectors outside that controlled by the state.[58] The increasingly commercialized economic environment in post-exilic Judah is evidenced by the appearance of imported ceramics at virtually every excavated site in Judah for the period. Also the types of native jars used for transport of goods, which heretofore had been concentrated along the coast, begin to appear inland in Judah during the post-exilic period, suggesting in K. Hoglund's view that agricultural products were being exported.[59]

In virtually any economic system, as commerce increases fortunes become volatile. We can assume this to have been the case in Achaemenid Judah. H.-G. Kippenberg has argued that the Persian

---

[55] Weinberg, "Die Agrarverhältnisse in der Bürger-Tempel-Gemeinde der Achämenidenzeit," 481–84.

[56] Note the prominence of the רָאשֵׁי הָאָבוֹת in contributing to the rebuilding of the temple and the maintenance of its treasury (Neh. 7:70–71; Ezra 2:68).

[57] "*Bürger-Tempel-Gemeinde*" is Weinberg's German equivalent for the Russian term used by G. Ch. Sarkisjan and I. D. Amussin (J. Weinberg, "Das *Beit ʾĀbōt* im 6.–4. Jh. v.u.Z.," 403 n. 2). It is difficult to render elegantly in English. "Civic-temple community" is the translation given in the English summary of Weinberg's article, "Das Wesen und die functionelle Bestimmung der Listen in 1 Chr 1–9," *ZAW* 93 (1981) 91–114 (see p.114).

[58] Weinberg, "Die Agrarverhältnisse in der Bürger-Tempel-Gemeinde der Achämenidenzeit," 473.

[59] K. Hoglund, "The Achaemenid Context," *Second Temple Studies: 1. Persian Period* (ed. P. Davies; JSOTSup 117; Sheffield: JSOT, 1991) 60–61.

innovation of requiring payment of imperial taxes in silver coinage contributed to economic class differentiation in the provinces. Hoglund doubts that such a requirement was imposed, noting the continuation of in-kind tax payments throughout the Achemenid empire, but both historians agree that the escalated commercial environment led to accumulating of debts, foreclosures, and intra-Judean economic strife. Neh 5 is the prime example of the Jerusalem leadership's attempt to deal with the situation: "We have borrowed money for the king's tax upon our fields," say the Judeans, "we are forcing our sons and our daughters to be slaves, ... for other men have our fields and our vineyards" (5:4–5).

Persian imperial strategy thus was a dominant factor in the shaping of the post-exilic Judean economy. The Persians aimed to maximize economic exploitation (i.e., tribute taking), allowing some degree of political autonomy without restoring the native monarchies of the provinces. The independence of local religious and legal institutions was encouraged.[60] Thus the temple, rebuilt and maintained under Persian authority (Ezra 1:1–4; 6:1–12; 7:12–26), assumed several key functions of the abolished monarchy, endowing the community with a collective identity as well as an economic and administrative center.[61] Prior royal land holdings were absorbed by the collective, so that the previously separable state, temple and private sectors were combined into a single economy.

Although land in this post-exilic civic-temple community was recognized formally as the property of YHWH (Lev 25:23; cf. Neh 9:8, 35, etc.), the Jerusalem temple held little if any land.[62] The real

---

[60] On Persian policy toward local religious-legal institutions, see P. Frei, "Zentralgewalt und Lokalautonomie im Achämenidenreich," *Reichsidee und Reichsorganisation im Perserreich* (ed. P. Frei and K. Koch; OBO 55; Freiburg: Universitätsverlag/Göttingen: Vandenhoeck & Ruprecht, 1984) 7–43.

[61] While Weinberg's model is meant to account for data throughout the Achaemenid empire, the post-exilic Judean community is his chief exemplar since the Hebrew Bible provides for this community the richest supply of documentation ("Die Agrarverhältnisse in der Bürger-Tempel-Gemeinde der Achämenidenzeit," 474; "Zentral- und Partikulargewalt im achämenidischen Reich," 26). M. A. Dandamayev discusses the evidence from Babylon in "Babylonia in the Persian Age," *The Cambridge History of Judaism*, 1.326–42, see esp. pp. 330–31; and "Social Stratification in Babylonia (7th-4th Centuries BC)," *Acta Antiqua* 22: 433–44. On Asia Minor, see J. Balcer, *Sparda by the Bitter Sea: Imperial Interaction in Western Anatolia* (Brown Judaic Studies 52; Chico: Scholars Press, 1984).

[62] For critique of Weinberg's view that there were no temple holdings, see J. Blenkinsopp, "Temple and Society in Achaemenid Judah," 49–50.

basis of the temple economy was the נַחֲלָה/אֲחֻזָּה, or inalienable property of the families who belonged to the collective.[63] The basic social unit within this economy was the בֵּת אָבוֹת "the house of the fathers," or paternal estate (Ezra 1:5; 10:16; Neh 7:70–71)—which functioned as a subordinate agnatic (extended family) collective, holding the land and parcelling it out among its own genealogical divisions.[64]

The members of each paternal estate were required to trace their lineage back to pre-exilic Israelite families. As Weinberg demonstrates, however, considerable dislocations occurred through the course of the exile and return, so that the structure of the post-exilic paternal estates was different from that of the pre-exilic clans.[65] In early pre-exilic Israel, the basic social unit seems to have been the בֵּת אָב, "house of the father" (singular), which consisted of an extended family numbering (by N. Gottwald's estimate) from fifty to one hundred persons.[66] An individual father's house was related to similar neighboring social units through membership in the clan, מִשְׁפָּחָה. The clan was simply an association of the extended family units that composed it, and this clan association was defined by a network of real or fictive kinship relations. The clan was responsible for maintaining and protecting each individual בֵּת אָב on its own property allotment, and for regulating inheritance and dispersal of clan property; i.e., all the landed property

---

[63] According to Weinberg, the studies of M. Dandamayev, G. Ch. Sarkisjan, and A. G. Perichanjan have shown that this is the pattern common to all civic-temple communities of the Achaemenid period, in Mesopotamia, Asia Minor, and Armenia. A high god was acknowledged as owner of the land, while it was in fact divided and used by the members of the community. See Weinberg, "Die Agrarverhältnisse in der Bürger-Tempel-Gemeinde der Achämenidenzeit," 484–85.

[64] The present discussion uses "father's house" for בֵּת אָב and "paternal estate" for בֵּת אָבוֹת. Weinberg uses the Hebrew term בָּתֵּי אָבוֹת to refer to more than one paternal estate, but as J. Scharbert has pointed out such a term is never used in the Hebrew Bible ("*Bēyt ʾāb* als soziologische Grösse im alten Testament," *Von Kanaan bis Kerala* fs. J. P. M. Van der Ploeg [ed. W. C. Delsman et al.; AOAT 21; Neukirchen: Neukirchener Verlag, 1982] 213–227, esp. 234). Granting Scharbert's linguistic point, the term "paternal estates," a translation of בֵּת אָבוֹת suggested by R. J. Williams (*Hebrew Syntax: An Outline*; 2nd. ed. [Toronto: University of Toronto Press, 1976] #14) is an adequate rendering.

[65] "Das *Bēit ʾĀbōt* im 6.–4. Jh. v.u.Z.," esp. 413.

[66] N. K. Gottwald, *The Tribes of Yahweh: A Sociology of Liberated Israel, 1250–1050 BCE* (Maryknoll: Orbis, 1979) 285; cf. B. Halpern, *The Emergence of Israel in Canaan* (SBLMS 29; Chico: Scholars Press, 1983) 242–3.

in the clan's territory. This meant, of course, that the clan adjudicated disputes between one father's house and another, and generally guided the relations among its member families to their common social and economic benefit.

In the post-exilic texts, the clan (מִשְׁפָּחָה) has lost all importance and the individual father's house (singular) is no longer mentioned. In place of both of them is the paternal estate, the "house of the fathers" (plural, בֵּת אָבוֹת). Thus, in the books of Ezra and Nehemiah, it is the paternal estates which themselves entitle members to participation in the temple cult and its economic administration, as well as to landed property. This signals a fundamental change in social and economic structure. Now the "heads of the fathers' houses" constitute a large middle class that controls all economic matters including the distribution of property, each within his own collective—that is, within the *house* of which he is the principle *father*.

Weinberg holds that the census lists of Neh 7:6–73a and Ezra 2:1–70 contain the names of the paternal estates who belonged to the civic-temple community, probably up to 458/7 BCE. From these lists and the record in Ezra 8:1–14, Weinberg concludes that the average size of the Judean paternal estate during the early Restoration period was comparable to that of similar social units in contemporary Persia, where the average paternal estate comprised ca. 600 adult male members, with subdivisions of approximately 70 members. Our sources are not sufficiently complete or reliable to plot the demographic contours of the civic-temple community as closely as Weinberg attempts to do, but it does seem clear that the early civic-temple community included only a fraction of the whole Judean population.[67] Weinberg's estimates assign membership in the civic-temple community to no more than twenty per cent of the population in Judah prior to the time of Nehemiah.

To summarize: The postexilic community was not, as often assumed, a purely religious association.[68] Under the Persian-sponsored civic-temple community, land tenure, participation in the temple cult, and full citizenship were combined and brought under the umbrella of a genealogical system that defined membership in terms of family

---

[67] For critique of Weinberg's reading of the census lists, see J. Blenkinsopp, "Temple and Society in Achaemenid Judah," 43–44.

[68] Typical of such an approach is the work of H. C. M. Vogt, *Studien zur nachexilischen Gemeinde in Esra-Nehemiah* (Werl: Dietrich-Coeble, 1966).

descent, within the "house of the fathers," and accorded positions of political and economic leadership to the largest landholders. Especially at first, the civic-temple community was narrowly defined, dominated by the families who had returned from Babylonian exile, and excluded large segments of the remaining population of Judah.

This background motivated one of the most striking instances of the post-exilic sages' engagement with economic concerns: the polemic of Prov 1–9 against the "Strange Woman" (אִשָּׁה זָרָה or "Foreign Woman" (נָכְרִיָּה; Prov 2:16–19; 5:1–23; 6:24–35; 7:5–27; cf. also 9:13–18). During the early post-exilic period, when chapters 1–9 were fashioned as an introduction to the book of Proverbs, the אִשָּׁה זָרָה/נָכְרִיָּה represented women who did not belong to the golah-community. Liaisons between Judean men and these "foreign" women posed economic problems: since genealogical lineage, land tenure, and cultic membership were linked in the post-exilic period, the prospect of exogamous marriages brought the danger of outside encroachment upon the land holdings of the Judean congregation.

Thus in Prov 2 the signal warning against the אִשָּׁה זָרָה/נָכְרִיָּה, whose "house sinks down to death" (2:18), is linked with possession of the land. In Prov 5:8–11 involvement with the Strange Woman is associated with the alienation of Judean wealth. The severe penalties of Ezra 10 illumine the sage's warning in Prov 5:14. Stay away from the Strange Woman, he says, lest at the end of your life in weakness and poverty you look back and say: "I was at the point of utter ruin in the assembled congregation" (קָהָל, 5:14). This plight of impoverishment combined with disgrace before the assembly is clearly reminiscent of the punishment stipulated in Ezra 10:8.[69]

Against the social-historical background that has been described here, where are the authors and audience of the Hebrew Proverbs to be located? In most critical discussion the identity of the post-exilic editors of Proverbs has remained understandably vague. The urban setting of Prov 1–9 (e.g., 1:20–21; 8:1–3) suggests Jerusalem, but to identify the class of people in the capital who would have been responsible for preserving the Proverbs is more difficult. R. Murphy surmises that the Proverbs may have been preserved in the post-exilic period by a

---

[69] For further details, see my study, "The Strange Woman (אִשָּׁה זָרָה/נָכְרִיָּה) of Proverbs 1–9 and Post-exilic Judean Society," *Second Temple Studies 2. Temple and Community in the Persian Period* (ed. T. C. Eskenazi and K. H. Richards; JSOTSup; Sheffield: JSOT, forthcoming).

"scribal (lay) class," without suggesting what their function in society might have been.[70] The professional scribal class of the Judean monarchy which had cultivated the international wisdom literature has all but disappeared under Achaemenid domination. Others have suggested that the post-exilic sages were attached to the Jerusalem temple.[71] The slight acknowledgment of the cult in Proverbs, however, makes a priestly editor very unlikely.[72]

It is clear that the social location and educational aims of the final editors of Proverbs were different from those of the Judean scribes who first brought international Instruction into contact with Hebrew proverbial wisdom.[73] The post-exilic civic-temple community placed two classes of people at the head of society, the priestly leadership of the temple and the lay heads of paternal estates. It becomes quickly apparent from an examination of Proverbs that the text presupposes a community whose profile coincides with the leading members of the post-exilic בֵּת אָבוֹת. They are educated, comprising especially in the early decades of the Restoration the descendants of the Judean elite who were deported to Babylon. They possess an ancient literary and didactic heritage, but apply it toward no professional end. The family metaphor becomes the dominant reference for the educational context. Despite their urban sophistication they are engaged in agriculture and combine practical farming advice with elegant poetic figures from the world of agriculture. These post-exilic sages were concerned with the education of a broader laity. Thus when instruction which was rooted originally in scribal training found wider application in the post-exilic community, elements specific to the scribal professional class were no longer pertinent.

---

[70] *Wisdom Literature: Job, Proverbs, Ruth, Canticles, Ecclesiastes, and Esther*, 8.

[71] E.g., Hermisson, *Studien zur israelitischen Spruchweisheit*, 131–2; Mettinger, *Solomonic State Officials*, 145.

[72] Cf. L. Perdue, *Wisdom and Cult: A Critical Analysis of the Views of Cult in the Wisdom Literature of Israel and the Ancient Near East* (SBLDS 30; Missoula, Montana: Scholars Press, 1977) 142–165.

[73] On the literary and teaching activity of this period see A. Demsky, "Education in the Biblical Period," col. 384; M. Fishbane, *Biblical Interpretation in Ancient Israel*, 36–37, 107–13; and J. L. Kugel, *Early Biblical Interpretation* (Library of Early Christianity 3; Philadelphia: Westminster, 1986) 52–61.

ATTENUATION OF THE PROFESSIONAL SCRIBAL ORIENTATION
IN THE POST-EXILIC CONTEXT

Before taking up the treatment of the theme of wealth and poverty in Proverbs, it is pertinent to mention briefly a few passages that reflect this crucial change in the social context of the material. For example, the difficult text of Prov 22:21 evidences the reinterpretation of scribal technical terminology into terms accessible to the laity at large: the term קֹשְׁט, orginally a Hebrew form of Egyptian *gśty*, "scribal palette," is now interpreted as the Aramaism, "truth".[74]

A second example is found in the skilled worker of Prov 22:29. Prov 22:29a-b reads:

חָזִיתָ אִישׁ מָהִיר בִּמְלַאכְתּוֹ
לִפְנֵי־מְלָכִים יִתְיַצָּב

Do you see one who is skillful in his work?
He will stand before kings.

Gressmann first noted the parallel verse in Amen 27.16–17:

The scribe who is skillful in his office,
He is found worthy to be a courtier.[75]

Most commentators take Prov 22:29 as a reference to the scribal office in pre-monarchic Israel. W. McKane, for example, comments:

There is no doubt that here is a case where the vocational character of the Egyptian Instruction is preserved in the biblical book of Proverbs.[76]

Since the verse belongs to the Words of the Wise (22:27–24:22), where the influence of Amenemope is especially prominent, it is indeed hard to deny that the verse derives from Amenemope 27.16–17, with its explicit reference to the scribal profession. If this is the case, however, it is extraordinary that the Hebrew writer has not used the

---

[74] I have set forth the details in an unpublished paper "An Unrecognized Egyptian Loan Word in Prov 22:21: BH קֹשְׁט, 'Truth' < Egyptian *gśty*, 'Scribal Palette'."

[75] "Die neugefundene Lehre des Amen-em-ope und die vorexilische Spruchdichtung Israels," *ZAW* n.s. 1 (1924) 276. For the form of v. 29a, cf. Prov 29:20, חָזִיתָ אִישׁ אָץ בִּדְבָרָיו Gressmann deletes חָזִיתָ because it has no equivalent in Amenemope and LXX, but the Targum supports MT. Oesterley deletes חָזִיתָ here but retains it at 29:20.

[76] *Proverbs: A New Approach*, 380.

expression סוֹפֵר מָהִיר, the obvious translation one would expect for the Egyptian *sš iw=f šs3 m-i3wt=f*, "a scribe skilled in his office." The appellation סוֹפֵר מָהִיר is a stock phrase in biblical Hebrew.[77] The best example is Ps 45:2: "my tongue is like the pen of a skilled scribe" (סוֹפֵר מָהִיר).[78] A later and extended use of the phrase is Ezra 7:6, where Ezra is designated a "scribe skilled in the law of Moses" (סֹפֵר מָהִיר בְּתוֹרַת מֹשֶׁה). Ahiqar bears the title ספר מהיר בתורת משה. Gressmann proposed emending the text, inserting ספר in agreement with Egyptian *sš*. But in this case the difference between the Hebrew and Egyptian versions of the saying is significant. By the time Proverbs was completed, the material no longer served the training of scribes; it was applied to the education of a much broader laity. While the saying likely had a professional scribal application in the pre-monarchic period, the original reference to a skilled scribe is now broadened to refer in general to people who are capable at their crafts. The reference to kings in v. 29b, לִפְנֵי־מְלָכִים יִתְיַצָּב, has little relevance in the post-exilic context. Thus, although the context calls for a two-line saying, a third is added:

בַּל־יִתְיַצֵּב לִפְנֵי חֲשֻׁכִּים

he will not stand before obscure people.

Commentators often delete v. 29c as an intrusive gloss. It is, however, a prime example of the adaptation of earlier scribal instruction materials by post-exilic editors.

A final example of this development is the emphasis in Proverbs upon the mother and father as the source of wisdom. As we saw in part one, traditionally in the Egyptian scribal Instruction, the teacher

---

[77] The Egyptian counterpart, *sš iw=f šs3 m-i3wt=f*, "a scribe skilled in his office," seems also to have been a standard formula. It occurs in Amenemope 1.13 as a designation of Amenemope. The Egyptian title *sš m-hr* in Papyrus Anastasi I, however, is not related (against Gressmann, "Die neugefundene Lehre des Amen-em-ope und die vorexilische Spruchdichtung Israels," 295; cf. W. McKane, *Prophets and Wise Men* [SBT 44; London: SCM, 1965] 30–33; A. F. Rainey, "The Soldier-Scribe in Papyrus Anastasi I," *JNES* 26 [1967] 58–60; A. R. Schulman, "Mhr and mskb, Two Egyptian Military Titles of Semitic Origin," *ZÄS* 93 [1966] 123–32). Papyrus Anastasi I 17,7 does contain a similar phrase as a loan from Semitic: *su-p[ ]-r ya-di-ʿa*=סופר יודע, "a knowledgeable scribe".

[78] M. Dahood compares to this the Punic PN *bn mhrbʿl spr*, "son of Mahirbaʿal, the scribe" (*Psalms* [AB 16; Garden City, N.Y.: Doubleday, 1966] 1.271).

addresses the student as "my son". There were cases, especially in the Old Kingdom, of actual father-son instruction, but in the Egyptian wisdom tradition the address "my son" became a purely literary formula, and "son" (or plural, "children"), simply designated students. Numerous texts make clear that in the educational setting this usage does not refer to natural offspring.

In the Hebrew Instruction this literary form is taken up and the address "my son" appears frequently. Very often in Prov 1-9 and five times in Prov 22:17-24:22 we find this address. But unique to the biblical material is the mention of the mother as well as the father as a source of wisdom. For example, Prov 1:8: "Hear, my son, your father's instruction, and reject not your mother's teaching." Nothing like this appears in the Egyptian Instruction tradition (cf. Prov 4:1-3; 6:20; 10:1; 15:20; and 31:1, the instruction of Lemuel's mother).

In Prov 23:22-25, between two passages which open with the address to "my son," we have a text which associates the mother and father together with the acquisition of wisdom:

> Hearken to your father who begot you,
> and do not despise your mother when she is old
> [or, "for she is an elder"] ...
> Acquire wisdom, instruction, and understanding ...
> let your father and mother be glad.

C. Camp relates the association of wisdom with the mother to the post-exilic period, when family values and education at the home became more important after the collapse of the monarchy and its institutions.[79] Camp maintains that these appeals to the mother as sage are grounded in post-exilic social reality:

> The final level of redaction that is evident in 1:8; 6:20; 23:22-25 and 31:10-31 all include the mother's instruction along with or even, in the case of 31:26, in place of the home setting. This probably indicates a home setting for this instruction. Even if the book were used in an extra-familial instructional setting in the post-exilic period, those instructors had as one of their explicit goals the inculcation of family values as the basis for a workable social organization. This goal has taken complete precedence in the final composition over whatever diplomatic training for which the book may previously have been used, even though traces of the latter still remain (cf. 23:1-3).[80]

---

[79] Camp draws here on R. Albertz's portrayal of familial piety during the post-exilic period, *Persönliche Frömmigkeit und offizielle Religion: Religionsinterner Pluralismus in Israel und Babylon* (Calwer Theologische Monographien, Reihe A, 9; Stuttgart: Calwer, 1978).

Here wisdom instruction, associated with the parents and family, is no longer restricted to a professional class, but inculcates values essential to the broader community. As we turn to the theme of wealth and poverty in the Hebrew Proverbs, we will see that much of the diversity in views of this topic results from the combination of teachings from the international scribal Instruction tradition with native Hebrew folk wisdom on wealth and poverty.

---

[80] Camp, *Wisdom and the Feminine in the Book of Proverbs*, 251-52.

IX
WEALTH AND POVERTY IN THE BOOK OF PROVERBS

THE FOLK TRADITION

Scholars have long held that some of the Hebrew Proverbs are of folk origin, far removed from the professional scribal circles where international wisdom was cultivated in Israel. The frequency with which characters in Hebrew narrative invoke traditional sayings (e.g., 1 Sam 24:14; 2 Sam 20:18; Judg 8:2, 21), and the ability of the prophets to invoke proverbs (e.g., Ezek 18:2=Jer 31:29; Hos 8:7, cf. Prov 22:8) suggest that proverbial expressions circulated at large in Israelite society, not just among the students of scribal didactic literature.

Since proverbial expressions about wealth and poverty are found in the traditional wisdom of virtually every culture whose folklore has been recorded,[1] we can assume that the folk wisdom of ancient Israel addressed this topic. It is difficult, however, to determine which of the sayings about wealth and poverty in the book of Proverbs may have originated in folk wisdom. To date there has been no real success, by form-critical or other means, in isolating the folk material in Proverbs.

O. Eissfeldt established the distinction between the "folk pro-

---

[1] This is visible at a glance in the proverb compendium of S. G. Champion, *Racial Proverbs: A Selection of the World's Proverbs arranged Linguistically* (New York: Macmillan, 1938; see the subject index, pp. 688–91).

verb" (*Volkssprichwort*), and the "wisdom saying" (*Weisheitsspruch*).[2] In the book of Proverbs, Eissfeldt identifies as folk proverbs the first lines of verses which occur elsewhere in the book with different second lines (e.g., 10:15a=18:11a; 14:31a=17:5a), arguing that these single-line sayings are stylistically primitive folk proverbs, elaborated into wisdom sayings by the addition of a second parallel colon.[3]

There is, however, no reason to assume, as Eissfeldt does, that variant second lines indicate the existence of an original one-line saying. Doublets can just as easily be alternate versions of two-line sayings. Even if original one-line sayings do lie behind some of the doublets in Proverbs, this does not necessarily mean that they can be assigned to a folk origin. Eissfeldt's evolutionary model of the development of the sophisticated wisdom saying out of the short, crude folk saying depends on the form-critical assumption that shorter units must be older. This principle can no longer be upheld in general, and has been shown to be false regaring the development of wisdom genres in particular.[4] Eissfeldt's other criteria for identifying folk proverbs concern sayings outside the book of Proverbs, so they are of no help here.[5]

R. B. Y. Scott has attempted systematically to compare Hebrew folk proverbs with the folk wisdom of ancient Egypt and Mesopotamia.[6] He proposes seven "idea patterns" or "proverb idioms" for the classification of ancient Near Eastern folk wisdom. These include the following categories: (1) "identity, equivalence, or

---

[2] *Der Maschal im Alten Testament* (BZAW 24; Giessen: A. Toepelmann, 1913) 12–13.

[3] *Der Maschal im Alten Testament*, 45–46.

[4] The basic study, demonstrating from the Egyptian material that literary units of extended length are ancient, is C. Bauer-Kayatz, *Studien zu Proverbien 1–9: Eine form- und motivgeschichtliche Untersuchung unter Einbeziehung Ägyptischen Vergleichsmaterials* (WMANT 22; Neukirchen: Neukirchener, 1966). See also on this question McKane, *Proverbs: A New Approach*, 4; and the R. Murphy's criticism of Eissfeldt: "The Interpretation of Old Testament Wisdom Literature," *Int* 23 (1969) 289–301; and "Wisdom Theses," *Wisdom and Knowledge*, fs. J. Papin, 2 vols. (ed. J. Armenti; Philadelphia: Villanova University, 1976) 2:194; and H. J. Hermisson, *Studien zur israelitischen Spruchweisheit*, 46–49.

[5] Eissfeldt identifies as folk proverbs: (1) sayings which are designated as מָשָׁל in the text of Hebrew narrative or prophecy (e.g., 1 Sam 10:12; Ezek 12:22); (2) sayings introduced by "and therefore they say," or a similar formula (e.g., Gen 10:9; Isa 40:27); and (3) passages which "sound like proverbs" (e.g., Judg 8:2; Jer 12:13). See *Der Maschal im Alten Testament*, 45–46.

[6] "Folk Proverbs of the Ancient Near East," *Transactions of the Royal Society of Canada* 55 (1961) 47–56; repr. in *SAIW* 417–26.

invariable association;" (2) "contrast, non-identity, paradox;" (3) "similarity, analogy, typology;" (4) "contrary to order, futile, absurd;" (5) "proverbs which classify and characterize persons, actions or situations;" (6) "value, lack of value, relative value, proportion or degree;" and (7) "cause and consequence."

Since these classifications combine categories of structure and content they are of little use for form-critical purposes.[7] Scott has, moreover, no reliable way to establish that the ancient Near Eastern sayings he examines are in fact folk wisdom. Biblical folk proverbs, Scott maintains, are "picturesque adages," "short and pithy," as opposed to the school sayings, which are moralistic, show a higher degree of literary development, and have an "air of ponderous authority."[8] The extra-biblical proverbs, however, do not lend themselves to such a contrast. Scott seems to assume that all proverbs in the Egyptian and Mesopotamian sources are of folk origin. Some of these ancient Near Eastern sayings, included by Scott in his classifications, are patently not folk wisdom; they are the specific property of scribal students. For example, Scott cites the "metaphor of parenthood" as a special type of his seventh class, the "cause and consequence" idiom. His only example of this type is a Babylonian saying, "The scribal art is the mother of orators and the father of scholars."[9] This saying obviously derives from the context of scribal education; if it had folk antecedents, they are now lost. The saying cannot be used to establish the existence of a folk wisdom pattern. Scott's categories do not help distinguish the folk proverbs from the rest of the material in the book of Proverbs.

In his *Studien zur israelitischen Spruchweisheit*, H.-J. Hermisson attempts to reassess the extent of folk material in Proverbs 10–29. Hermisson's view is that most of these proverbs were produced in the "wisdom schools," but his criteria for identifying folk proverbs seem already to reflect this judgment.[10] The main mark of folk origin, according to Hermisson, is the absence of didactic intent. The folk proverb, he maintains, "must draw a conclusion from a sum of experiences, or simply confirm a state of affairs, an 'order', without thereby indicating what someone should or should not do."[11] Thus any

---

[7] C. Fontaine, *Traditional Sayings in the Old Testament: A Contextual Study* (Bible and Literature Series 5; Sheffield: Almond, 1982), 20–21; cf. Fontaine, "Proverb Performance in the Old Testament," *JSOT* 32 (1985) 91.

[8] "Folk Proverbs of the Ancient Near East," *SAIW*, 417–18.

[9] "Folk Proverbs of the Ancient Near East," *SAIW*, 427.

[10] Cf. C. Fontaine, *Traditional Sayings in the Old Testament*, 10–13.

[11] *Studien zur israelitischen Spruchweisheit*, 36.

proverbs which are explicitly didactic must, according to Hermisson, derive from a cultivated didactic setting.

The folklores of other cultures, however, show that the absence of didactic intent is not an appropriate criterion for identifying folk sayings. Folk proverbs often instruct in proper behavior, although usually one must know the situation in which a proverb could be cited in order to describe its didactic application. For example, a folk proverb current among African slaves in the coastal plantations of antebellum South Carolina stated: "Promising talk don't cook rice." The saying derives from a Hausa proverb of the western Sudan: "Chattering doesn't cook the rice."[12] The proverb could be used with didactic intent in variety of ways. It might be cited, for example, to instruct a youth on the necessity of hard work in place of ambitious talk. It could be used to advise someone not to rely on the promises of friend, until they are fulfilled. This sort of proverb usage, in the clan or family setting, is a likely background for many Hebrew wisdom sayings.[13] The presence of didactic import is not a dividing line between folk and school wisdom.

Also according to Hermisson, a certain "profundity and complexity of thought" shows that many Hebrew proverbs (e.g., 14:10; 14:12; 14:13; 19:3; 22:2), could not have originated among the folk.[14] Since folk wisdom, in Hermisson's view, gives prosaic, simple-minded reports of the result of everyday experience, any saying which presupposes the ability to engage in critical reflection must be the product of a more educated class.

To gauge the depth of thought embodied in a proverb, however, is surely a subjective matter. Consider the following two Hebrew proverbs:

The heart knows its own bitterness,
and no stranger knows its joy (14:10).

Hope deferred makes the heart sick,
but a desire fulfilled is a tree of life (13:12).

---

[12] C. Joyner, *Down by the Riverside: A South Carolina Slave Community* (Urbana, Illinois: University of Illinois, 1984) 210.

[13] Cf. J. Crenshaw, "Prolegomenon," *SAIW*, 14; "Education in Ancient Israel," 614.

[14] *Studien zur israelitischen Spruchweisheit*, 55.

Hermisson judges the first proverb to be sufficiently profound to qualify as a school saying, while the second, he maintains, is from a folk background.[15] Such assessments are too subtle; they give no objective basis for separating folk wisdom from traditions related to formal education.

Hermisson's assumption, moreover, that the Israelite "peasant folk" lacked sophistication of thought reflects a long-standing Western prejudice against pre- or nonliterate societies. With the more adequate appreciation of such cultures which the ethnographic disciplines have provided, it is impossible to sustain such an attitude.[16] Folk wisdom is typically full of startling insights. We may take another example from the folklore of the African-American slave communities. The following Gullah proverb makes a trenchant response to the legacy of slavery in America:

> If white people are never thieves,
> how come black people are here?[17]

The assumption that folk wisdom is dull and unreflective will mislead the search for Hebrew folk proverbs. On the other hand, a familiarity with known folk traditions can provide an instructive basis for comparison. There is now a large body of cross-cultural evidence

---

[15] *Studien zur israelitischen Spruchweisheit*, 53–55.

[16] The literature is, of course, vast. In connection with Hebrew wisdom, see C. Fontaine, *Traditional Sayings in the Old Testament*, 12, 30–32; "Proverb Performance in the Old Testament," 94. Especially helpful is the essay of A. Dundes: "Who Are the Folk?," *Frontiers of Folklore* (ed. W. R. Bascom; American Association for the Advancement of Science, Selected Symposium no. 5; Boulder, Co.: Westview Press, 1977) 17–35. For additional criticism of Hermisson on this point, see F. W. Golka, "Die israelitische Weisheitsschule oder 'Des Kaisers neue Kleider'," *VT* 33 (1983) 257–70; and "Die Königs- und Hofsprüche und der Ursprung der israelitischen Weisheit," *VT* 36 (1986) 13–36 (but Golka's conclusions, especially regarding the relation of Hebrew to international wisdom, are extreme).

[17] Gullah is the half-English, half-African creole spoken by blacks inhabiting the coastal areas and sea islands of South Carolina, Georgia and northeast Florida. The proverb is recorded in E. D. Genovese, *Roll, Jordan, Roll: The World the Slaves Made* (New York: Pantheon, 1974) 605; cf. Joyner, *Down by the Riverside*, 194. Folklorists have explored in depth the socially critical function of proverbs and traditional story telling in African American culture. See e.g. D. C. Simmons, "Protest Humor: Folkloristic Reaction to Prejudice," *American Journal of Psychiatry* 120 (1963) 567–70; R. A. and A. H. Bauer, "Day to Day Resistance to Slavery," *Journal of Negro History* 27 (1942) 388–419.

available for such comparison. Folklore has always been an object of prime interest to ethnographers and cultural anthropologists. The folk proverbs of a large number of traditional societies have been collected and preserved.[18] Paroemiology, the social-scientific study of proverbs, has emerged as a distinct subdiscipline in the comparative study of folklore.[19]

It is axiomatic in anthropological research that the social context of folklore must be grasped before its significance in a culture can be understood. Besides providing amusement and conveying basic information, folklore serves a variety of social functions. These include: education, the maintenance of social control, the validation of culture, and the release of psychological pressure through projection.[20] It is particularly true of folk proverbs that one must know the social setting in which a proverb is quoted to interpret its significance. People in traditional societies often make this point about folk proverbs themselves.[21]

---

[18] For an overview of ethnographic work on folk proverbs, see R. Finnegan, *Oral Literature in Africa* (London: Oxford University Press, 1970), chapter 14, "Proverbs," 389–425. For present purposes, the term "traditional societies" will designate non-Western, pre-industrial societies, in particular those with tribal or chieftainship (i.e., non-state) forms of social organization. Folk proverbs in these cultures are typically oral traditions, although traditional societies are not necessarily completely non-literate. See J. Goody, ed., *Literacy in Traditional Societies* (Cambridge: Cambridge University Press, 1968), especially the Introduction by Goody, p. 25.

[19] C. Fontaine defines paroemiology as "that 'branch' of folklore studies which collects and collates proverbs, analyzes local and international variants and makes some attempt at tracing the cross-cultural diffusion of proverbs" (*Traditional Sayings in the Old Testament*, 29). W. Mieder (*International Proverb Scholarship: An Annotated Bibliography*; Garland Folklore Bibliographies 3 [New York: Garland, 1982]) surveys hundreds of entries in the field.

[20] See W. R. Bascom, "Four Functions of Folklore," *Journal of American Folklore*, 67 (1954) 333–49 (repr. in A. Dundes, ed., *The Study of Folklore* [Englewood Cliffs, N.J.: Prentice-Hall, 1965] 279–97).

[21] A tribal elder of the Fante people in southern Ghana, after being asked to discuss a proverb in the abstract, responded to ethnographer J. B. Christensen: "There is no proverb without the situation" ("The Role of Proverbs in Fante Culture," *Africa* 28 [1958] 232). Similarly, a young member of the Ibo tribe, who had left Nigeria to study at the University of California at Berkeley, and consequently was losing touch with his native culture, replied to an ethnographer's queries: "I know the proverbs, but I don't know how to apply them" (A. Dundes and E. Ojo Arewa, "Proverbs and the Ethnography of Speaking Folklore," in A. Dundes, ed., *Analytic Essays in Folklore*, 2. [The Hague: Mouton, 1975] 35).

The social functions of proverbs in traditional societies can be highly specialized and to an extent formalized. Some proverbs, for example, function juridically in traditional societies. Traditional sayings may be invoked with rhetorical force to support a legal argument, or may be cited, much as legal precedents are cited in Western jurisprudence, in support of a judgment.[22]

C. Fontaine's *Traditional Sayings in the Old Testament* is the first attempt to use comparative ethnographic data to investigate the role of folk proverbs in ancient Israelite society.[23] Fontaine bases her model of "proverb performance" on P. Seitel's analysis of proverb use among the Ibo in Nigeria.[24] Using this model she analyzes the situations of social interaction in Hebrew narrative where proverbs are invoked.[25] Proverb performance in Hebrew narrative, she concludes, operates to resolve conflict among characters. The use of traditional sayings provides the characters with "a form of verbal behavior which might diffuse potentially aggressive situations."[26] Fontaine describes the patterns of conflict resolution through proverb quotation found in the ethnographic data, and tests the Hebrew narratives for agreement with these patterns. Individuals of inferior social status, for example, typically use indirect proverbial references to criticize their superiors,

---

[22] For the juridical use of proverbs among the Anang people of southeastern Nigeria, see J. C. Messenger, "The Role of Proverbs in a Nigerian Judicial System," *The Study of Folklore* (ed. A. Dundes; Englewood Cliffs, N. J.: Prentice-Hall, 1965) 300–307; on proverb use in the legal proceedings of the Iabo, a Kru-speaking people of southeastern Liberia; see Finnegan, *Oral Literature in Africa*, 419; Christensen discusses proverbs in Fante judicial proceedings, "Role of Proverbs in Fante Culture," 233–35.

[23] Fontaine summarizes her method and results in "Proverb Performance in the Hebrew Bible," *JSOT* 32 (1985) 87–103.

[24] See P. Seitel, "Proverbs: A Social Use of Metaphor," *Genre* 2 (1969) 143–61 (repr. in *Folklore Genres* [ed. D. Ben-Amos; Austin: University of Texas Press, 1976] 125–43).

[25] Fontaine's method, in a nutshell, is to analyze "the Interaction Situation, in which the item is quoted; the Proverb Situation, which consists of the relationship between topic and comment; and the Context Situation, to which the text is applied." "Ethnography," she continues, "stresses the importance of asking questions about the status of proverb user (X, the Source) and proverb hearer (Y, the Receiver), the presence of other persons, the 'historical' background and causation of the context situation, and so on" ("Proverb Performance," 95–96). Fontaine applies this analysis in detail to Judg 8:2; 8:21; 1 Sam 16:7; 24:14; and 1 Kgs 20:11.

[26] Fontaine, "Proverb Performance in the Old Testament," 99.

while those in positions of power are more likely to issue direct challenge.[27]

Fontaine's analysis is illuminating, but it is questionable methodologically to assume that biblical narrative describes proverb use as it actually occurred in Israelite society. Fontaine addresses this problem, noting that folklorists sometimes use literary sources when direct field observation is not possible.[28] The relations between the proverb speaker and proverb referents which are predicted on the basis of Swahili and Ibo field studies, however, do not always hold true for Fontaine's analysis of Hebrew traditional sayings.[29] This may be because Fontaine's analysis deals with an artificial literary environment, as opposed to the ethnographic observation of proverb use in real life. Fontaine observes that the *literary* function of proverb performance in the Hebrew Bible is to bring about a denouement of plot.[30] This literary function could result in a picture somewhat different from actual everyday proverb use in ancient Israel.

Fontaine's research does confirm, however, the importance of folk wisdom in ancient Israel.[31] There is little reason to doubt that folk proverbs circulated in Israel and served functions similar to those we observe in traditional societies today. Thus it is likely that proverbs originating from this Hebrew folk material were incorporated into collections ultimately included in the book of Proverbs. We still have no objective means of identifying these sayings, however. There is no "proverb performance" in Proverbs; the book gives no narrative context for the sayings. We have access to folk sayings in Proverbs only at a secondary stage, after their incorporation into a literary collection.[32] For this reason it is not productive to speculate about the

---

[27] "Proverb Performance," 97. On the preeminence of indirect reference in the use of proverbs in various social situations see also E. Albert, "'Rhetoric,' 'Logic,' and 'Poetics,' in Burundi: Culture Patterning of Speech Behavior," *American Anthropologist* 66 (1964) Special Publication, Part 2, Number 6, 50; and Finnegan, *Oral Literature in Africa*, 411.

[28] For example, Seitel's work on the Ibo uses the novels of Nigerian author Chinua Achebe for examples of proverb use in traditional contexts, in addition to ethnographic reports based on direct observation (*Traditional Sayings in the Old Testament*, 54–62, 72–76).

[29] "Proverb Performance in the Old Testament," 99; *Traditional Sayings in the Old Testament*, 163; see p. 67, 72ff.

[30] *Traditional Sayings in the Old Testament*, 154.

[31] *Traditional Sayings in the Old Testament*, 166–68.

[32] Two scholars have used African folk proverbs to explore the ways in which

original function of a particular saying in Proverbs which may appear to have had a folk origin.

It is illuminating, however, to compare the content of sayings on wealth and poverty in Proverbs with the large body of evidence collected in cross-cultural studies of the folk proverb. Certain themes appear with regularity in folk cultures; thus a comparison of content will show that many sayings found in the Hebrew proverbs are likely to have a folk origin. The extent of the material available for comparison is immense. From African traditional societies alone, some four thousand proverbs have been published in the Rundi language, about three thousand in Nkundo, around two thousand in Luba and Hausa.[33] My use of this material makes no claim to exhaustiveness, but several thousand folk proverbs have been surveyed to give a sufficiently large basis for comparison. I have used for the most part, but not exclusively, sayings from African traditional societies, especially from collections in translation of proverbs in Swahili, Hausa, and the Bantu languages.[34]

Expressions on wealth and poverty in Proverbs can be grouped into variations on a number of themes, such as "wealth is an unqualified good," as opposed to "wealth is a liability"; "poverty is a disgrace," as opposed to "the disgrace of X (dishonesty, cruelty, etc.) is worse than poverty," and so on. Comparison with the folk proverbs of traditional societies shows that some of these themes are frequent in the folk setting, while others which are prominent in the Hebrew Proverbs are almost never found in known folk proverb traditions. Likewise, some important motifs in the Hebrew proverbs are absent from folk traditions, but are prominent in the wisdom traditions of ancient Near Eastern scribal education.

---

the transition from oral to written tradition may influence the material. See C. Westermann, "Weisheit im Sprichwort," *Schalom: Studien zu Glaube und Geschichte Israels, Alfred Jepsen zum 70. Geburtstag* (ed. C.-H. Bernhardt; Stuttgart: Calwer, 1971) 73-85; T. R. Schneider, "From Wisdom Sayings to Wisdom Texts, Part I," *BT* 37 (1986) 128-35; "Part II," *BT* 38 (1987) 101-117.

[33] Finnegan, *Oral Literature in Africa*, 389. W. R. Bascom lists approximately thirty other African peoples for whom 500 or more proverbs have been recorded ("Folklore Research in Africa," *Journal of American Folklore* 77 [1964] 16-17).

[34] In the following paragraphs the published sources of the traditional sayings cited are identified by short title in parentheses following the quotation. For full publication details, see the bibliography.

Thus, while the provenance of any particular saying must remain uncertain, the aggregate pattern of these comparisons shows that certain motifs regarding wealth and poverty in Proverbs are likely to be of folk origin, while others probably belonged to the context of scribal education before their inclusion in the book of Proverbs.

Prominent among the folk sayings which have parallels in the Hebrew Proverbs are those which describe the social isolation of the poor. The poor are spurned by their neighbors, friends, even relatives:

> The poor are disliked even by their neighbors,
> but the rich have many friends (Prov 14:20).

> Wealth brings many new friends,
> but the poor are left friendless (Prov 19:4).

> If the poor are hated even by their kin,
> how much more are they shunned by their friends (Prov 19:7).

To these may be compared the following sayings from contemporary traditional societies:

> A poor man has no friends (Walser, *Luganda Proverbs* #4469; Rattray, *Hausa Folk-Lore* #119).

> A poor man is not a friend, though you like him you will hate him on a feast day (Whitting, *Hausa-Fulani Proverbs* #91).

> The poor man gets a friend; the rich man takes him away (Thomas, *Ibo-Speaking Peoples* #396).

> How can one make friends if he is poor?
> (Knappert, *Proverbs from the Lamu* #193).

> A pauper has no kin (Scheven, *Swahili Proverbs* #1598).

> Relations love each other; as long as both parties are rich (Walser, *Luganda Proverbs* #81).

> Brethren love each other when they are equally rich (Ganda #53, Champion, *RP* p. 530).

On the other hand people of means attract favor and flattery:

> Many seek the favor of the generous,
> and everyone is a friend to a giver of gifts (Prov 19:6).

> A rich man possessing riches is told pleasant things (Walser, *Luganda Proverbs* #2825).

> He that has success, people say nice things to him (Knappert, *Proverbs from the Lamu* #40).

He who is greased never lacks someone to finish polishing him
(Ruanda #13, Champion, *RP* p. 578).

The words of the poor command no hearing:

The poor use entreaties,
but the rich answer roughly (Prov 18:23).

The voice of the poor is not audible
(Nyembezi, *Zulu Proverbs* p. 210).

What the poor man says is not listened to
(Zulu #28, Champion, *RP* p. 608).

Whatever a poor man says is wrong
(Scheven, *Swahili Proverbs* 1591A).

The poor man's word is considered last
(Nyembezi, *Zulu Proverbs* p. 209).

There is no right for a destitute person
(Scheven, *Swahili Proverbs* #1583A).

Some ostensibly free economic relations are tantamount to slavery:

The rich rule over the poor,
and the borrower is the slave of the lender (Prov 22:7).

Debts make slaves (Bantu #6, Champion, *RP* p. 509).

The poor lack the means to preserve their lives:

Wealth is a ransom for a person's life,
but the poor have no means of redemption (Prov 13:8).

The poor man makes his neck pay the fine
(i.e., if he cannot pay, they put a rope around his neck.
Walser, *Luganda Proverbs* #4463).

The life of the poor is unremitting trouble:

All the days of the poor are hard (Prov 15:15a).

There is no rest for the poor man (Merrick, *Hausa Proverbs* #88).

Meanwhile the rich enjoy security:

The wealth of the rich is their fortress;
the poverty of the poor is their ruin (Prov 10:15).

> You can do everything, if you have money
> (Scheven, *Swahili Proverbs* #1622).

Even when the poor manage to provide for themselves, they are dispossessed:

> The fallow ground of the poor yields much food,
> but it is swept away through injustice (Prov 13:23).

> The mighty fasts, the poor pays
> (Scheven, *Swahili Proverbs* #1405).

> The children of the poor man make fat those of the rich one
> (Walser, *Luganda Proverbs* #42).

The folklore of traditional societies is rich in proverbial commentary on the futility of life for the poor. Compare the following sayings to Prov 18:23; 13:23; 10:15. etc.:

> The trade of a poor man brings no profit, and if it brings a profit,
> it is just an accident (Scheven, *Swahili Proverbs* #1621).

> A poor man's pipe does not sound (Accra, Champion, *RP* p. 527).

> A poor potter's clay dries at once beneath his hand
> (Pedi #29, Champion, *RP* p. 576).

> A poor man is overlooked when they divide food;
> but he is not overlooked when they give out work
> (Walser, *Luganda Proverbs* #4462).

> The eyes of a poor man let in the dirt
> (Nyang #37, Champion, *RP* p. 571).

> The eye of the poor man does not see,
> even if it sees it does not guide
> (Scheven, *Swahili Proverbs* #1580).

> The poor man's [beast] does not bring forth a heifer
> (Giryama #34).

> When a poor man thinks he has found something (i.e., to eat),
> he finds a jackal (i.e., uneatable; Walser, *Luganda Proverbs* 4277).

> The poor man does not cook a chicken,
> except in the year of the chicken pest
> (Scheven, *Swahili Proverbs* #1597).

> The poor man's chicken cannot lay eggs
> (Knappert, *Proverbs from the Lamu* #339).

The hen of a poor man lays no eggs,
and even if she lays eggs, she never hatches,
and if she hatches, she never rears the chicks,
and when she rears, the chicks are taken by the hawk
(Scheven, *Swahili Proverbs* #1582).

The boat of a poor man never sails close to the winds
(Scheven, *Swahili Proverbs* #1572, Knappert, *Proverbs from the Lamu* #108)

The poor man's boat can't tack, if it tacks it sinks
(Scheven, *Swahili Proverbs* #174, *RP* p. 587).

The poor man's boat sank already in the river
(Scheven, *Swahili Proverbs* #1586).

Given the social context of these sayings among people who live close to poverty themselves, I would suggest that the humor of some of the proverbs, far from mocking the situation of the poor, expresses the futility of poverty. Although these sayings could of course be applied derisively, in principle at least they do not reflect class conceit. This is important for the interpretation of the Hebrew Proverbs, because as a rule the ancient Near Eastern scribal didactic literature does not contain such fatalistic maxims on the plight of the poor.[35] Rather, above all in the Instruction of Amenemope, compassion and divine favor for the poor are expressed. Thus the set of Hebrew sayings which describe objectively the situation of the poor without ethical evaluation most likely belong to folk tradition. It should be recalled that these are the sayings which have often led to the suggestion by biblical scholars that the Proverbs lack social concern and reflect a limited "class ethic". If these sayings originated as folk observations of certain harsh realities, their lack of compassion can not be attributed to superior social location. In a relatively non-stratified village society, moreover, such sayings are not as open to abuse as they would be in urban society.

The same is true of the class of Hebrew Proverbs which are sometimes referred to as the "sluggard sayings". Compare the following Hebrew Proverbs with examples of folk wisdom from contemporary traditional societies:

---

[35] The single exception of which I am aware is a Sumerian proverb which must be of folk origin: "When a poor man has died, do not try to revive him; when he has salt, he has no bread; when he has bread, he has no salt; when he has meat, he has no condiment; when he has condiment, he has no meat" (E. I. Gordon and T. Jacobsen, *Sumerian Proverbs* [Philadelphia: University Museum of the University of Pennsylvania, 1959] 1:55).

A little sleep, a little slumber,
a little folding of the hands to rest;
And poverty will come upon you like a robber,
and want, like an armed warrior (Prov 24:33–34; cf. 6:10–11).

He who stretches out his legs will never be rich
(Ewe #40, Champion, *RP* p. 526).

For the drunkard and the glutton will come to poverty,
and drowsiness will clothe them with rags (Prov 23:21).

The beggar is the companion of the loafer
(Merrick, *Hausa Proverbs* #286).

A slack hand causes poverty,
but the hand of the diligent makes rich (Prov 10:4).

Riches are like perspiration;
if you rest, they dry up (Walser, *Luganda Proverbs* #1222).

One who loves pleasure will be poor;
one who loves wine and oil will not be rich (Prov 21:17)

Where you have drunk oil, you will drink poverty
(Herskovits-Tagbwe, *Kru Proverbs* #77).

The appetite of the sluggard craves and gets nothing (Prov 13:4a).

The heart of lazy man desires and has nothing
(Thomas, *Ibo-Speaking Peoples* #504).

Those who till their land will have plenty of food (Prov
12:11a=28:19a).

The sluggard does not plough in autumn;
he will seek at harvest and have nothing (Prov 20:4).

He who gets blisters from the hoe-handle will not die of hunger
(Scheven, *Swahili Proverbs* #1959).

Love not sleep, lest you come to poverty;
open your eyes, and you will have plenty of bread (Prov 20:13).

Sleep on, we shall do the hoeing, you just do the eating!
(Doke, *Lamba Folk-Lore* #562).

In all toil there is profit,
but mere talk leads only to poverty (Prov 14:23).

Babbling is the source of hunger
(Scheven, *Swahili Proverbs* #1136).

A lazy person talks his tongue dry
(Walser, *Luganda Proverbs* #4268).

The way of the lazy is overgrown with thorns,
but the path of the upright is a level highway (Prov 15:19).

Laziness begets weakness (Walser, *Luganda Proverbs* #3420).

Laziness brings on deep sleep (Prov 19:15a).

Laziness lends a helping hand to fatigue
(Yoruba #96, Champion, *RP* p. 605).

The plain truth stated by these sayings is undeniable: labor is
necessary, and those who are not inclined to labor may go hungry. It is
equally clear that the proverbs could be misused to blame victims of
oppression and exploitation. The origin of the sayings, however, was
among people living at a subsistence or near-subsistence level. In such
a context, one must work or starve, and this is the brute fact stated in
the proverbs. The Hebrew sages handed on this folk wisdom, but only,
as we shall now see, when it was tempered by an equally august
tradition enjoining care for the poor. The sources of this teaching are
found in the international ancient Near Eastern tradition; hence the
diversity of the teachings in the Hebrew Proverbs on wealth and
poverty can be attributed to the combining of traditions of originally
disparate origins, both village folk wisdom and the international
sapiential literary tradition.

THE INFLUENCE OF INTERNATIONAL WISDOM

With the substratum of native Hebrew folk wisdom on wealth
and poverty in view, we may now compare those instances in Proverbs
where the Hebrew text relies on the international tradition as
represented in the Instruction of Amenemope. The close parallels from
the sub-collection known as the "Words of the Wise" (Prov 22:17–
24:22) will be examined first.

Prov 22:22–23: "Do not rob the poor."

The sub-collection of the "Words of the Wise" begins with a
prologue patterned closely after the Egyptian antecedent:

Incline your ear, and hear the words of the wise (Prov 22:17).

Compare Amenemope 3.9:

Give your ears, hear the sayings.

After the prologue, Prov 22:22a continues,

אַל־תִּגְזָל־דָּל

Do not rob the poor.

Amenemope opens the instruction proper likewise:

Beware of robbing a poor person (4.4).

The Hebrew text thus duplicates Amenemope, not only in the form of the prologue but in placing the prohibition against oppressing the poor at the head of the ethical instruction in the text.[36]

Prov 22:22b–23a sets the prohibition in a forensic context:

וְאַל־תְּדַכֵּא עָנִי בַשָּׁעַר
כִּי־יְהוָה יָרִיב רִיבָם

and do not crush the lowly in the gate,
for the Lord will plead their case.

Commentators recognize the dependence of this section upon Amenemope, but they typically view the legal setting as unique to the Hebrew text.[37] The forensic motivation, however, is also already present in Amenemope. After the opening admonitions in 4.4ff, Amenemope says of the wrongdoer:

i^{c}ḥ s:^{c}ḥ^c bt3=f

It is the Moon who declares his crime (4.19).

The Moon represents Thoth, patron divinity of scribes and also symbol of the administration of justice and the court. The verb of which Thoth is subject in 4.19, s:^{c}ḥ^c, is a forensic term, frequently used in the sense of "to accuse" or "to convict" someone of a crime.[38]

---

[36] M. Schwantes, *Das Recht der Armen* (BET 4; Frankfurt: Lang, 1977) 237, recognizes the programmatic significance of placing the prohibition at the beginning of the instruction.

[37] E.g., Gemser (*Sprüche Salomos*, 84), remarks that the motivation clause is "typisch israelitisch." Ringgren (*Sprüche/Prediger*, 91): "echt israelitisch". McKane (*Proverbs: A New Approach*, 377) sees the motivation as unique to Proverbs; also G. H. Wittenberg, "The Lexical Context of the Terminology for Poor in the Book of Proverbs," *Scriptura* 2 (1986) 79.

[38] Representative citations and basic bibliography in R. O. Faulkner, *A Concise*

This Hebrew text also echoes Amenemope 20.21–21.8, which expressly forbids oppression in the courts. These strophes refer back to Amenemope 4.4–5 by reference the poor (*iȝd*, 21.8; 4.4), and the weak (*sȝw-ʿ*, 21.4; 4.5), terms which otherwise do not occur in Amenemope.[39] The admonition, "Do not confound a person in law court (*ḳnbt*)" (Amenemope 20.21), lies behind the command of Prov 22:22b. The term for the law court, *ḳnbt*, is the semantic equivalent to Hebrew שַׁעַר,[40] and here again Amenemope asserts that divine justice, *maʿat*, will deliver the poor (21.8). In Prov 22:22–23, Thoth and Maat as divine advocates of the poor are replaced by Yhwh, otherwise the prohibition and motivation are the same.

The single phrase in these verses which has no precedent in Amenemope is Prov 22:22aᵇ, כִּי דַל־הוּא, "because he is poor". Commentators have claimed that this phrase indicates a special emphasis in the Hebrew proverb.[41] On the contrary, the Hebrew author alludes here to Ptahhotep 74–77, (again a forensic context):

> If you encounter an opponent in court,
> A poor man, not your equal,
> Do not abuse him, because he is weak.[42]

Prov 22:28 = 23:10: "Do not remove the ancient landmark."

The moving of landmarks is of course condemned elsewhere in the Hebrew Bible (Hos 5:10; Deut 24:17; Job 24:2), but commentators agree that the theme appears in this section of Proverbs because of its prominence in Amenemope. As we saw above, Amenemope censures all types of dishonesty among scribes, especially the falsification of land boundaries:

Dictionary of Middle Egyptian (Oxford: Griffith Institute, 1962) 215.

[39] On the law court as the *Sitz-im-Leben* of both passages in Amenemope, see Grumach, *Untersuchungen zur Lebenslehre des Amenope*, 32, 137.

[40] The term *ḳnbt* denotes literally a "corner" in the street where the magistrates convene, and by extension the judicial assembly itself (see Gardiner, *EG*³, 497.) The hieroglyphic sign for *ḳnbt* serves as the determinative for Middle Egyptian *ʿrrt*, "gate". In using the term שַׁעַר the Hebrew author has simply given an appropriate translation for the term.

[41] Wittenberg, "The Lexical Context of the Terminology for Poor," 79; Schwantes, *Das Recht der Armen*, 238.

[42] My translation, cf. Lichtheim, *AEL* 1.64; Zába, *Les maximes de Ptahhotep*, 73.

Do not move the markers on the borders of fields,
nor shift the position of the measuring cord (7.12).

Beware of destroying the borders of the fields,
lest a terror carry you away (8.9-10).

The moving of boundaries by measurement officials in the
Egyptian agricultural bureaucracy would have benefitted not only the
scribes themselves, but the clients whom they favored. Thus the
socially weak, such as widows (7.15), who were not capable of
offering bribes, deserved special protection.[43] Amenemope also warns
against adding unjustly to one's own property, urging honest relations
with one's neighbors: "Do not be greedy for a cubit of land" (7.14).

Prov 23:10a, אַל־תַּסֵּג גְּבוּל עוֹלָם, is probably based on Amenemope 7.15, "Do not encroach on the boundaries of a widow." The
Hebrew text would originally have read אַל־תַּסֵּג גְּבוּל אַלְמָנָה supplying a
better parallel to יְתוֹמִים in 23:10b. The corruption to עוֹלָם in 23:10a
may have occurred by attraction to 22:28, where עוֹלָם suits the parallel
structure.[44]

Prov 23:11 supplies the motive clause for 23:10, again using the
forensic terminology of the רִיב:

Do not remove an ancient landmark,
or enter the fields of the fatherless,
for their Redeemer is strong;
he will plead their case against you.

כִּי־גֹאֲלָם חָזָק הוּא־יָרִיב אֶת־רִיבָם אִתָּךְ

This motive clause too has been claimed as a unique feature of the
Hebrew tradition.[45] Egyptian society apparently had no counterpart to
the Hebrew legal institution of the גֹּאֵל; but Amenemope uses forensic
language to describe divine intervention against the offender here as
well:

Do not move the markers on the borders of fields ...
Nor encroach the boundaries of a widow ...
He who falsifies it [the furrow] in the fields,

---

[43] Cf. Grumach, *Untersuchungen zur Lebenslehre des Amenope*, 61.

[44] This is the argument of Sellin, review of Erman, "Eine ägyptische Quelle der
'Sprüche Salomos'," *DLZ* 45 (1924) 1326; Gressmann, "Die neugefundene Lehre
des Amen-em-ope und die vorexilische Spruchdichtung Israels," 276; and Gemser,
Sprüche Salomos, 84.

[45] Especially Wittenberg, "The Lexical Context of the Terminology for Poor,"
81.

When he has snared it by false oaths,
He will be caught by the might of the Moon (7.12-19).

The Moon again represents Thoth, so the threat, "He will be caught by
the might of the Moon" is materially identical to the Hebrew warning,
"Their Redeemer is strong, he will plead their case against you" (Prov
23:11). The Hebrew passage adapts the expression to the Israelite
cultural context.

Prov 23:4-5: "Do not toil to acquire wealth."

Although the Hebrew passage is textually difficult, its
dependence on Amenemope is nonetheless clear. Proverbs 23:4-5
reads:

> Do not toil to acquire wealth,
> be wise enough[46] to desist,
> When[47] your eyes light upon it,[48] it is gone,
> for suddenly it takes to itself wings
> flying like an eagle toward heaven.

Compare these sentences in Amenemope:

> Do not set your heart on wealth,...
> Do not strain to seek increase,
> What you have, let it suffice you....
> [Riches] will not stay the night with you.
> Comes day they are not in your house.
> Their place is seen, but they are not there.
> They made themselves wings like geese,
> and flew away to the sky (9.10-10.5).

The Hebrew text changes the Egyptian goose, *rɜ*, to an eagle, (or per-

---

[46] Reading with MT מִבִּינָתְךָ, or as emended by Sellin (review of Erman, "Eine
ägyptische Quelle der 'Sprüche Salomos'," 1326), מִבְּיָזְתְךָ, "from your robbery,"
cf. BHS.

[47] This phrase is difficult. McKane (*Proverbs: A New Approach*, 382) follows
Gemser in taking the ה as introducing a condition (cf. LXX ἐάν), not as
interrogative ה, but there is no real evidence for this apart from the LXX reading.
For the verb one must assume that the Qere תָעִיף, "cause to fly," can mean
something like "cast a glance," "set one's eyes," or alternatively is a denominative
from עֲפַף, "eyelid," thus "blink".

[48] Erman ("Eine ägyptische Quelle der 'Sprüche Salomos'," 87), pointed out
that the 3ms suffix on בּו has no antecedent in the Hebrew. He suggested that the
superfluous עֲשֹׂה may be a misplaced corruption of עֹשֶׁר, "wealth," which supplied
the necessary noun subject.

haps vulture), נֶשֶׁר;[49] otherwise the image and its import are the same as in Amenemope: wealth is undependable and not worth the expense of great exertion in its pursuit.

We have seen, then, that this sub-collection of Proverbs adopts from Amenemope a consistent view of wealth and poverty characterized by explicit concern for the poor, condemnation of unjust gain, and only a qualified acknowledgement of the value of wealth. The doctrine that prosperity is a reward for righteousness is absent here.

In view of the large number of sources upon which the author of this section of Proverbs draws for the treatment of other themes, the heavy reliance on Amenemope for sayings about wealth and poverty is significant.

We can also discern, however, in Proverbs 22:17-24:22 a pattern of selectivity in the use of Amenemope's material which may be attributed to the attenuation of scribal professional orientation in Proverbs as outlined above. Amenemope, even in discussions of wealth and poverty, is addressed specifically to the concerns of the scribal profession. The biblical book of Proverbs adopts those aspects of the Instruction which will be pertinent to the biblical community as a whole, but screens out features which apply only to the scribal guild.

For example, the strictures in this set of Proverbs against unjust acquisition of wealth are taken directly from Amenemope. Proverbs repeats Amenemope's warnings against altering land boundaries, because this concern applies to the biblical community equally well. Proverbs does not, however, preserve the repeated strictures in Amenemope not to "cheat with the pen" (Amenemope 15.20, 16.4, 17.6-7, 17.11), because these admonitions are particular to the scribal guild.

Finally we may note the role of the "better"-sayings in the Hebrew Proverbs, especially the following examples:

> Better is a little with fear of the Lord
> than great treasure and trouble with it (15:16).

> Better is a dinner of vegetables where love is
> than a fatted ox and hatred with it (15:17).

---

[49] Either for "poetical" reasons (so Erman, "Eine ägyptische Quelle der 'Sprüche Salomos'," 87), or because the נֶשֶׁר was more familiar in Israel than the goose (H. Grimme, "Weiteres zu Amen-em-ope und Proverbien," *OLZ* 28 [1925] col. 61).

Better is a little with righteousness
than great revenues with injustice (16:8)

Commentators have long recognized the influence of the *3ḥ*-sayings in Amenemope (9.5-8, 16.11-12) upon the biblical טוֹב-sayings.[50] The Hebrew Proverbs adopt both the form of the "better"-saying from Amenemope, as well as the thematic focus of the form upon the question of wealth and poverty. In addition to highlighting the relative praise of poverty from the Egyptian tradition, this Hebrew use of the form results in an exquisite extended word-play, because טוֹב in biblical Hebrew can have the concrete sense of prosperity, or material wealth (cf. especially Prov 28:10). The complex of "better"-sayings thus illustrates the self-subverting strategy of Hebrew proverbial wisdom: despite the praise of wealth and its association with wisdom in Proverbs, the sages slyly indicate that a life of integrity without luxury is "better than" (טוֹב מִן) the enjoyment of material prosperity (טוֹב). This feature of the sayings points to the fact that individual sayings can sometimes be shown to interact with one another in the larger context established by the book of Proverbs. We will examine this aspect of the book of Proverbs in the final section of this chapter.

CONTEXTUAL READING OF THE SAYINGS ON WEALTH AND POVERTY

In the previous section it became apparent that Proverbs relies on the international scribal tradition to qualify some teachings about wealth and poverty that originated among the native Hebrew folk. The theme of wealth and poverty is only one of many topics which receive conflicting treatments in Proverbs.[51] The question thus arises whether it

---

[50] E.g., Erman, "Eine ägyptische Quelle der Sprüche Salomos," 87; Gressmann, "Die neugefundene Lehre des Amen-em-ope und die vorexilische Spruchdichtung Israels," 278-9; D. Herzog, "Die Sprüche des Amen-em-ope und Proverbien Kapp. 22,17-24,35," *Zeitschrift für Semitistik und verwandte Gebiete* 7 (1929) 128; D. C. Simpson, "The Hebrew Book of Proverbs and the Teaching of Amenophis," *JEA* 12 (1926) 234; H. Wiesmann, *Das Buch der Sprüche, übersetzt und erklärt* (Bonn: P. Hanstein, 1923) 47; G. Bryce, *A Legacy of Wisdom*, 71-75; G. Bryce, "'Better'-Proverbs: An Historical and Structural Study," *SBLSP* 108 (1972) 343-54.

[51] The classic example is the opposing advice on "answering a fool according to his folly," in Prov 26:4 and 5. According to the Talmud the contradictory teachings in Proverbs, especially these two verses, jeopardized the book's admission into the canon (*b. Sabb. 30b*). On the history of attempts to reconcile 26:4 and 26:5, see K. G. Hoglund, "The Fool and the Wise in Dialogue," *The*

is possible to interpret the book as a whole: are these varying expressions presented randomly, with the simple purpose of giving a variety of perspectives on a subject,[52] or does the arrangement of proverbs sometimes suggest the commendation of one view over another? Does literary context, in other words, influence the import of particular sayings in the sub-collections of Proverbs?

Modern commentators typically assume that the sentence collections of Proverbs are assembled in a haphazard fashion. Only a few formal patterns of arrangement are generally acknowledged. For example, it is recognized that Prov 10–15 are chiefly in antithetic parallelism, while chs. 16–22 are primarily in synonymous parallelism. Paranomasia, catchwords, synonym sequences, and word plays have been shown to work as mnemonic devices linking halves of verses or associating one verse with the next.[53] Beyond these stylistic features, most interpreters see no evidence of more substantive, or content-related, principles of arrangement.[54]

Listening Heart: Essays in Wisdom and the Psalms in Honor of Roland E. Murphy, O. Carm. (eds. K. G. Hoglund et al; JSOTSup 58; Sheffield: Sheffield Academic Press, 1987) 161–80.

[52] This is the view established by W. Zimmerli ("Concerning the Structure of Old Testament Wisdom," *SAIW*, 175–207, originally published in *ZAW* 10 [1933] 177–204). For Zimmerli, Hebrew wisdom constitutes עֵצָה, or debatable counsel, open to the vicissitudes of experience and thus subject to change, as distinguished from authoritative מִצְוָה, or command. For reviews of the continuing debate over the intellectual structure of Hebrew wisdom *vis à vis* order and authority, see J. L. Crenshaw, "Prolegomenon," *SAIW*, 1–45; and "Murphy's Axiom: Every Gnomic Saying Needs a Balancing Corrective," *The Listening Heart: Essays in Wisdom and the Psalms in Honor of Roland E. Murphy, O. Carm.* (eds. K. G. Hoglund et al; JSOTSup 58; Sheffield: Sheffield Academic Press, 1987) 1–17.

[53] The basic study is G. Boström, *Paronomasi i den äldre hebreiska Maschalliteraturen* (LUA N.F. Avd. 1 Bd. 23, Nr. 8; Lund: Gleerup, 1928). Some account of Boström's work is given by H. J. Hermisson, *Studien zur israelitischen Spruchweisheit*, 171–72; and R. C. van Leeuwen, *Context and Meaning in Proverbs 25–27*, 10–11.

[54] See for example Oesterley, *The Book of Proverbs*, xii, and his remarks on 14:20 and 18:11 (pp. 112, 148). McKane (*Proverbs: A New Approach*, 10) asserts that "there is, for the most part, no context in the sentence literature". R. B. Y. Scott (*Proverbs, Ecclesiastes*, 17) sees the subcollections as the result of a long process of random accretion, producing no meaningful patterns of arrangement. Cf. the commentaries of B. Gemser, *Sprüche Salomos*; A. Barucq, *Le livre des Proverbes* (Sources Bibliques; Paris: J. Gabalda, 1964); H. Ringgren, *Sprüche-Prediger*.

There are passages, however, where proverbs which originated as independent sayings create, by virtue of their juxtaposition with other proverbs, a critical or qualifying context for the sayings with which they are placed. Traditional Jewish exegesis recognizes this potential in Proverbs. Even in the absence of stylistic linking devices, the great medieval commentators frequently draw illuminating connections between separate proverbs. A particular saying may be interpreted as a comment, critical or complementary, upon a preceding proverb.[55]

A few modern scholars have pursued the question of literary context in the sentence collections. H.-J. Hermisson's study of Proverbs treats the organization of the sayings in chapters 10–15.[56] Hermisson combines Boström's examination of stylistic features with thematic analysis, and concludes that significant groupings can be found in this collection, where originally independent sayings are complemented or corrected by the proverbs which follow. O. Plöger has made a similar attempt in Prov 11 to identify significant groupings of proverbs on the basis of theme.[57] Both Hermisson and Plöger suggest that an intentional disputational technique is applied in these groupings. R. N. Whybray has argued that the Yahweh-sayings in Prov 10–22 are deliberately placed in order to modify or correct older secular wisdom sayings.[58] R. C. van Leeuwen's monograph on *Context and Meaning in Proverbs 25–27* is a thorough structural, poetic, and semantic analysis of the features which establish literary context for the interpretation of the individual sayings in chs. 25–27.[59] T. Hildebrandt

---

[55] E.g., Ibn Ezra on 23:8–9, 24:10–11, 27:1–2; Rashi on 26:9–10; Saadia on 20:20–21; Jonah b. Abraham Gerondi on 14:27–28. For bibliographical details on these commentators see A. Cohen, *Proverbs: Hebrew Text and English Translation with an Introduction and Commentary* (Hindhead, Surrey: Soncino, 1945); and J. H. Greenstone, *Proverbs with Commentary* (Philadelphia: Jewish Publication Society, 1950).

[56] *Studien zur israelitischen Spruchweisheit,* 171–83.

[57] "Zur Auslegung der Sentenzensammlungen des Proverbiabuches," *Probleme biblischer Theologie. Gerhard von Rad zum 70. Geburtstag* (ed. H. W. Wolff; Munich: Kaiser, 1971) 402–16.

[58] "Yahweh-sayings and their Contexts in Proverbs 10,1–22,16," *La Sagesse de l'Ancien Testament* (ed. M. Gilbert; BETL 51; Gembloux: Duculot,1979) 153–65. R. Murphy remains skeptical of these attempts to identify true contexts out of which individual sayings are to be interpreted (*Wisdom Literature: Job, Proverbs, Ruth, Canticles, Ecclesiastes, and Esther,* 63–4).

[59] SBLDS 96 (Atlanta: Scholars Press, 1988).

has proposed the "proverbial pair" as "a literary form which evinces the literary and editorial craftsmanship of the proverbial collectors."[60]

R. Gordis has shown that outside the book of Proverbs the disputational technique of "virtual quotation" is favored especially by the wisdom authors.[61] A frequently used strategy is the citation of contrasting proverbs, where the second member of the pair represents the author's view. Qohelet, for example, quotes the traditional wisdom that folly and destructive sloth go together,

> Fools fold their hands,
> and eat their own flesh (4:5);

but then gives the rejoinder:

> Better is a handful with quiet,
> than two handfuls with toil,
> and a striving after wind (4:6).[62]

These two verses are linked stylistically by the synonymous catchword references to the "hands" in vv. 5 and 6, but the association of the two verses is more than formal. For Qohelet, all striving after achievement is vain. He thus uses the traditional form of the "better" (טוֹב) saying in v. 6 to refute the approbation of diligence and hard work which is characteristic of conventional wisdom (v. 5). We will see that several sayings on wealth and poverty in the book of Proverbs have a similar disputational relation to one another.

Commentators have often recognized that the Instruction of Prov 1–9 sets an interpretive frame for the diverse sayings of chapters 10–31.[63] This especially holds true for the themes of wealth, poverty, and

---

[60] "Proverbial Pairs: Compositional Units in Proverbs 10–29," *JBL* 107 (1988) 208; cf. p. 218: "The goal of this study is simply to establish that binding of individual sentences into pairs is a discrete level of composition that should not be ignored in analysis."

[61] "Quotations in Biblical, Oriental, and Rabbinic Literature," *Poets, Prophets, and Sages: Essays in Biblical Interpretation* (Bloomington: Indiana University Press, 1971) 104–159; "The Use of Quotations in Job," *The Book of God and Man: A Study of Job* (Chicago: University of Chicago Press, 1965) 169–89.

[62] Gordis, "The Use of Quotations in Biblical, Oriental, and Rabbinic Literature," 138–9.

[63] See especially B. Childs, "Chapters 1–9 as a framework," *Introduction to the Old Testament as Scripture* (Philadephia: Fortress, 1979) 552–55. Childs observes that "Zimmerli spoke of these chapters providing the 'hermeneutical guide' for understanding the rest of the book" (p. 553).

social equity. The prologue of Prov 1:2–6 sets as the object of instruction not only "wisdom" (חָכְמָה), "insight" (בִּינָה), and "wise dealing" (שֵׂכֶל, vv. 2–3), but also the cardinal values of "righteousness, justice, and equity" (צֶדֶק וּמִשְׁפָּט וּמֵישָׁרִים , v. 3). The word pair צֶדֶק וּמִשְׁפָּט (cf. Prov 2:9; 21:3) reflects the emergent canonical awareness of the postexilic author-redactor, and commits the reader, in interpreting the subsequent sayings about wealth and poverty, to the social values of צֶדֶק וּמִשְׁפָּט which Wisdom now shares with the Law (Deut 33:21) and the Prophets (Isa 9:6; 16:5; Jer 22:15–16). The programmatic statement of v. 7a which crowns the prologue has a similar effect:

יִרְאַת יְהוָה רֵאשִׁית דָּעַת

The fear of the Lord is the beginning of knowledge
(cf. Prov 1:29; 2:5; 8:13; 9:10; 10:27; 14:26–27; 15:16, 33;
16:6; 19:23; Job 28:28; Ps 111:10).[64]

"Fear of God" receives special emphasis in the book of Deuteronomy (Deut 4:10; 5:26; 6:2, 13, 24; 8:6; 10:12, 20; 13:5; 14:23; 17:19; 28:58; 31:12–13), where its basic connotation is covenantal loyalty, including the social stipulations of Deuteronomic Law.[65] Given the extent of reverence for Law which we have identified in Proverbs, it is fair to assume that the phrase יִרְאַת יְהוָה has the same association here.

The socio-economic emphasis of the sages is clear as the instruction proper begins, in 1:8–19, with a warning against falling in with murderous plotters whose only aim is unjust gain:

We shall find all kinds of costly things;
We shall fill our houses with booty (1:13).

Little do such thieves know, says the sage, that they

set an ambush—for their own lives!
such is the end of all who are greedy for gain;
it takes away the life of its possessors (1:18b–19).

In a short essay on Proverbs 22:1–9, R. Murphy, while recognizing the tensions in the teaching of Proverbs concerning wealth and poverty, states:

---

[64] Often referred to as the "motto" of the book of Proverbs (e.g., Plöger, *Sprüche Salomos*, 8; Delitzsch, *Biblical Commentary on the Proverbs of Solomon*, 58).

[65] See M. Weinfeld, *Deuteronomy and the Deuteronomic School*, 274–281.

> Nevertheless we think a fairly consistent and pertinent teaching
> about poverty and the poor emerges from the Book of Proverbs....
> Within the Book of Proverbs itself the rich person and possession
> of riches are qualified in many ways that suggest a certain caution
> if not negativity. Many ambiguities attach to the possession of
> wealth, and the sayings are tilted in favor of the poor (a
> "preferential option"?).[66]

Without denying the conflicting elements of Proverbs' teachings and
the rich and poor, we can acknowledge with Murphy that there is a
tendency in Proverbs to qualify the ethically problematic sayings and
place relative stress on concern for the poor. Often this is done through
contextual clues to the sense in which a proverb should be viewed.

A common pattern in the disputational arrangment of sayings is
the qualification of ethically neutral proverbs, those which simply
observe facts of human experience, by the addition of ethically
evaluative sayings. A model for this use of proverbs is found in the
Instruction of Proverbs 1–9. In chapter 9 Folly is personified as a
prostitute seducing young men to their destruction. In an appeal to the
passer-by, who is "deficient in intelligence" (חֲסַר לֵב, 9:16), Folly
quotes a proverb. It is an ethically neutral maxim, an observation of the
universal fact of human psychology that illicit pleasure can be
especially intense:

> Stolen water is sweet,
> and bread eaten in secret is pleasant (9:17).

These words are quoted by the sage, however, only to expose their
deceitfulness and the danger they pose to the passer-by:

> But he does not know that the dead are there,
> that her guests are in the depths of Sheol (9:18).

Much of the proverbial material about wealth and poverty is
treated in a similar fashion: an ethically neutral observation is qualified
by placing the statement in an ethically evaluative context. Here it is
necessary to disagree with R. N. Whybray's assertion that "only in the
so-called 'better'-proverbs is there a possibility of introducing a
comparative standard of values".[67] In some cases the simple juxtaposition of sayings suggests the editor's preference for an evaluative
statement over neutral description. In other instances, the definitive
option of the sages is explicitly marked by reference to Yhwh, or to the

---

[66] "Proverbs 22:1–9," *Int* 41 (1987) 400–401.

[67] *Wealth and Poverty in the Book of Proverbs*, 63.

righteous (צַדִּיק) in contrast to the wicked (רָשָׁע), or by other ethically evaluative language.

For example, Prov 14:20 and 14:21 both treat the theme of wealth and poverty. The verses are linked by the catchword רֵעַ, "neighbor,":

(14:20a) גַּם־לְרֵעֵהוּ יִשָּׂנֵא רָשׁ

(14:21a) בָּז־לְרֵעֵהוּ חוֹטֵא

and by the similarity of their syntactic structure.[68] The effect of the juxtaposition of these two verses is to qualify the ethically neutral observation of a social fact, that the poor are friendless while the rich are esteemed (14:20), with the ethical evaluation that those who despise their neighbors are sinners (and generosity to the poor is to be commended, 14:21):

> The poor are disliked even by their neighbors,
> but the rich have many friends (14:20).
>
> Those who despise their neighbors are sinners,
> but happy are those who are kind to the poor (14:21).

As O. Plöger observes, v. 21 provides a critical corrective to v. 20.[69] The moral language of sin (חוֹטֵא, v. 21a) as opposed to blessedness (אַשְׁרֵי, v. 21b) clarifies the ethical choice of the sages.

It is not necessary for sayings to be immediately adjacent in order to suggest an interactive reading; proximity can achieve the same effect. Prov 19:4, 6–7 presents a series of sayings similar to Prov 14:20, describing the social isolation of the poor:

> Wealth brings many friends,
> but the poor are left friendless (19:4).
>
> Many seek the favor of the generous,
> and everyone is a friend to a giver of gifts (19:6).
>
> If the poor are hated even by their kin,
> how much more are they shunned by their friends! (19:7ab).

We saw earlier in this chapter that these sayings probably derive from traditional Hebrew folk wisdom, because similar sayings appear with regularity in the folklore of contemporary traditional societies. While

---

[68] The pair is identified as an editorial unit by T. Hildebrandt, "Proverbial Pairs: Compositional Units in Proverbs 10–29," 209.

[69] *Sprüche Salomos*, 173.

village wisdom of this sort acknowledges an indisputable social fact, it holds little redemptive potential for the poor. Thus it is significant that the present section of Proverbs is introduced by a טוֹב-saying which asserts the relative value of poverty, and presents the poor person as one of dignity and moral worth:

> Better the poor walking in integrity
> than one perverse of speech who is a fool (19:1).

A sensitive reader of the Proverbs will recognize, moreover, that sayings such as Prov 14:20; 19:4, 6-7, which describe the tendency of people to despise the poor, are set in a critical light by the presence of sayings such as the following, wherever they may appear in the sub-collections:

> Those who oppress the poor insult their Maker;
> but those who are kind to the needy honor him (14:31).

> Those who mock the poor insult their Maker;
> those who are glad at calamity will not go unpunished (17:5).

> The rich and the poor have this in common:
> The Lord is the maker of them all (22:2).

> The poor and the oppressor have this in common:
> The Lord gives light to the eyes of both (29:13).[70]

This emphasis on the common humanity of rich and poor can only have a salutary import for reflection on social-ethical questions in light of the Proverbs.

Prov 10:4-5 presents a pair of sayings enjoining diligence:

> A slack hand causes poverty
> but the hand of the diligent makes rich (10:4).

> A child who gathers in summer is prudent,
> but a child who sleeps in harvest brings shame (10:5).[71]

---

[70] On the proverbial motif of the poor as God's creatures, cf. R. N. Whybray, *Wealth and Poverty in the Book of Proverbs*, 41–42; and P. Doll, *Menschenschöpfung und Weltschöpfung in der alttestamentlichen Weisheit*; Stuttgarter Bibelstudien 117 (Stuttgart: Katholisches Bibelwerk, 1985).

[71] T. Hildebrandt analyzes Prov 10:4-5 as a deliberately constructed proverbial pair: "a bi-proverbial chiasm AB/BA (lax hands/diligent hands//working wise son/otiose shameful son)" (T. Hildebrandt, "Proverbial Poetry: Its Settings and Syntax" [Th.D. diss., Grace Theological Seminary, 1985] 655). Hildebrandt also notes here the suggestion of Boström that the editors may have intended a wordplay in this context of חָרוּצִים, "diligent" upon חָרוּץ, "gold" (G. Boström, *Paronomasi I den Äldre Hebreiska Maschalliteraturen*, 120).

These sayings too are likely to have originated in a village folk setting.
In the circumstances of near-subsistence agriculture, such teachings
emphasize the fact that survival depends on hard work. In an urban situation, or among the prosperous, however, a saying such as Prov 10:4
might lend itself to misuse. The proverb could be applied to blame the
poor and justify the complacency of the rich. Thus the editorial setting
of Prov 10:1-5 militates against such an application. Various commentators have recognized that the opening verses of chapter 10 establish a
meaningful context larger than the individual sentence. F. Delitzsch,
for example, introduces the passage in this way: "There follows now a
series of proverbs which place possessions and goods under a moral-
religious point of view".[72] O. Plöger describes Prov 10:1-5 as a
compositionally unified "field" of key themes, noting that chiastic
order is uniform regular in this sequence, but not apparent in the rest of
the chapter:

> positive elements: 1a, 2b, 3a, 4b, 5a
>
> negative elements: 1b, 2a, 3b, 4a, 5b.[73]

The unit constructed from these diverse sayings undermines the self-
satisfaction of the rich by challenging them to examine the ethical basis
of their comfort:

> Treasures gained by wickedness do not profit,
> but righteousness delivers from death (10:2).

Likewise the traditional teaching that the honest will be sustained by
God is invoked:

> The Lord does not let the righteous go hungry,
> but he thwarts the craving of the wicked (10:3; cf. Ps 37:25).

A similar qualification of the folk teaching about diligence is achieved
in Prov 19:15-17. The first verse of this group repeats the traditional
wisdom:

---

[72] *Biblical Commentary on the Proverbs of Solomon*, 1.209.

[73] *Sprüche Salomos*, 124. Cf. T. Hildebrandt's characterization of 10:2-5 as a
"quatrain centering on the theme of various character relationships to material
benefits" ("Proverbial Poetry: Its Setting and Syntax," 656.) Hildebrandt also
observes that while Prov 10:1 does not address the theme of wealth and poverty, it
is integrated compositionally by the chiastic structure and by the double reference
to the "son" (בֵּן) in 10:1a, b and 10:5a, b, forming an *inclusio* to the five-verse
unit.

Laziness brings on deep sleep;
an idle person will suffer hunger (19:15).

Lest the reader be misled, however, into blaming the poor for their suffering, this saying is immediately placed in the ethical context of post-exilic legal piety:

The one who keeps the commandment (שֹׁמֵר מִצְוָה) will live;
those who are heedless of his (i.e., Yhwh's) ways will die (19:16);

and lest one overlook the fact that "keeping the commandment" includes kindness to the poor, the next verse stipulates:

Whoever is kind to the poor lends to the Lord,
and will be repaid in full (19:17).

Prov 22.7 offers a stark social observation:

The rich rules over the poor,
and the borrower is the slave of the lender.

These sad economic facts of life, however, are immediately set in an ethical context:

Whoever sows injustice will reap calamity,
and the rod of their anger will fail (22:8).[74]

Those who are generous are blessed,
for they share their bread with the poor (22:9).

A comparable transformation of the individual saying is achieved by the context of Prov 10:15:

The wealth of the rich is their fortress;
the poverty of the poor is their ruin (10:15).

This saying is often taken to illustrate the ethical aloofness of the sages. C. Toy, for example, comments on 10:15:

There is probably no ethical thought in the proverb—the sense is that wealth smooths one's path in life ... while the poor man is exposed to bodily and social privations.... It seems to be simply a recognition of the value of money.[75]

---

[74] R. Murphy, despite his interest in the significance of this group for the topic of wealth and poverty, fails to connect the two sayings, taking v. 8 as a simple statement of the fact that one must live with the consequences of one's actions ("Proverbs 22:1–9," 399).

[75] *A Critical and Exegetical Commentary on the Book of Proverbs*, 208.

Similarly Scott asserts that the saying gives no hint that the writers consider the division of rich and poor unjust.[76] J. H. Greenstone likewise comments:

> There is apparently no intention to express any moral lesson in this verse; it is simply a statement of a fact which prevails in all conditions of society.[77]

But Greenstone takes the additional step of connecting Prov 10.15 to the following verse:

> The wage of the righteous leads to life,
> the gain of the wicked to sin (10:16).

Greenstone concludes that the editor, by creating this context, deliberately curtails the application of the former saying.[78] As H.-J. Hermisson observes, Prov 10:15 seems at first to be a saying with the tenor, "so it goes in the world," but the saying is not adequately understood without the addition of v. 16.[79] Hildebrandt likewise takes the two verses together:

> Prov 10:15-16 is a good example of a non-catchword proverbial pair.... Wealth without morality is death. Because of the nexus of these two verses, one can see the necessity of wealth's being accompanied by righteousness if one is to secure one's existence. Thus recognizing the pair as a collectional literary unit that is hermeneutically interactive leads to a higher level of interpretation and recognition of canonical intent.[80]

Of course these two verses do not settle the question whether in a particular situation it is possible to acquire wealth ethically, or whether the just acquisition of wealth is possible in principle. For these questions one must reflect on other sayings (e.g. Prov 30:8-9), as well as on one's contigent situation. An interpreter who would absolutize a saying such as Prov 10:15, however, surely lacks the discernment which the Proverbs are intended to teach.

---

[76] R. B. Y. Scott, *Proverbs, Ecclesiastes*, 84.

[77] *Proverbs with Commentary*, 104.

[78] Greenstone refers here to the Hebrew commentary on Proverbs of Joseph ibn Nachmias: "The greatest good is righteousness and the greatest evil is wickedness."

[79] Hermisson, *Studien zur altisraelitischen Spruchweisheit*, 182.

[80] T. Hildebrandt, "Proverbial Pairs: Compositional Units in Proverbs 10-29," 214-15; cf. Hildebrandt, "Proverbial Poetry: Its Settings and Syntax," 667-69.

The reliance of the wealthy upon the security of their riches is criticized again in Prov 18:10–11, where the assurance that the name of Yhwh is a strong tower (מִגְדַּל־עֹז) precedes the description of the rich person's illusory perception that wealth is a "strong city" (קִרְיַת עֻזּוֹ).

> The name of the Lord is a strong tower;
> the righteous run into it and are safe (18:10).
>
> The wealth of the rich is their strong city;
> in their imagination it is like a high wall (18:11).[81]

The editorial arrangement of the Hebrew Proverbs does not resolve all the tensions among sayings about wealth and poverty in the manner examined here. It would be an overstatement to suggest that the book of Proverbs offers a unified social ethic. Too often, however, commentators misconstrue the outlook of the sages by focusing on isolated sayings. R. B. Y. Scott, for example, remarks on Prov 10:15: "The wisdom teachers, unlike the prophets, were socially conservative."[82] Prophetic and sapiential discourse, to be sure, typically employ different strategies, but the attentive reader of the book of Proverbs will discern not only the sages' willingness to look unflinchingly at the social inequities of the world around them, but also their interest in criticizing those inequities as violations of the moral order. The book as a whole does not simply reflect the class conceit of a sapiential elite; rather it embodies the broader social concern of the post-exilic sages, whose social location was more diffuse than that of their scribal-bureaucratic predecessors, and whose social function concerned the instruction and well-being of the entire Judean lay community. One of the aims of the collection of Hebrew Proverbs is to mirror instructively the ambiguities of the natural world and human society. The editorial tendencies disclosed above, however, demonstrate the sages' desire to teach a Wisdom consonant with the social values of the Hebrew Law and Prophets.

---

[81] R. N. Whybray, *Wealth and Poverty in the Book of Proverbs*, 67 n. 1 (Whybray's observation here is in tension with his earlier assertion that only in the 'better'-sayings are relative values expressed). Other commentators who have argued that the two sayings are to be linked, thus stressing that the advantages of wealth are illusory, include J. H. Greenstone, *Proverbs with Commentary*, 195; A. Cohen, *Proverbs: Hebrew Text and English Commentary*, 120; cf. T. Hildebrandt, "Proverbial Pairs: Compositional Units in Proverbs 10–29," 209.

[82] *Proverbs-Ecclesiastes*, 84.

X
SUMMARY OF RESULTS

Although the contents of the book of Proverbs developed gradually over a course of centuries, the final composition can be dated on the basis of linguistic, structural, and thematic features to the Persian period in Judah. Close affinities between Proverbs and Amenemope indicate a relationship of literary dependence. While literary influence in both directions has been argued, it is clear that Proverbs is dependent upon the Instruction of Amenemope. The influence of Amenemope was mediated through scribal education in the capital city of Jerusalem, perhaps as early as the period of the United Monarchy.

Some five centuries later, when Judah was under Achaemenid rule, the book of Proverbs finally assumed its present shape. In the Judean civic-temple community of the Persian period (Weinberg's *Bürger-Tempel-Gemeinde*), leadership of the community fell to the priesthood and the lay heads of the בֵּת אָבוֹת. The sages who completed the book of Proverbs are presumably to be found among these lay leaders of the Restoration community. Meanwhile the professional scribal class which had cultivated international didactic literature had all but disappeared from local Judean society. Consequently the professional scribal orientation of the antecedent literature diminishes in Proverbs.

Proverbs is shown to be a product of the Restoration era social-historical background. Against this background the teachings on wealth and poverty in the book of Proverbs are examined. In the book of Proverbs, the folk wisdom of Judean village society, which stressed hard work and communal interdependence, is combined with the ancient Near Eastern tradition emphasizing care for the poor. The Instruction of Amenemope is one of the primary sources of this latter teaching. The final editing of the book does not resolve all the tensions among the various formulations concerning wealth and poverty, but contextual clues point toward an affirmative ethic of social equity.

CONCLUSION

Discarded hypotheses can sometimes shed an interesting light on the result of an inquiry: as I began working on this study, my expectation was that an elite upper-class perspective in the ancient Near Eastern international scribal literature, exemplified in the Egyptian Instruction, could be shown to have been tempered in the Hebrew Proverbs by the socially salutary emphases of Israelite folk wisdom and Yahwist piety. I found almost the opposite to be true. A "democratization of wisdom" is already well advanced in the Egyptian tradition. By the late New Kingdom period, when Amenemope was composed, the Instruction genre is addressing the concerns of an increasingly widened socio-economic spectrum. This democratizing tendency in the Egyptian tradition is completed some eight centuries later in the demotic Instruction of Ankhsheshonq. Although the narrative frame of Ankhsheshonq places the composition within the tradition of royal scribal Instruction, the teaching itself concerns the life of a small rural farmer.

The Instruction of Amenemope unmistakably assumes a posture of advocacy on behalf of the poor. This is a consequence of the broadened audience of the Instruction genre in the late New Kingdom period, of sensitivity to the socio-economic distress experienced by Ramesside society, and last but not least, of a religious piety of the most authentic sort—that which tends toward compassion and active concern for others. The book of Proverbs is most in accord with the ancient Near Eastern texts that influenced it, above all with Amenemope, when it defends the poor. The Hebrew sayings that might appear to blame the poor for their own poverty originated, in all likelihood, as native Hebrew village wisdom.

This work demonstrates the value of ancient Near Eastern background and of social-historical context for understanding the antecedents to Proverbs and the development of Hebrew sapiential thought. For the great body of New Kingdom Egyptian literature, whose influence on Hebrew wisdom has not yet been fully appreciated, we have access to a well documented social-historical background which greatly aids our grasp of the social function of the texts. As for Proverbs, the origins of portions of the book in monarchic Judah have been overemphasized. The book of Proverbs is finally a document of the Persian period, and it should be interpreted more thoroughly in that context.

This study illustrates the problems involved in attempting to apply biblical texts to ethical questions. Like the Hebrew canon as a whole, the book of Proverbs refuses to yield an entirely consistent social ethic. Rather, a diverse range of historically contingent points of view are held in creative tension with one another. Yet it is precisely the appreciation of this creative tension that the ancient sages sought to teach, along with the discernment necessary to adjudicate among contingencies and the willingness to submit sensitively and humbly to the instruction of tradition. In its capacity for self-criticism, the intellectual tradition of the ancient Near East and Israel served a vital social-critical purpose. For this reason among others, sapiential thought is essential to the moral vision of the Hebrew Bible.

BIBLIOGRAPHY

Egyptological Studies

Albright, W. F. *The Vocalization of the Egyptian Syllabic Orthography.* American Oriental Series 5. New Haven: American Oriental Society, 1934.

_____. "Some Oriental Glosses on the Homeric Problem." *AJA* 54 (1950) 162–76.

_____. "Northwest-Semitic Names in a List of Egyptian Slaves from the Eighteenth Century BC." *JAOS* 74 (1954) 222–33.

Albright, W. F. and T. Lambdin. "New Material for the Egyptian Syllabic Orthography." *JSS* 2 (1957) 113–27.

Aldred, C. A. "Egypt: The Amarna Period and the End of the Eighteenth Dynasty." *Cambridge Ancient History.* 3rd edition. Vol. 2, Part 2. *History of the Middle East and the Aegean Region c. 1380–1000 B.C.*, 49–97. Edited by I. E. S. Edwards, C. J. Gadd, N. G. L. Hammond, and E. Sollberger. Cambridge: Cambridge University Press, 1975.

Allam, S. *Das Verfahrensrecht in der Arbeitersiedlung von Deir el-Medineh.* Untersuchungen zum Rechtsleben im alten Ägypten 1. Tübingen: S. Allam, 1973.

_____. *Hieratische Ostraka und Papyri aus der Ramessidenzeit.* Urkunden zum Rechtsleben im alten Ägypten 1. Tübingen: S. Allam, 1973.

_____. "L'apport des documents juridiques de Deir-el-Medineh." *Le droit égyptien ancien*, 139–62. Colloque organisee par l'Institut des Hautes Etudes de Belgique, 1974.

_____. "Familie und Besitzverhältnisse in der altägyptischen Arbeitersiedlung von Deir el-Medineh." *Revue Internationale des Droit de l'Antiquité* 30 (1983) 17–39.

_____. "Justice in an Ancient Egyptian Village." *Everyday Life in Ancient Egypt.* Prism Archaeological Series 1. Cairo: Prism Publications, 1985.

Alt, A. "Zur literarischen Analyse der Weisheit des Amenemope." *Wisdom in Israel and the Ancient Near East: Presented to Professor Harold Henry Rowley*, 16–25. Edited by M. Noth and D. Winton Thomas. VTSup 3. Leiden: E. J. Brill, 1955.

Altenmueller, A. "Bemerkungen zu Kapitel 13 des Lehre des Amenemope (Am. 15,19–16,14)." *Fontes atque Pontes: Studien zu Geschichte, Kultur und Religion Ägyptens und des Alten Testaments*, fs. H. Brunner, 1–17. Edited by M. Görg. Ägypten und Altes Testament 5. Wiesbaden: Harrassowitz, 1983.

Assmann, J. *Ägyptische Hymnen und Gebete.* Zurich and Munich: Artemis, 1975.

_____. "Weisheit, Loyalismus, und Frömmigkeit." *Studien zu altägyptischen Lebenslehren*, 11–72. Edited by E. Hornung and O. Keel. OBO 28. Göttingen: Vandenhoeck & Ruprecht, 1979.

Baines, J. "Literacy and Ancient Egyptian Society." *Man* n.s. 18 (1983) 572–99.

Baines, J. and C. J. Eyre. "Four Notes on Literacy." *GM* 61 (1983) 65–96.

Barta, W. "Das Schulbuch Kemit." *ZÄS* 105 (1978) 6–14.

Bierbrier, M. L. *The Late New Kingdom in Egypt (c. 1300–664 B.C): A Genealogical and Chronological Investigation.* Warminster: Aris and Phillips, 1975.

_____. *The Tomb-Builders of the Pharaohs.* London: British Museum Publications, 1982.

Bissing, Fr. W. von. *Altägyptische Lebensweisheit.* Zurich: Artemis, 1955.

Blackman, A. M. "The Use of the Egyptian Word *ḥet* 'House' in the Sense of 'Stanza'." *Or* 7 (1938) 64–67.

Bonnet, C., and D. Valbelle. "Le village de Deir el-Médineh. Reprise de l'étude archéologique." *BIFAO* 75 (1975) 429–446.

_____. "Le village de Deir el-Médineh. Etude archéologique (suite)." *BIFAO* 76 (1976) 317–42.

Boochs, W. "Über den Strafzweck des Pfählens." *GM* 69 (1983) 7–10.

Borghouts, J. F. "Divine Intervention in Ancient Egypt and its Manifestation (*b3w*)." *Gleanings from Deir el-Medîna*, 1–69. Edited by R. J. Demarée and J. J. Janssen. Leiden: Nederlands Instituut voor het Nabije Oosten, 1982.

Botti, G. and T. E. Peet. *Il Giornale della Necropoli di Tebe*. Turin: Fratelli Bocca, 1928.

Breasted, J. H. *Development of Religion and Thought in Ancient Egypt*. New York: Harper, 1912.

Brunner, H. "Die Weisheitsliteratur." *Handbuch der Orientalistik*, Vol. 1, pt. 2, *Ägyptologie*. Edited by B. Spuler. Leiden: Brill, 1952.

_____. "Die Methode des Anfängerunterrichts im alten Ägypten und ihre Bedeutung." *Erziehung zur Menschlichkeit: Die Bildung im Umbruch der Zeit*; fs. E. Spranger, 207–218. Tübingen: Max Niemeyer, 1957.

_____. *Altägyptische Erziehung*. Wiesbaden: Harrassowitz, 1957.

_____. "Gerechtigkeit als Fundament des Thrones." *VT* 3 (1958) 426–428.

_____. "Die religiöse Wertung der Armut im Alten Ägypten." *Saeculum* 12 (1961) 319–44.

_____. "Die 'Weisen,' ihre 'Lehren' und 'Prophezeiungen' in altägyptischer Sicht." *ZÄS* 93 (1966) 29–35.

_____. "Der freie Wille Gottes in der ägyptischen Weisheit." *Les sagesses du Proche-Orient ancien, Colloque de Strasbourg 17–19 mai 1962*, 103–120. Bibliothèque des Centres d'Etudes Supérieures spécialisés. Paris: Presses universitaires, 1963.

_____. "Zitate aus Lebenslehren." *Studien zu altägyptischen Lebenslehren*, 105–71. Edited by E. Hornung and O. Keel. OBO 28. Freiburg: Universitätsverlag/Göttingen: Vandenhoeck & Ruprecht, 1979.

_____. "Die religiöse Antwort auf die Korruption in Ägypten." *Korruption im Altertum*, 71–77. Edited by W. Schuler. Munich/Vienna: Oldenbourg, 1982.

_____. "Schreibunterricht und Schule als Fundament der Ägyptischen Hochkultur." *Schulgeschichte im Zusammenhang der Kulturentwicklung*, 62–75. Edited by L. Kriss-Rettenbeck and M. Liedtke. Bad Heilbrunn: Julius Klinkhardt, 1983.

_____. *Altägyptische Weisheit: Lehren für das Leben*. Zurich and Munich: Artemis, 1988.

Bruyère, B. *Rapport sur les fouilles de Deir el Médineh*; 17 vols. Cairo: Institut français d'archéologie orientale, 1924-53.

Budge, E. A. W. *By Nile and Tigris: A Narrative of Journeys in Egypt and Mesopotamia on Behalf of the British Museum between the Years 1886 and 1913.* London: J. Murray, 1920.

_____. "The Precepts of Life, by Amen-em-Apt, the Son of Ka-nekht." *Recueil d'études égyptologiques dédiées à la mémoire de Jean-François Champollion.* Paris: E. Champion, 1922.

_____. *Facsimiles of Egyptian Hieratic Papyri in the British Museum with Descriptions, Summaries of Contents, Etc.* Second Series. London: Harrison and Sons, 1923.

_____. *The Teaching of Amen-em-Apt, Son of Kanekht.* London: Martin Hopkinson, 1924.

Burchardt, M. *Die altkanaanäischen Fremdworte und Eigennamen im Ägyptischen.* Leipzig: J. C. Hinrichs, 1909-1910.

Caminos, R. *Late Egyptian Miscellanies.* Brown Egyptological Studies 1. London: Oxford University Press, 1954.

Capart, J., A. Gardiner, and B. van de Walle. "New Light on the Ramesside Tomb-Robberies." *JEA 22* (1936) 169-93.

Černý, J. "Le culte d'Aménophis Ier chez les ouvriers de la nécropole thébaine." *BIFAO 27* (1927) 159-203.

_____. "Papyrus Salt 124 (Brit. Mus. 10055)." *JEA 15* (1929) 244.

_____. "Fluctuations in Grain Prices During the Twentieth Egyptian Dynasty." *Archiv Orientální 6* (1934) 173-78.

_____. "Une famille de scribes de la nécropole royale de Thèbes." *Chron. d'Eg 22* (1936) 247-50.

_____. *Late Ramesside Letters.* Bibliotheca Aegyptiaca 9. Brussels: 1939.

_____. *Ostraca hiératiques non littéraires de Deir el Medineh.* Cairo: Institut français d'archéologie orientale, 1951.

_____. *Paper and Books in Ancient Egypt.* London: H. K. Lewis, 1952.

_____. "Prices and Wages in Egypt in the Ramesside Period." *Journal of World History 1* (1954) 903-21.

_____. *Papyrus Hieratiques de Deir el-Medineh*, Vol I. Documents de Fouilles 8. Cairo: Institut français d'archéologie orientale, 1959.

_____. *A Community of Workmen at Thebes in the Ramesside Period*. Cairo: Institut français d'archéologie orientale, 1973.

_____. "Egypt: From the Death of Ramesses III to the End of the Twenty-First Dynasty." *Cambridge Ancient History*. 3rd edition. Vol. 2, Part 2. *History of the Middle East and the Aegean Region c. 1380-1000 B.C.*, 606-57. Edited by I. E. S. Edwards, C. J. Gadd, N. G. L. Hammond, and E. Sollberger. Cambridge: Cambridge University Press, 1975.

Černý, J. and S. I. Groll. *A Late Egyptian Grammar*. Rome: Biblical Institute Press, 1975.

Clère, J. J. "Un monument de la réligion populaire de l'époque ramesside." *RdE* 27 (1975) 70-77.

Couroyer, B. "Amenemopé I,9; III,13: Egypte ou Israel?." *RB* 68 (1961) 394-400.

_____. "L'origine égyptienne de la Sagesse d'Amenemopé." *RB* 70 (1963) 208-224.

Crum, W. E., ed. *A Coptic Dictionary*. Oxford: Clarendon, 1939.

Curtis, J. W. "Coinage of Pharaonic Egypt." *JEA* 43 (1957) 71-76.

De Buck, A. "Het religieus karakter der oudste egyptische Wijsheid." *NTT* 21 (1932) 322-49.

Drioton, E. "Sur la sagesse d'Aménémopé." *Mélanges bibliques rédigés en l'honneur de André Robert*, 254-80. Travaux de l'Institut catholique de Paris 4. Paris: Bloud and Gay, 1957.

Dunham, D. "The Biographical Inscriptions of Nekhebu in Boston and Cairo." *JEA* 24 (1938) 1-8.

Edel, E. "Neue Keilschriftlichen Umschreibungen Ägyptischer Namen aus den Bogazköytexten." *JNES* 7 (1948) 11-24.

_____. "Neues Material zur Beurteilung der syllabischen Orthographie des Ägyptischen." *JNES* 8 (1949) 44-47.

Edgerton, W. F. *Medinet Habu Graffiti Facsimiles*. Oriental Institute Publications 36. Chicago: University of Chicago Press, 1937.

_____. "The Strikes in Ramses III's Twenty-Ninth Year." *JNES* 10 (1951) 139-45.

_____. "Egyptian Phonetic Writing, from its Invention to the Close of the Nineteenth Dynasty." *JAOS* 60 (1940) 473–506.

_____. "The Nauri Decree of Seti I: A Translation and Analysis of the Legal Portion." *JNES* 6 (1947) 219–230.

Edgerton, W. and J. A. Wilson. *Historical Records of Ramses III*. Chicago: Oriental Institute, 1936.

Eggebrecht, A. "Die frühen Hochkulturen: Das Alte Ägypten." *Geschichte der Arbeit: Vom Alten Ägypten bis zur Gegenwart*, 24–93. Edited by A. Eggebrecht et al. Cologne: Kiepenheuer & Witsch, 1980.

Erman, A. "Das Weisheitsbuch des Amen-em-ope." *OLZ* 27 (1924) cols. 241–52.

_____. "Eine ägyptische Quelle der 'Sprüche Salomos'." *Sitzungsberichte der Preussischen Akademie der Wissenschaften zu Berlin: Phil.-hist. Klasse* 15 (1924) 86–93.

_____. *Die ägyptische Schülerhandschriften*. APAW 1925, Phil-hist. Kl. 2. Berlin: Akademie der Wissenschaften, 1925.

Erman, A. and H. Grapow. *Wörterbuch der ägyptischen Sprache*. 7 vols. Leipzig, J. C. Hinrichs, 1926–63.

Eyre, C. J. "A 'Strike' Text from the Theban Necropolis." *Glimpses of Ancient Egypt: Studies in Honour of H. W. Fairman*, 80–91. Edited by J. Ruffle, G. A. Gaballa and K. A. Kitchen. Warminster: Aris & Phillips, 1979.

_____. "Work and the Organisation of Work in the New Kingdom." *Labor in the Ancient Near East*, 166–221. Edited by M. A. Powell. American Oriental Series 68. New Haven, Conn.: American Oriental Society, 1987.

_____. "Work and the Organisation of Work in the Old Kingdom." *Labor in the Ancient Near East*, 5–47. Edited by M. A. Powell. American Oriental Series 68. New Haven, Conn.: American Oriental Society, 1987.

Faulkner, R. O. "The Installation of the Vizier." *JEA* 41 (1955) 18–29.

_____. *A Concise Dictionary of Middle Egyptian*. Oxford: Griffith Institute, 1962.

_____. "Egypt: From the Inception of the Nineteenth Dynasty to the Death of Ramesses III." *Cambridge Ancient History*. 3rd edition. Vol. 2, Part 2. *History of the Middle East and the Aegean Region c. 1380–1000 B.C.*, 217–51. Edited by I. E. S. Edwards, C. J. Gadd, N. G. L. Hammond, and E. Sollberger. Cambridge: Cambridge University Press, 1975.

Fischer-Elfert, H.-W. *Die Satirische Streitschrift des Papyrus Anastasi I.* Kleine Ägyptische Texte. Wiesbaden: O. Harrassowitz, 1983.

_____. *Literarische Ostraka der Ramessidenzeit in Übersetzung.* Klein Ägyptische Texte. Wiesbaden: Harrassowitz, 1986.

Fox, M. V. "Two Decades of Research in Egyptian Wisdom Literature." *ZÄS* 107 (1980) 120-35.

_____. "The Social Setting of the Wisdom Instruction: The Egyptian Example." Paper presented to the Hebrew Scriptures and Cognate Literature Section of the Society of Biblical Literature Annual Meeting, November 19, 1989, Anaheim, California.

Gardiner, A. H. *The Admonitions of an Egyptian Sage.* Leipzig: J. C. Hinrichs, 1909.

_____. *Egyptian Hieratic Texts. Series I: Literary Texts of the New Kingdom. Part I: The Papyrus Anastasi I and the Papyrus Koller, Together with the Parallel Texts.* Leipzig: J. C. Hinrichs, 1911.

_____. "A Lawsuit Arising from the Purchase of Two Slaves." *JEA* 21 (1935) 140-6.

_____. *Late-Egyptian Miscellanies.* Bibliotheca Aegyptiaca 7. Brussels: Fondation Egyptologique, 1937.

_____. "Ramesside Texts Relating to the Taxation and Transport of Corn." *JEA* 27 (1941) 19-73.

_____. *Ancient Egyptian Onomastica.* London: Oxford University Press, 1947.

_____. *Ramesside Administrative Documents.* Oxford: Oxford University Press, 1948.

_____. "A Pharaonic Encomium." *JEA* 41 (1955) 30 and pls. 7-11.

_____. "A Pharaonic Encomium, II." *JEA* 42 (1956) 8-20.

_____. *Egyptian Grammar.* Third edition, revised. Oxford: Griffith Institute, 1957.

_____. *Egypt of the Pharaohs.* Oxford: Oxford University Press, 1961.

Gauthier, H. *La grande inscription dédicatoire d'Abydos.* Cairo: Imprimerie de l'Institut français d'archéologie orientale, 1912.

Goedicke, H. "A Neglected Wisdom Text." *JEA* 48 (1962) 25-35.

Goetze, A. "The Struggle for the Domination of Syria (1400-1300 B.C.)." *Cambridge Ancient History*. 3rd edition. Vol. 2, Part 2. *History of the Middle East and the Aegean Region c. 1380-1000 B.C.*, 1-20. Edited by I. E. S. Edwards, C. J. Gadd, N. G. L. Hammond, and E. Sollberger. Cambridge: Cambridge University Press, 1975.

Griffith, F. Ll. "The Teaching of Amenophis the Son of Kanakht. Papyrus B.M. 10474." *JEA* 12 (1926) 191-231.

_____. "The Abydos Decree of Seti I at Nauri." *JEA* 13 (1927) 193-208.

Grumach, I. *Untersuchungen zur Lebenslehre des Amenope*. Münchner ägyptologische Studien 23. Munich: Deutscher Kunstverlag, 1970.

Gunn, B. "The Religion of the Poor in Ancient Egypt." *JEA* 3 (1916) 81-94.

Gutgesell, M. *Die Datierung der Ostraka und Papyri aus Deir el-Medineh und ihre ökonomische Interpretation, Teil I: Die 20. Dynastie*. Hildesheimer Ägyptologische Beiträge 18. Hildesheim: Gerstenberg, 1983.

Helck, H. W. *Der Einfluss der Militärführer in der 18. ägyptischen Dynastie*. Leipzig: J. C. Hinrichs, 1939.

_____. *Materialien zur Wirtschaftsgeschichte des Neuen Reiches*. Wiesbaden: Harrassowitz, 1961-70.

_____. *Die Beziehungen Ägyptens zu Vorderasien im 3. und 2. Jahrtausend v. Chr.*. Ägyptologische Abhandlungen 5. Wiesbaden: Harrassowitz, 1962.

_____. *Geschichte des alten Ägypten*. Handbuch der Orientalistik, I, Vol 1, Section 3. Leiden: E. J. Brill, 1968.

_____. *Die Lehre des Dw3-Htjj*. Wiesbaden: Harrassowitz, 1970.

_____. *Wirtschaftsgeschichte des alten Ägypten im 3. und 2. Jahrtausend vor Chr.*. Leiden: E. J. Brill, 1975.

_____. "Zur Buchmalerei im alten Ägypten." *Studien zur Geschichte und Kultur des Vorderen Orients*, fs. Bertold Spuler, 167-70. Edited by H. R. Roemer and A. North. Leiden: E. J. Brill, 1981.

_____. "'Korruption' im Alten Ägypten." *Korruption im Altertum*, 65-70. Edited by W. Schuler. Munich/Vienna: Oldenbourg, 1982.

Helck, H. W., and E. Otto, eds. *Lexicon der Ägyptologie*. Wiesbaden: Harrassowitz, 1972.

Hornung, E. *Untersuchungen zur Chronologie und Geschichte des Neuen Reiches*. Ägyptologische Abhandlungen 11. Wiesbaden: Harrassowitz, 1964.

James, T. G. H. *The Hekanakhte Papers and Other Early Middle Kingdom Documents.* New York: Metropolitan Museum of Art, 1962.

James, T. G. H. *Pharaoh's People: Scenes from Life in Imperial Egypt.* Chicago: University of Chicago Press, 1984.

_____. *Two Ancient Egyptian Ship's Logs: Papyrus Leiden I 350 verso and Papyrus Turin 2008+2016.* Leiden: Brill, 1961.

_____. "Semitic Loan-Words in Egyptian Ostraca." *JEOL* 19 (1966) 443–48.

_____. *Commodity Prices from the Ramessid Period: An Economic Study of the Village of Necropolis Workmen at Thebes.* Leiden: E. J. Brill, 1975.

_____. "Prolegomena to the Study of Egypt's Economic History during the New Kingdom." *SAK* 3 (1975) 127–85.

_____. "Background Information on the Strikes of Year 29 of Ramesses III." *OrAnt* 18 (1979) 301–308.

_____. "The Role of the Temple in the Egyptian Economy During the New Kingdom." *State and Temple Economy in the Ancient Near East: Proceedings of the International Conference Organized by the Katholieke Universiteit Leuven from the 10th to the 14th of April 1978*, 2.505–15. Orientalia Lovaniensia Analecta 5–8. Leuven: Department Oriëntalistik, 1979.

_____. "Absence from Work by the Necropolis Workmen of Thebes." *SAK* 8 (1980) 127–152.

_____. "Die Struktur der pharaonischen Wirtschaft." *GM* 48 (1981) 59–77.

_____. "The Mission of the Scribe Pesiur." *Gleanings from Deir el-Medîna*, 133–48. Edited by R. J. Demarée and J. J. Janssen. Leiden: Nederlands Instituut voor het Nabije Oosten, 1982.

Jequier, G. *Le Papyrus Prisse et ses variants.* Paris: Libraire Paul Geuthner, 1911.

Kadry, A. *Officers and Officials in the New Kingdom.* Studia Aegyptiaca 8. Budapest: Université Loránd Eötvös de Budapest, 1982.

Kaplony-Heckel, U. "Schüler und Schulwesen in der Ägyptischen Spätzeit." *SAK* 2 (1974) 227–46.

Katary, S. "Cultivator, Scribe, Stablemaster, Soldier: The Late-Egyptian Miscellanies in Light of *P. Wilbour.*" *Egyptological Miscellanies: A Tribute to Professor Ronald J. Williams*, 71–94. Edited by J. K. Hoffmeier et al. Chicago: Ares, 1983.

Kees, H. "Die Laufbahn des Hohenpriesters Onhurmes von Thinis." *ZÄS* 73 (1937) 77-90.

Kemp, B. J. "Imperialism and Empire in New Kingdom Egypt (c. 1575-1087 B.C.)." *Imperialism in the Ancient World*, 7-57. Edited by P. D. Garnsey and C. R. Whittaker. Cambridge: Cambridge University Press, 1978.

_____. "Old Kingdom, Middle Kingdom and Second Intermediate." *Ancient Egypt: A Social History*, 71-182. Edited by B. G. Trigger et al. Cambridge: Cambridge University Press, 1983.

Kitchen, K. A. *Suppiluliuma and the Amarna Pharaohs*. Liverpool: Liverpool University Press, 1962.

_____. *The Third Intermediate Period in Egypt*. Warminster: Aris and Phillips, 1973.

_____. Review of I. Grumach, *Untersuchungen zur Lebenslehre des Amenope. Or* 43 (1974) 127-8.

_____. *Pharaoh Triumphant: The Life and Times of Ramesses II, King of Egypt*. Warminster: Aris & Phillips, 1982.

Knudtzon, J. A. *Die El-Amarna Tafeln mit Einleitung und Erläuterungen*. Leipzig: J. C. Hinrichs, 1908-1915.

Lambdin, T. "Egyptian Loan Words in the Old Testament." *JAOS* 73 (1953) 145-55.

_____. "Egyptian Words in Tell El Amarna Letter No. 14." *Or* n.s. 22 (1953) 367.

Lange, H. O. "En ny Visdomsbog fra det Gamle Aegypten." *Nordisk Tidskrift* (1924) 94-107.

_____. *Das Weisheitsbuch des Amenemope aus dem Papyrus 10,474 des British Museum herausgegeben und erklärt*. Det Kgl. Danske videnskabernes Selskab, Historisk-filologiske Meddelelser 11,2. Copenhagen: Andr. Fred. Høst, 1925.

Leclant, J. "Documents nouveaux et points de vue recents sur les Sagesses de l'Egypte ancienne." *Les sagesses du Proche-Orient ancien, Colloque de Strasbourg 17-19 mai 1962*, 5-26. Bibliothèque des Centres d'Etudes Supérieures spécialisés. Paris: Presses universitaires, 1963.

Lesko, L. H. and B. S. Lesko. *A Dictionary of Late Egyptian*. Berkeley, California: Scribe Publications, 1982-88.

Lichtheim, M. *Ancient Egyptian Literature*, Vols. I–III. Berkeley: University of California Press, 1976–1980.

_____. "Some Corrections to My *Ancient Egyptian Literature*, I–III." *GM* 41 (1980) 67–74.

Luria, S. "Die Ersten werden die Letzten sein." *Klio* 22 (1929) 405–431.

Mariette, A. *Abydos, description des fouilles executées sur l'emplacement de cette ville*. Paris: A. Franck, 1869–80.

Maspero, G. *La trouvaille de Deir el-Bahari*. Cairo: Imprimerie Nouvelle du "Moniteur Egyptien," 1883.

_____. *Les momies royales de Deir el-Bahari*. Cairo: Memoires ... mission archéologique au Caire I,2, 1887.

Morenz, S. *Egyptian Religion*. Ithaca, N.Y.: Cornell University Press, 1960.

_____. *Prestige-Wirtschaft im alten Ägypten*. Bayerische Akademie der Wissenschaften, Philosophisch-Historische Klasse, Sitzungsberichte 4. Munich: Bayerische Akademie der Wissenschaften, 1969.

Mueller, W. M. *Asien und Europa nach altägyptischen Denkmälern*. Leipzig: W. Engelman, 1893.

_____. *Die Liebespoesie der alten Ägypter*. Leipzig: J. C. Hinrichs, 1899.

O'Connor, D. "New Kingdom and Third Intermediate Period, 1552–644 BC." *Ancient Egypt: A Social History*, 183–278. Edited by B. G. Trigger et al. Cambridge: Cambridge University Press, 1983.

Otto, E. "Bildung und Ausbildung im alten Ägypten." *ZÄS* 8 (1956) 41–48.

Peet, T. E. "A Historical Document of Ramesside Age." *JEA* 10 (1924) 116–27.

_____. "Fresh Light on the Tomb Robberies of the Twentieth Dynasty at Thebes: Some New Papyri in London and Turin." *JEA* 11 (1925) 37–55.

_____. *The Great Tomb-Robberies of the Twentieth Egyptian Dynasty*. Oxford: Oxford University Press, 1930.

Pestman, P. W. and J. J. Janssen, "Burial and Inheritance in the Community of the Necropolis Workmen at Thebes." *JESHO* 11 (1968) 137–70.

Peterson, B. "A New Fragment of *The Wisdom of Amenemope*." *JEA* 52 (1966) 120–128; Pls. 31–31a.

_____. "A Note of the Wisdom of Amenemope 3.9-4.10." *Studia Aegyptiaca* 1 (1974) 323-27.

Pflüger, K. "The Edict of King Haremhab." *JNES* 5 (1946) 260-276.

Posener, G. *Littérature et politique dans l'Egypte de la xiie dynastie.* Bibliothèque de l'Ecole des Hautes Etudes 307. Paris: Ecole des Hautes Etudes, 1956.

_____. "Aménémopé 21,13 et *bj3j.t* au sens d''oracle'." *ZÄS* 90 (1963) 98-102.

_____. "Quatre tablettes scolaires de basse époque (Aménémopé et Hardjedef)." *RdE* 18 (1966) 45-65.

_____. "Amon juge du pauvre." *Beiträge zur Ägyptischen Bauforschung und Altertumskunde* 12, fs. H. Ricke (Wiesbaden: Harrassowitz, 1971) 59-63.

_____. "Une nouvelle tablette d'Aménémopé." *RdE* 25 (1973) 251-2.

_____. "La piété personelle avant l'âge amarnien." *RdE* 27 (1975) 195-210.

Rainey, A. F. "The Soldier-Scribe in *Papyrus Anastasi I.*" *JNES* 26 (1966) 58-60.

Ranke, H. *Die ägyptischen Personennamen.* Glueckstadt: J. J. Augustin, 1935-52.

Renouf, L. Le Page. "Is אַבְרֵךְ (Gen. xli,43) Egyptian? The Thematic Vowel in Egyptian." *Proceedings of the Society of Biblical Archaeology* 11 (1888-89) 6-8.

Römheld, D. *Wege der Weisheit: Die Lehren Amenemopes und Proverbien 22,17-24,22.* BZAW 184. Berlin: de Gruyter, 1989.

Sadek, A. I. *Popular Religion in Egypt during the New Kingdom.* HÄB 27. Hildesheim: Gerstenberg, 1987.

Säve-Söderbergh, T. *Ägypten und Nubien: Ein Beitrag zur Geschichte altägyptischer Aussenpolitik.* Lund: 1941.

Schenkel, W. "Eine neue Weisheitslehre?" *JEA* 50 (1964) 6-12.

_____. *Materialien zur Vorlesung: "Einführung in die klassisch-ägyptische Sprache und Schrift".* Tübingen: W. Schenkel, 1985.

Schulman, A. R. "*Mhr* and *mskb*, Two Egyptian Military Titles of Semitic Origin." *ZÄS* 93 (1966) 123-32.

Sethe, K., ed. *Urkunden der 18. Dynastie.* Urkunden des ägyptischen Altertums 4. Leipzig: J. C. Hinrichs, 1906-58.

_____. *Urkunden des alten Reichs.* Urkunden des ägyptischen Altertums. Leipzig: J. C. Hinrichs, 1906–58.

Simpson, W. K. *The Literature of Ancient Egypt: An Anthology of Stories, Instructions, and Poetry.* 2nd edition. New Haven: Yale University Press, 1973.

Spiegelberg, W. *Arbeiter und Arbeiterbewegung im Pharaonenreich unter den Ramessiden (ca. 1400–1100 v. Chr.) eine kulturgeschichtliche Skizze.* Strassburg: K. J. Trübner, 1895.

_____. Review of Budge, *Facsimiles of Egyptian Hieratic Papyri, Second Series, OLZ* 27 (1924) col. 185.

Steindorff, G. and K. C. Seele, *When Egypt Ruled the East.* Revised ed. Chicago: University of Chicago Press, 1957.

Stoof, M. "Untersuchungen zur Bevorratung und Lagerung von Getreide im alten Ägypten." *Ethnographisch-Archäologische Zeitschrift* 23 (1982) 453–464.

Strobel, A. *Der spätbronzezeitliche Seevölkersturm.* BZAW 145. Berlin/New York: de Gruyter, 1976.

Suys, E. *La Sagesse d'Ani.* Analecta Orientalia 11. Rome: Pontifical Institute, 1935.

te Velde, H. "Scribes and Literacy in Ancient Egypt." *Scripta Signa Vocis: Studies about Scripts, Scriptures, Scribes and Languages in the Near East,* fs. J. H. Hospers, 253–64. Edited by H. L. J. Vanstiphout et al. Groningen: Egbert Forsten, 1986.

Tresson, P. *La stèle de Koubân.* Cairo: Imprimerie de l'Institute français d'archéologie orientale, 1922.

Trigger, B. G., B. J. Kemp, D. O'Connor, A. B. Lloyd, eds. *Ancient Egypt: A Social History.* Cambridge: Cambridge University Press, 1983.

Tylor, J. J. and F. Ll. Griffith. *The Tomb of Paheri.* London: Kegan, Paul, Trench, Trübner, 1894.

van de Walle, B. *La transmission des textes littéraires égyptiens.* Brussels: Fondation égyptologique Reine Elisabeth, 1948.

_____. "Problèmes relatifs aux méthodes d'enseignement dans l'Egypte ancienne." *Les sagesses du Proche-Orient ancien, Colloque de Strasbourg 17–19 mai 1962,* 191–207. Bibliothèque des Centres d'Etudes Supérieures spécialisés. Paris: Presses universitaires, 1963.

van Seters, J. "A Date for the 'Admonitions' in the Second Intermediate Period." *JEA* 50 (1964) 13-23.

Vandier, J. *La famine dans l'Egypte ancienne.* Recherches d'archéologie, de philologie et d'histoire 7. Cairo: Institut français d'archéologie orientale, 1936.

Vercoutter, J. "The Gold of Kush. Two Gold-Washing Stations at Faras East." *Kush* 7 (1959) 129-35.

Ward, "Notes on Egyptian Group-Writing." *JNES* 16 (1957) 198-203.

Wente, E. *Late Ramesside Letters.* Studies in Ancient Oriental Civilization 33. Chicago: University of Chicago Press, 1967.

Wiedemann, A. Review of E. A. W. Budge, *The Teaching of Amen-em-apt. OLZ* 28 (1925) 300-301.

Williams, R. J. "The Alleged Semitic Original of the *Wisdom of Amenemope.*" *JEA* 47 (1961) 100-106.

_____. "Scribal Training in Ancient Egypt."*JAOS* 92 (1972) 214-221.

_____. "Piety and Ethics in the Ramessid Age." *JSSEA* 8 (1978) 131-37.

_____. "The Sages of Ancient Egypt in the Light of Recent Scholarship." *JAOS* 101 (1981) 1-19.

Wilson, J. *The Burden of Egypt: An Interpretation of Ancient Egyptian Culture.* Chicago: University of Chicago Press, 1951.

Zába, Z. *Les maximes de Ptahhotep.* Prague: Académie tchécoslovaque des sciences, 1956.

Biblical Studies

Ackroyd, P. *Exile and Restoration: A Study of Hebrew Thought of the Sixth Century B.C..* Old Testament Library. Philadelphia: Westminster, 1968.

Aitken, H. T. *Proverbs.* Philadelphia: Westminster, 1986.

Albertz, R. *Persönliche Frömmigkeit und offizielle Religion: Religionsinterner Pluralismus in Israel und Babylon.* Calwer Theologische Monographien, Reihe A, 9. Stuttgart: Calwer, 1978.

Albright, W. F. "The Egyptian Correspondence of Abimilki, Prince of Tyre." *JEA* 23 (1937) 190-203.

_____. "Some Canaanite-Phoenician Sources of Hebrew Wisdom." *Wisdom in Israel and in the Ancient Near East: Presented to Professor Harold Henry Rowley*, 1–15. Edited by M. Noth and D. W. Thomas. VTSup 3. Leiden: E. J. Brill, 1955.

Amiran, D. H. K. "Land Use in Israel." *Land Use in Semi-Arid Mediterranean Climates*, 101–112. Paris: Unesco, 1964.

Andersen, F. I. "Who Built the Second Temple?" *Australian Biblical Review* 6 (1958) 1–35.

Auscher, D. "Les relations entre la Grèce et la Palestine avant la conquête d'Alexandre." *VT* 17 (1967) 8–30.

Balcer, J. *Sparda by the Bitter Sea: Imperial Interaction in Western Anatolia.* Brown Judaic Studies 52. Chico: Scholars Press, 1984.

Barr, J. Review of M. Wagner, *Die lexicalischen und grammatikalischen Aramaismen im alttestamentalichen Hebräisch. JSS* 14 (1969) 252–56.

Barucq, A. *Le livre des Proverbes.* Sources Bibliques. Paris: J. Gabalda, 1964.

Bauer H., and P. Leander *Historische Grammatik der hebräischen Sprache.* Halle: Niemeyer, 1922.

Bauer-Kayatz, C. *Studien zu Proverbien 1–9: Eine form- und motivgeschichtliche Untersuchung unter Einbeziehung Ägyptischen Vergleichsmaterials.* WMANT 22. Neukirchen-Vluyn: Neukirchener, 1966.

Baumgartner, A. J. *Etude Critique sur l'état du livre des Proverbes d'apres les principales traductions anciennes.* Leipzig: W. Drugulin, 1890.

Baumgartner, W. *Israelitische und altorientalische Weisheit.* Tübingen: Mohr, 1933.

Begrich, J. "Sofer und Mazkir. Ein Beitrag zur inneren Geschichte des davidisch-salomonischen Grossreiches und des Königsreiches Juda." *ZAW* 58 (1940–41) 1–29.

Behnke, P. "Spr. 10,1.25,1." *ZAW* 16 (1896) 122.

Beyse, K.-M. *Serubbabel und die Königserwartungen der Propheten Haggai und Sacharja.* Stuttgart: Calwer, 1972.

Blenkinsopp, J. "The Mission of Udjahorresnet and Those of Ezra and Nehemiah." *JBL* 106 (1987) 409–21.

_____. *Ezra-Nehemiah: A Commentary.* OTL. Philadelphia: Westminster, 1988.

_____. "Temple and Society in Achemenid Judah." *Second Temple Studies: 1. Persian Period*, 22–53. Edited by P. R. Davies. JSOTSup 117. Sheffield: JSOT, 1991.

Boström, G. *Paronomasi i den äldre hebreiska Maschalliteraturen*. LUA N.F. Avd. 1 Bd. 23, Nr. 8. Lund: Gleerup, 1928.

Bright, J. *A History of Israel*, 3rd edition. Philadelphia: Westminster, 1981.

Bryce, G. E. *A Legacy of Wisdom: The Egyptian Contribution to the Wisdom of Israel*. Lewisburg: Bucknell University Press, 1979.

_____. "Another Wisdom-'Book' in Proverbs." *JBL* 91 (1972) 145–57.

_____. "'Better'-Proverbs: An Historical and Structural Study." *SBL Seminar Papers* 108 (1972) 2.343–54.

Buchanan, G. "Midrashim Prétannaites, à propos de Prov. I–IX." *RB* 72 (1965) 227–39.

Camp, C. *Wisdom and the Feminine in the Book of Proverbs*. Bible and Literature Series 11. Sheffield: JSOT Press, 1985.

_____. "What's So Strange About the Strange Woman?" *The Bible and the Politics of Exegesis: Essays in Honor of Norman K. Gottwald on His Sixty-Fifth Birthday*, 17–32. Edited by D. Jobling et al. Cleveland: Pilgrim, 1991.

Childs, B. *Introduction to the Old Testament as Scripture*. Philadelphia: Fortress, 1979.

Clements, R. E. "Wisdom." *It is Written: Scripture Citing Scripture: Essays in Honour of Barnabas Lindars, SSF*, 67–83. Edited by D. A. Carson and H. G. Williamson. Cambridge: Cambridge University Press, 1988.

Clines, D. J. A. "Nehemiah 10 as an Example of Early Jewish Biblical Exegesis." *JSOT* 21 (1981) 111–117.

Cody, A. "Le titre égyptien et le nom propre du scribe de David." *RB* 72 (1965) 381–393.

Cohen, A. *Proverbs: Hebrew Text and English Translation with an Introduction and Commentary*. Hindhead, Surrey: Soncino, 1945.

Coogan, M. D. "*ʾlp*, 'To be an Abecedarian'." *JAOS* 110 (1990) 322.

Cook, J. M. *The Persian Empire*. London: J. M. Dent & Sons, 1983.

Cox, D. *Proverbs, with an Introduction to the Sapiential Books*. Old Testament Message 17. Wilmington, Del.: Michael Glazier, 1982.

Crenshaw, J. L., ed. *Studies in Ancient Israelite Wisdom*. New York: Ktav, 1976 [=*SAIW*].

_____. "Prolegomenon." *SAIW*, 1-62.

_____. "Method in Determining Wisdom Influence upon 'Historical' Literature." *SAIW* 481-94.

_____. "Education in Ancient Israel." *JBL* 104 (1985) 601-15.

_____. "Murphy's Axiom: Every Gnomic Saying Needs a Balancing Corrective." *The Listening Heart: Essays in Wisdom and the Psalms in Honor of Roland E. Murphy, O. Carm.*, 1-17. Edited by K. G. Hoglund et al. JSOTSup 58. Sheffield: Sheffield Academic Press, 1987.

Cross, F. M. Jr. "The Discovery of the Samaria Papyri." *BA* 26 (1963) 110-21.

_____. "Aspects of Samaritan and Jewish History in Late Persian and Hellenistic Times." *HTR* 59 (1966) 201-211.

_____. "Papyri of the Fourth Century BC from Dâliyeh." *New Directions in Biblical Archaeology*, 45-9. Edited by D. N. Freedman and J. C. Greenfield. Garden City, N.Y.: Doubleday, 1969.

_____. "The Papyri and Their Historical Implications." *Discoveries in the Wâdî ed-Dâliyeh*, 17-29. Edited by P. W. Lapp and N. L. Lapp. AASOR 41. Cambridge, Mass.: American Schools of Oriental Research, 1974.

_____. "Samaria Papyrus I: An Aramaic Slave Conveyance of 335 B.C.E." *EI* 18 (1985) 7*-17*.

_____. "A Report on the Samaria Papyri." *Congress Volume: Jerusalem*, 17-26. VTSup 40. Leiden: E. J. Brill, 1988.

Dahood, M. *Proverbs and Northwest Semitic Philology*. Rome: Pontifical Institute, 1963.

_____. *Psalms*. AB 16-17A. Garden City, N.Y.: Doubleday, 1966-70.

Dandamayev, M. "Babylonia in the Persian Age." *The Cambridge History of Judaism*, vol. I, *Introduction; The Persian Period*, 326-41. Edited by W. D. Davies and L. Finkelstein. Cambridge: Cambridge University Press, 1984.

Delitzsch, F. *Biblical Commentary on the Proverbs of Solomon*. Edinburgh: T. & T. Clark, vol. 1, 1874; vol. 2, 1875.

Demsky, A. "Education in the Biblical Period." *Encyclopaedia Judaica.* Jerusalem: Keter, 1971. vol. 6, cols. 382–98.

Demsky, A. and M. Bar-Ilan, "Writing in Ancient Israel and Early Judaism." *Mikra: Text, Translation, Reading and Interpretation of the Hebrew Bible in Ancient Judaism and Early Christianity,* 1–38. Edited by M. J. Mulder. Philadelphia: Fortress/Assen-Maastricht: Van Gorcum, 1988.

Doll, P. *Menschenschöpfung und Weltschöpfung in der alttestamentlichen Weisheit.* Stuttgarter Bibelstudien 117. Stuttgart: Katholisches Bibelwerk, 1985.

Donald, T. "The Semantic Field of Rich and Poor in the Wisdom Literature of Hebrew and Accadian." *Oriens Antiquus* 3 (1964) 27–41.

Drioton, E. "Le livre des Proverbes et la sagesse d'Aménémopé." *Sacra Pagina: Miscellanea Biblica Congressus internationalis Catholici de Re Biblica,* 1.229–241. Edited by J. Coppens, A. Descamps, and E. Massaux. Bibliotheca ephemeridum theologicarum Lovaniensium 12–13. Gembloux: J. Duculot, 1959.

_____. "Un livre hébreu sur couverture égyptienne." *La Table ronde* (October 1960) 81–91.

_____. "Une colonie israélite en Moyenne Egypte à la fin du VIIe siecle av. J.-C." *A la Rencontre de Dieu: Mémorial Albert Gelin,* 181–91. Bibliothèque de la faculté catholique de théologie de Lyon 8. Le Puy: Xavier Mappus, 1961.

Driver, G. R. "Hebrew Poetic Diction." *Congress Volume: Copenhagen,* 26–39. VTSup 1. Leiden: E. J. Brill, 1953.

Ehrlich, A. B. *Randglossen zur Hebräischen Bibel: Textkritisches, Sprachliches, und Sachliches.* 6r Band. *Psalmen, Sprüche, und Hiob.* Leipzig: Hinrichs, 1913.

Eissfeldt, O. *Der Maschal im Alten Testament.* BZAW 24. Giessen: A. Toepelmann, 1913.

_____. *The Old Testament: An Introduction.* New York: Harper & Row, 1965.

Elayi, J. *Pénétration grecque en Phénicie sous l'Empire perse.* Nancy: Presses Universitaires de Nancy, 1988.

Erman, A. "Eine ägyptische Quelle der 'Sprüche Salomos'." *SPAW* 15 (1924) 86–93.

Eskenazi, T. C. *In An Age of Prose: A Literary Approach to Ezra-Nehemiah.* SBLMS 36. Atlanta: Scholars Press, 1988.

Fensham, F. C. "Widow, Orphan, and the Poor in Ancient Near Eastern Legal and Wisdom Literature." *SAIW* 161–174.

Fichtner, J. *Die altorientalische Weisheit in ihrer israelitisch-jüdischen Ausprägung; Eine Studie zur Nationalisierung der Weisheit in Israel.* BZAW 42. Giessen: A. Toepelmann, 1933.

Fishbane, M. "Torah and Tradition." *Theology and Tradition in the Old Testament*, 275–300. Edited by D. Knight. Philadelphia: Fortress, 1977.

_____. *Biblical Interpretation in Ancient Israel.* Oxford: Clarendon, 1985.

Fohrer, G. *Introduction to the Old Testament.* Philadelphia: Fortress, 1970.

Fontaine, C. *Traditional Sayings in the Old Testament: A Contextual Study.* Bible and Literature Series 5. Sheffield: Almond, 1982.

_____. "Proverb Performance in the Hebrew Bible." *JSOT* 32 (1985) 87–103.

Fox, M. V. *The Song of Songs and the Ancient Egyptian Love Songs.* Madison: University of Wisconsin Press, 1985.

_____. *Qoheleth and His Contradictions.* JSOTSup 71. Sheffield: Almond, 1989.

Frei, P. "Zentralgewalt und Lokalautonomie im Achämenidenreich". *Reichsidee und Reichsorganisation im Perserreich*, 7–43. Edited by P. Frei and K. Koch. OBO 55. Freiburg: Universitätsverlag and Göttingen: Vandenhoeck & Ruprecht, 1984.

Funck, B. "Zur Bürger-Tempel-Gemeinde im nachexilischen Juda." *Klio* 59 (1977) 492–96.

Galling, K. "Erwägungen zur antiken Synagoge." *ZDPV* 72 (1956) 163–78.

_____. *Studien zur Geschichte Israels im persischen Zeitalter.* Tübingen: Mohr, 1964.

Garbini, G. *History and Ideology in Ancient Israel.* New York: Crossroad, 1988.

Gemser, B. *Sprüche Salomos.* 2nd ed. HAT 16. Tübingen: Mohr, 1962.

Gerleman, G. "The Septuagint Proverbs as a Hellenistic Document." *OTS* 8 (1950) 15–27.

_____. *Studies in the Septuagint, III, Proverbs.* Lunds Universitets Arsskrift, N.F., Avd. I, Bd. 52, Nr. 3 (1956).

Gese, H. *Lehre und Wirklichkeit in der alten Weisheit: Studien zu den Sprüchen Salomos und zu dem Buche Hiob*. Tübingen: Mohr, 1958.

_____. "Wisdom Literature in the Persian Period." *The Cambridge History of Judaism*, Vol 1, *Introduction; The Persian Period*, 189–218. Edited by W. D. Davies et al. Cambridge: Cambridge University Press, 1984.

Gevaryahu, H. M. "Privathaüser als Versammlungsstätten von Meister und Jüngern." *ASTI* 12 (1983) 5–12.

Giese, R. "Wisdom and Wealth in the Septuagint of Proverbs." Ph.D. dissertation, University of Wisconsin, Madison, 1990.

Gilbert, M., ed. *La Sagesse de l'Ancien Testament*. BETL 51. Gembloux: Duculot, 1979.

Giveon, R. *The Impact of Egypt on Canaan: Iconographical and Related Studies*. OBO 20. Göttingen: Vandenhoeck & Ruprecht, 1978.

Glare, P. G. W., ed. *Oxford Latin Dictionary*. Oxford: Clarendon, 1982.

Golka, F. W. "Die israelitische Weisheitsschule oder 'Des Kaisers neue Kleider'." *VT* 33 (1983) 257–70.

_____. "Die Königs- und Hofsprüche und der Ursprung der israelitischen Weisheit." *VT* 36 (1986) 13–36.

Gordis, R. "The Social Background of Wisdom Literature." *HUCA* 18 (1944) 77–118.

_____. "Quotations as a Literary Usage in Biblical, Oriental, and Rabbinic Literature." *Poets, Prophets, and Sages: Essays in Biblical Interpretation*, 104–159. Bloomington: Indiana University Press, 1971.

_____. "The Use of Quotations in Job." *The Book of God and Man: A Study of Job*, 169–89. Chicago: University of Chicago Press, 1965.

Gordon, E. I. and T. Jacobsen. *Sumerian Proverbs: Glimpses of Everyday Life in Ancient Mesopotamia*. Philadelphia: University Museum of the University of Pennsylvania, 1959.

Gottwald, N. *The Tribes of Yahweh: A Sociology of Liberated Israel, 1250–1050 BCE*. Maryknoll: Orbis, 1979.

_____. *The Hebrew Bible: A Socio-Literary Introduction*. Philadelphia: Fortress, 1985.

Green, A. R. "Solomon and Siamon: A Synchronism between Dynastic Israel and the Twenty-First Dynasty of Egypt." *JBL* 97 (1978) 353–67.

_____. "Israelite Influence at Shishak's Court?" *BASOR* 233 (1979) 59–62.

Greenstone, J. H. *Proverbs with Commentary.* Philadelphia: Jewish Publication Society, 1950.

Gressmann, H. "Die neugefundene Lehre des Amen-em-ope und die vorexilische Spruchdichtung Israels." *ZAW* n.s. 1 (1924) 272–81.

_____. *Israels Spruchweisheit im Zusammenhang der Weltliteratur.* Berlin: C. Curtius, 1925.

Grimme, H. "Weiteres zu Amen-em-ope und Proverbien." *OLZ* 28 1925) col. 58.

Halpern, B. *The Emergence of Israel in Canaan.* SBLMS 29. Chico: Scholars Press, 1983.

Hamp, V. *Das Buch der Sprüche.* Echter Bibel 8. Wurzburg: Echter, 1949.

Haran, M. "On the Diffusion of Literacy and Schools in Ancient Israel." *Congress Volume: Jerusalem 1986,* 81–95. VTSup 40. Leiden: E. J. Brill, 1988.

Helck, W. "Proverbia 22,17 ff. und die Lehre des Amenemope." *AfO* 22 (1968) 26–27.

Hengel, M. *Judaism and Hellenism: Studies in their Encounter in Palestine during the Early Hellenistic Period.* Philadelphia: Fortress, 1974.

Hermisson, H.-J. *Studien zur israelitischen Spruchweisheit.* WMANT 28. Neukirchen: Neukirchener, 1968.

Herzog, D. "Die Sprüche des Amen-em-ope und Proverbien Kapp. 22,17–24,35." *Zeitschrift für Semitistik und verwandte Gebiete* 7 (1929) 124–60.

Hildebrandt, T. "Proverbial Poetry: Its Settings and Syntax." Th.D. dissertation, Grace Theological Seminary, 1985.

_____. "Proverbial Pairs: Compositional Units in Proverbs 10–29." *JBL* 107 (1988) 207–224.

Hill, A. E. "Dating the Book of Malachi: A Linguistic Reexamination." *And the Word of the Lord Shall Go Forth: Essays in Honor of David Noel Freedman in Celebration of his Sixtieth Birthday,* 77–89. Edited by C. L. Meyers and M. O'Connor. Winona Lake: Eisenbrauns, 1983.

Hitzig, F. *Die Sprüche Salomo's.* Zurich: Orell, Fuessli, 1858.

Hoglund, K. G. "The Fool and the Wise in Dialogue." *The Listening Heart: Essays in Wisdom and the Psalms in Honor of Roland E. Murphy, O. Carm.*, 161–80. Edited by K. G. Hoglund et al. JSOT Sup 58. Sheffield: Sheffield Academic Press, 1987.

————. "Achaemenid Imperial Administration in Syria-Palestine and the Missions of Ezra and Nehemiah." Ph.D. dissertation, Duke University, 1989.

————. "The Achaemenid Context." *Second Temple Studies: 1. Persian Period*, 54–72. Edited by P. R. Davies. JSOTSup 117. Sheffield: JSOT, 1991.

Humbert, P. *Recherches sur les sources Egyptiennes de la littérature sapientiale d'Israel*. Neuchatel: Secrétariat de l'universitairé, 1929.

Humphreys, W. L. "The Motif of the Wise Courtier in the Book of Proverbs." *Israelite Wisdom: Theological and Literary Essays in Honor of Samuel Terrien*, 177–90. Edited by J. G. Gammie et al. New York: Union Theological Seminary, 1978.

Hurvitz, A. "The Chronological Significance of 'Aramaisms' in Biblical Hebrew." *IEJ* 18 (1968) 234–40.

Israelit-Groll, S. "The Egyptian Administrative System in Syria and Palestine in the 18th Dynasty." *Fontes atque Pontes: Studien zu Geschichte, Kultur und Religion Ägyptens und des Alten Testaments, Festgabe H. Brunner*, 334–42. Edited by M. Görg. Ägypten und Altes Testament 5; Wiesbaden: O. Harrassowitz, 1983.

Jamieson-Drake, D. W. *Scribes and Schools in Monarchic Judah: A Socio-Archeological Approach*. Social World of Biblical Antiquity Series 9. Sheffield: JSOT, 1991.

Janssen, E. *Juda in der Exilszeit*. FRLANT 69. Göttingen: Vandenhhoeck & Rupprecht, 1956.

Joüon, P. *Grammaire de l'hébreu biblique*. Rome: Pontifical Biblical Institute, 1923.

Kasher, R. "The Interpretation of Scripture in Rabbinic Literature." *Mikra: Text, Translation, Reading and Interpretation of the Hebrew Bible in Ancient Judaism and Early Christianity*, 547–594. Edited by M. Mulder. Philadelphia: Fortress/Assen-Maastricht: Van Gorcum, 1988.

Keller, C.-A. "Zum sogenannten Vergeltungsglauben im Proverbienbuch." *Beiträge zur alttestamentliche Theologie*, fs. W. Zimmerli, 223–238. Edited by H. Donner et al. Göttingen: Vandenhoeck & Ruprecht, 1977.

Kellermann, U. *Nehemiah: Quellen, Überlieferung und Geschichte.* BZAW 102. Berlin: Töpelmann, 1967.

Kevin, R. O. "The Wisdom of Amen-em-apt and its Possible Dependence upon the Hebrew Book of Proverbs." *JAOS* 14 (1930) 115–57.

Khanjian, J. "Wisdom." *Ras Shamra Parallels* 2, 371–400. Edited by L. Fisher. Analecta Orientalia 50. Rome: Pontifical Biblical Institute, 1975.

Kidner, D. *The Proverbs: an Introduction and Commentary.* London: Tyndale, 1964.

Kindler, A. "Addendum to the Dated Coins of Alexander Janneus." *IEJ* 18 (1968) 188–91.

Kippenberg, H. J. *Religion und Klassenbildung im antiken Judaea: Eine religionssoziologische Studie zum Verhältnis von Tradition und gesellschaftlicher Entwicklung.* SUNT 14. Göttingen: Vandenhoeck und Ruprecht, 1978.

Kitchen, K. A. Review of I. Grumach, *Untersuchungen zur Lebenslehre des Amenope.* Or 43 (1974) 127–8.

Koch, K. "Gibt es ein Vergeltungsdogma im Alten Testament?" *ZTK* 52 (1955) 1–42. Reprinted in *Um das Prinzip der Vergeltung in Religion und Recht des Alten Testaments.* Edited by K. Koch; Wege der Forschung 125; Darmstadt: Wissenschaftliche Buchgesellschaft, 1972). Abridged English translation in *Theodicy in the Old Testament*, 57–87. Edited by J. Crenshaw. Issues in Religion and Theology 4. Philadelphia: Fortress, 1983.

Koehler, L., W. Baumgartner, B. Hartmann, and E. Y. Kutscher, *Hebräisches und Aramäisches Lexikon zum Alten Testament.* Leiden: E. J. Brill, 1967–1990.

Kovacs, B. "Is There a Class-Ethic in Proverbs?" *Essays in Old Testament Ethics. J. P. Hyatt, In Memoriam*, 171–89. Edited by J. L Crenshaw and J. T. Willis. New York: Ktav, 1974.

Kraeling C. H. and R. M. Adams, eds. *City Invincible: A Symposium on Urbanization and Cultural Development in the Ancient Near East.* Chicago: University Press of Chicago Press, 1960.

Kreissig, H. *Die sozialökonomische Situation in Juda zur Achämenidenzeit.* Schriften zur Geschichte und Kultur des Alten Orients 7. Berlin: Akademie-Verlag, 1973.

Kugel, J. L. *Early Biblical Interpretation.* Library of Early Christianity 3. Philadelphia: Westminster, 1986.

Lambdin, T. O. "Egyptian Loan Words in the Old Testament." *JAOS* 73 (1953) 145-55.

Lambert, W. G. *Babylonian Wisdom Literature*. Oxford: Clarendon, 1960.

Lang, B. *Die weisheitliche Lehrrede: Eine Untersuchung von Sprüche 1-7*. Stuttgart: Katholisches Bibelwerk, 1972.

_____. "Schule und Unterricht im alten Israel." *La Sagesse de l'Ancien Testament*, 182-201. Edited by M. Gilbert. BETL 51. Gembloux: Editions Duculot, 1979.

_____. *Wisdom and the Book of Proverbs: An Israelite Goddess Redefined*. New York: Pilgrim, 1986.

Lemaire, A. *Les écoles et la formation de la Bible dans l'ancien Israél*. OBO 39. Göttingen: Vandenhoeck & Ruprecht, 1981.

_____. "Sagesse et écoles." *VT* 34 (1984) 270-81.

Liddell, H. G., R. Scott, and H. S. Jones, eds. *A Greek-English Lexicon*. Oxford: Clarendon, 1968.

Lindenberger, J. *The Aramaic Proverbs of Ahiqar*. Baltimore: Johns Hopkins, 1983.

Lipiński, E. "Royal and State Scribes in Ancient Jerusalem." *Congress Volume: Jerusalem 1986*, 157-64. VTSup 40. Leiden: E. J. Brill, 1988.

Mack-Fisher, L. R. "A Survey and Reading Guide to the Didactic Literature of Ugarit: Prolegomenon to a Study on the Sage;" and "The Scribe (and Sage) in the Royal Court at Ugarit." *The Sage in Israel and the Ancient Near East*, 67-80, 109-115. Edited by J. G. Gammie and L. G. Perdue. Winona Lake, Indiana: Eisenbrauns, 1990.

Malamat, A. "The Kingdom of David and Solomon in its Contact with Egypt and Aram Naharaim." *BA* 21 (1958) 96-102.

_____. "Aspects of the Foreign Policies of David and Solomon." *JNES* 22 (1963) 1-17.

_____. "A Political Look at the Kingdom of David and Solomon and its Relations with Egypt." *Studies in the Period of David and Solomon and Other Essays: Papers Read at the International Symposium for Biblical Studies, Tokyo, 5-7 December, 1979*, 189-204. Edited by T. Ishida. Winona Lake, Indiana: Eisenbrauns, 1982.

_____. *Das davidische und salomonische Königsreich und seine Beziehungen zu Ägypten und Syrien.* Österreichische Akademie der Wissenschaften Philosophisch-historische Klasse Sitzungsberichte 407. Vienna: Verlag der Österreichschen Akademie der Wissenschaften, 1983.

McGlinchey, J. M. *"The Teaching of Amen-em-ope and The Book of Proverbs."* Doctor of Sacred Theology dissertation. Catholic University of America, Washington, D.C., 1938.

McKane, W. *Prophets and Wise Men.* SBT 44. London: SCM, 1965.

_____. *Proverbs: A New Approach.* OTL. Philadelphia: Westminster, 1970.

Meshel, Z. "Kuntillet ʿAjrûd, 1975-1976." *IEJ* 27 (1977) 52-53.

_____. "Kuntillet ʿAjrûd, A Religious Center from the Time of the Judean Monarchy on the Sinai Border." *Israel Museum* (Jerusalem: 1978; Hebrew) catalogue no. 175.

Mettinger, T. *Solomonic State Officials: A Study of the Civil Government Officials of the Israelite Monarchy.* CB OT Series 5. Lund: Gleerup, 1971.

Meyers, E. M. "The Shelomith Seal and the Judean Restoration: Some Additional Considerations." *Eretz Israel* 18 (1985) 33*-38*.

Meyers, C. L. and E. M. Meyers. *Haggai, Zechariah 1-8.* Anchor Bible 25B. Garden City, N.Y.: Doubleday, 1987.

Millard, A. R. "The Practice of Writing in Ancient Israel." *BA* 35 (1972) 98-111.

_____. "An Assessment of the Evidence for Writing in Ancient Israel." *Biblical Archaeology Today: Proceedings of the International Congress on Biblical Archaeology, April 1984,* 301-312. Edited by A. Biran. Jerusalem: Israel Exploration Society, 1985.

Miller, P. D., Jr. *Sin and Judgment in the Prophets.* SBLMS 27; Chico, California: Scholars Press, 1982.

Morenz, S. "Ägypten und die Bibel." *RGG,* 1, cols. 117-21.

_____. "Ägyptologische Beiträge zur Erforschung der Weisheitsliteratur Israels." *Les sagesses du Proche-Orient ancien, Colloque de Strasbourg 17-19 mai 1962,* 63-71. Bibliothèque des Centres d'Etudes Supérieures spécialisés. Paris: Presses universitaires, 1963.

Murphy, R. "Assumptions and Problems in Old Testament Wisdom Research." *CBQ* 29 (1967) 102-112.

_____. "The Interpretation of Old Testament Wisdom Literature." *Int* 23 (1969) 289–301.

_____. "Wisdom Theses." *Wisdom and Knowledge*, fs. J. Papin. 2 vols. Edited by J. Armenti. Philadelphia: Villanova University Press, 1976.

_____. "Wisdom—Theses and Hypotheses." *Israelite Wisdom: Theological and Literary Essays in Honor of Samuel Terrien*, 35–42. Edited by J. L. Gammie et al. Missoula, Montana: Scholars Press, 1978.

_____. *Wisdom Literature: Job, Proverbs, Ruth, Canticles, Ecclesiastes, and Esther*. FOTL 13. Grand Rapids: Eerdmans, 1981.

_____. "Proverbs 22:1–9." *Int* 41 (1987) 398–402.

Naveh, J. "Dated Coins of Alexander Janneus." *IEJ* 18 (1968) 20–26.

Nel, P. J. "The Concept 'Father' in the Wisdom Literature of the Ancient Near East." *JNWSL* 5 (1977) 53–66.

_____. "Israelite Wisdom in the Persian Period: The Motivation of its Ethos." *OTWSA* 25 (1982) 1–15.

O'Brien, J. M. *Priest and Levite in Malachi*. SBLDS 121. Atlanta: Scholars Press, 1990.

Oesterley, W. O. E. "The 'Teaching of Amen-em-ope' and the Old Testament." *ZAW* 45 (1927) 9–24.

_____. *The Wisdom of Egypt and the Old Testament in the Light of the Newly Discovered "Teaching of Amen-em-ope"*. London: SPCK, 1927.

_____. *The Book of Proverbs*. London: Methuen & Co., 1929.

Olivier, J. P. J. "Schools and Wisdom Literature." *JNWSL* 4 (1975) 49–60.

Olmstead, A. T. *History of the Persian Empire*. Chicago: University of Chicago Press, 1948.

Perdue, L. *Wisdom and Cult: A Critical Analysis of the Views of Cult in the Wisdom Literature of Israel and the Ancient Near East*. SBLDS 30. Missoula, Montana: Scholars Press, 1977.

Petersen, D. L. *Haggai and Zechariah 1–8: A Commentary*. OTL. Philadelphia: Westminster, 1984.

Plöger, O. "Zur Auslegung der Sentenzensammlungen des Proverbiabuches." *Probleme biblischer Theologie. Gerhard von Rad zum 70. Geburtstag*, 402–416. Edited by H. W. Wolff. Munich: Kaiser, 1971.

_____. *Sprüche Salomos (Proverbia)*. BKAT 17. Neukirchen-Vluyn: Neukirchener, 1984.

Pleins, J. D. "Biblical Ethics and the Poor: The Language and Structures of Poverty in the Writings of the Hebrew Prophets." Ph.D. dissertation, University of Michigan, 1986.

_____. "Poverty in the Social World of the Wise." *JSOT* 37 (1987) 67–78.

Polzin, R. *Late Biblical Hebrew: Toward an Historical Typology of Biblical Hebrew Prose*. HSM 12. Missoula, Montana: Scholars Press, 1976.

Pritchard, J., ed. *Ancient Near Eastern Texts Relating to the Old Testament*. 3rd edition with supplement. Princeton: Princeton University Press, 1969.

Puech, E. "Les écoles dans l'Israel préexilique: données épigraphiques." *Congress Volume: Jerusalem 1986*, 189–203. VTSup 40. Leiden: E. J. Brill, 1988.

Rabin, C. "Hebrew." *Current Trends in Linguistics*, 6, 304–46. Linguistics in South West Asia and North Africa. Edited by T. A. Sebeok. The Hague: Mouton, 1970.

Redford, D. B. "Studies in Relations Between Palestine and Egypt During the First Millennium B.C. I. The Taxation System of Solomon." *Studies on the Ancient Palestinian World*, 141–46. Edited by J. W. Wevers and D. B. Redford. Toronto: University of Toronto Press, 1972.

Rendsburg, G. A. "Late Biblical Hebrew and the Date of 'P'." *JANES* 12 (1980) 65–80.

_____. "Bilingual Wordplay in the Bible." *VT* 38 (1988) 354–57.

Rendtorff, R. "Esra und das 'Gesetz'." *ZAW* 56 (1984) 165–84.

_____. *The Old Testament: An Introduction*. Philadelphia: Fortress, 1986.

Richter, W. *Recht und Ethos: Versuch einer Ortung des weisheitlichen Mahnspruches*. SANT 15. Munich: Kösel, 1966.

Ringgren, H. *Sprüche/Prediger*. Das Alte Testament Deutsch 16/1. Göttingen: Vandenhoeck & Ruprecht, 1962.

Robert, A. "Les attaches littéraires Bibliques de Prov. I–IX." *RB* 43 (1934) 42–68, 172–204, 374–84; 44 (1935) 344–65, 502–25.

Rost, L. *Die Vorstufen von Kirche und Synagoge im alten Testament*. BWANT 24. Stuttgart: Kohlhammer, 1938.

Roth, W. M. W. *Numerical Sayings in the Old Testament*. VTSup 13. Leiden: Brill, 1965.

Rudolph, W. *Esra und Nehemia*. HAT 20. Tübingen: Mohr, 1949.

Ruffle, J. "The Teaching of Amenemope and its Connexion with the Book of Proverbs." M.A. thesis, University of Liverpool, 1964.

Rylaarsdam, J. *Revelation in Jewish Wisdom Literature*. Chicago: University of Chicago Press, 1946.

Les sagesses du Proche-Orient ancien, Colloque de Strasbourg 17-19 mai 1962. Bibliothèque des Centres d'Etudes Supérieures spécialisés. Paris: Presses universitaires, 1963 [=*SPOA*].

Scharbert, J. "*Bĕyt 'āb* als soziologische Grösse im alten Testament," *Von Kanaan bis Kerala* fs. J. P. M. Van der Ploeg, 213-227. Edited by W. C. Delsman et al. AOAT 21. Neukirchen: Neukirchener Verlag, 1982.

Schmid, H. H. *Wesen und Geschichte der Weisheit: Eine Untersuchung zur altorientalischen und Israelitischen Weisheitsliteratur*. BZAW 101. Berlin: Toepelmann, 1966.

_____. *Gerechtigkeit als Weltordnung: Hintergrund und Geschichte des alttestamentlichen Gerechtigkeitsbegriffes*. BHT 40. Tübingen: Mohr, 1968.

Schnabel, E. J. *Law and Wisdom from Ben Sira to Paul: A Tradition Historical Enquiry into the Relation of Law, Wisdom, and Ethics*. WUNT 2. Reihe, 16. Tübingen: Mohr, 1985.

Schneider, H. *Die Sprüche Salomos, Das Buch des Predigers, Das Hohelied*. Herders Bibelkommentar 7/1. Freiburg: Herder, 1962.

Schneider, T. R. "From Wisdom Sayings to Wisdom Texts, Part I." *BT* 37 (1986) 128-35; "Part II." *BT* 38 (1987) 101-117.

Schottroff, W. "Zur Sozialgeschichte Israels in der Perserzeit." *VF* 27 (1982) 47-68.

Schwantes, M. *Das Recht der Armen*. BET 4. Frankfurt: Lang, 1977.

Scott, R. B. Y. "Folk Proverbs of the Ancient Near East." *Transactions of the Royal Society of Canada* 55 (1961) 47-56. Reprinted in *SAIW*, 417-26.

_____. *Proverbs-Ecclesiastes*, 2nd ed. AB 18. Garden City, New York: Doubleday, 1965.

_____. "Wise and Foolish, Righteous and Wicked." *Studies in the Religion of Ancient Israel*, 146-65. Edited by G. W. Anderson et al. VTSup 23. Leiden: Brill, 1972.

Segal, M. H. *A Grammar of Mishnaic Hebrew*. Oxford: Clarendon, 1958.

Sellers, O. *The Citadel of Beth Zur: A Preliminary Report of the First Excavation Conducted by the Presbyterian Theological Seminary, Chicago, and the American School of Oriental Research, Jerusalem, in 1931 at Khirbat et Tubeiqa*. Philadelphia: Westminster, 1933.

Sellin, E. "Die Neugefundene 'Lehre des Amen-em-ope' in ihrer Bedeutung für die jüdische Literatur- und Religionsgeschichte." *DLZ* 26 (1924) cols. 1873-84.

Shupak, N. "The 'Sitz im Leben' of the Book of Proverbs in the Light of a Comparison of Biblical and Egyptian Wisdom Literature." *RB* 94 (1987) 98-199.

Simpson, D. C. "The Hebrew Book of Proverbs and the Teaching of Amenophis." *JEA* 12 (1926) 232-39.

Skehan, P. *Studies in Ancient Israelite Poetry and Wisdom*. CBQMS 1. Washington, D.C.: Catholic Biblical Association, 1971; 9-45:="The Seven Columns of Wisdom's House in Proverbs 1-9," *CBQ* 9 (1947) 190-98; "A Single Editor for the Whole Book of Proverbs," *CBQ* 10 (1948) 115-30; "Wisdom's House," *CBQ* 29 (1967) 468-86.

Skladny, U. *Die ältesten Spruchsammlungen in Israel*. Göttingen: Vandenhoeck & Ruprecht, 1961.

Smith, D. E. "Wisdom Genres in RS 22.439." In *Ras Shamra Parallels* 2, 215-47. Edited by R. R. Fisher. Analecta Orientalia 50. Rome: Pontifical Biblical Institute, 1975.

Smith, D. L. *The Religion of the Landless: The Social Context of the Babylonian Exile*. Bloomington, Indiana: Meyer-Stone, 1989.

Smith, M. "On the Differences Between the Culture of Israel and the Major Cultures of the Ancient Near East." *JNES* 5 (1974) 389-95.

_____. *Palestinian Parties and Politics that Shaped the Old Testament*. 2nd edition. London: SCM, 1987.

Snaith, J. G. "Biblical Quotations in the Hebrew of Ecclesiasticus." *JThS* 18 (1967) 1-12.

Soggin, J. A. *Introduction to the Old Testament*. 3rd edition. Louisville: Westminster/Knox, 1989.

236   WEALTH AND POVERTY IN AMENEMOPE AND PROVERBS

Stern, E. *Material Culture of the Land of the Bible in the Persian Period, 538-332 B.C.*. Warminster: Aris and Phillips, 1982.

Steuernagel, C. *Sprüche.* Edited by E. Kautzsch and A. Bertholet. Die heilige Schrift des alten Testaments 4. Tübingen: J. C. B. Mohr, 1923.

Stone, M. E. *Scriptures, Sects, and Visions: A Profile of Judaism from Ezra to the Jewish Revolts.* Philadelphia: Fortress, 1980.

Story, C. I. K. "The Book of Proverbs and Northwest-Semitic Literature." *JBL* 64 (1945) 319-337.

Talmon, S. "The Emergence of Jewish Sectarianism in the Early Second Temple Period." *Ancient Israelite Religion: Essays in Honor of Frank Moore Cross,* 587-616. Edited by P. D. Miller, Jr., Paul D. Hanson, and S. Dean McBride. Philadelphia: Fortress, 1987.

Toy, C. H. *A Critical and Exegetical Commentary on the Book of Proverbs.* ICC. New York: Charles Scribner's Sons, 1899.

Ullendorff, E. "The Knowledge of Languages in the Old Testament." *BJRL* 44 (1962) 455-65.

Van der Weiden, W. A. *Le livre des Proverbes: Notes philologiques.* Rome: Biblical Institute Press, 1970.

Van Leeuwen, C. *Le Développement du Sens Social in Israël avant l'ère Chrétienne.* Studia Semitica Neerlandica 1. Assen: Van Gorcum, 1955.

Van Leeuwen, R. C. "Prov 30:21-23 and the Biblical World Upside Down." *JBL* 105 (1986) 599-610.

_____. *Context and Meaning in Proverbs 25-27.* SBLDS 96. Atlanta: Scholars Press, 1988.

Vaux, R. de. "Titres et fonctionnaires égyptiens à la cour de David et de Salomon." *RB* 48 (1939) 394-405.

Vermes, G. "The Torah is a Light." *VT* 8 (1958) 436-37.

Vogt, H. C. M. *Studien zur nachexilischen Gemeinde in Esra-Nehemiah.* Werl: Dietrich-Coeble, 1966.

Von Rad, G. *Old Testament Theology.* New York: Harper, 1962.

_____. *Wisdom in Israel.* Nashville: Abingdon, 1972.

Wagner, M. *Die lexicalischen und grammatikalischen Aramaismen im alttestamentlichen Hebräisch.* BZAW 96. Berlin: Toepelmann, 1966.

Waldman, N. M. *The Recent Study of Hebrew: A Survey of the Literature with Selected Bibliography*. Cinncinati: Hebrew Union College/Winona Lake, Indiana: Eisenbrauns, 1989.

Waltke B. K. and M. O'Connor. *An Introduction to Biblical Hebrew Syntax*. Winona Lake, Indiana: Eisenbrauns, 1990.

Washington, H. C. "The Strange Woman (אִשָּׁה זָרָה/נָכְרִיָּה) of Proverbs 1–9 and Post-Exilic Judean Society." *Second Temple Studies 2. Temple and Community in the Persian Period* (ed. T. C. Eskenazi and K. H. Richards; JSOTSup; Sheffield: JSOT, forthcoming).

_____. "An Unrecognized Egyptian Loan Word in Proverbs 22:21: Biblical Hebrew קֹשֶׁט < Egyptian *gśty*, 'Scribal Palette'." Paper presented to Kolloquium für Graduierte, Universität Tübingen, April 27, 1987; and Old Testament Section, Central States Regional Meeting of the Society of Biblical Literature, Kansas City, April 19, 1989.

_____. "The Case of the Drunken Scribe: Proverbs 23:31–35 and Ancient Egyptian Scribal Instruction." Paper presented to the Israelite and Early Christian Wisdom Section, Annual Meeting of the Society of Biblical Literature, Chicago, November 21, 1988.

Watson, W. G. E. *Classical Hebrew Poetry: A Guide to Its Techniques*. JSOTSup 26. Sheffield: JSOT, 1984.

Weill, R. "Les transmissions littéraires d'Egypte à Israel." *Revue d'Egyptologie, Cahier complémentaire* 1 (1950) 43–61.

Weinberg, J. P. "Demographische Notizen zur Geschichte der nachexilischen Gemeinde in Juda." *KLIO* 54 (1972) 45–58.

_____. "Das *Bēit 'Ābōt* im 6.–4. Jh. v.u.Z." *VT* 23 (1973) 400–14.

_____. "Der *ʿam hāʾāreṣ* des 6.–4. Jh. v.u.Z." *KLIO* 56 (1974) 325–35.

_____. "Die Agrarverhältnisse in der Bürger-Tempel-Gemeinde der Achämenidenzeit." *Wirtschaft und Gesellschaft im Alten Vorderasien*, 473–86. Edited by J. Harmatta and G. Komoróczy. Budapest: Akademiai Kiadö, 1976.

_____. "Zentral- und Partikulargewalt im achämenidischen Reich." *KLIO* 59 (1976) 24–43.

_____. "Das Wesen und die functionelle Bestimmung der Listen in 1 Chr 1–9." *ZAW* 93 (1981) 91–114.

Weinberg, S. "Post-Exilic Palestine: An Archaeological Report." *Proceedings of the Israel Academy of Sciences and Humanities* 4 (1970) 78–97.

Weinfeld, M. *Deuteronomy and the Deuteronomic School.* Oxford: Oxford University Press, 1972.

Weinstein, J. M. "The Egyptian Empire in Palestine: A Reassessment." *BASOR* 241 (1981) 1-28.

Wenning, R. "Attische Keramik in Palästina. Ein Zwischenbericht." *Transeuphratène* 2 (1990) 157-168.

Westermann, C. "Weisheit im Sprichwort." *Schalom: Studien zu Glaube und Geschichte Israels, Alfred Jepsen zum 70. Geburtstag*, 73-85. Edited by C.-H. Bernhardt. Stuttgart: Calwer, 1971.

Whedbee, J. W. *Isaiah and Wisdom.* Nashville: Abingdon, 1971.

Whybray, R. N. *Wisdom in Proverbs: The Concept of Wisdom in Proverbs 1-9.* SBT 45. London: SCM, 1965.

_____. *The Book of Proverbs.* NEB. Cambridge: Cambridge University Press, 1972.

_____. *The Intellectual Tradition in the Old Testament.* BZAW 135. Berlin: de Gruyter, 1974.

_____. "Yahweh-sayings and their Contexts in Proverbs 10,1-22,16." *La Sagesse de l'Ancien Testament*, 153-65. Edited by M. Gilbert. BETL 51. Gembloux: Duculot, 1979.

_____. *Wealth and Poverty in the Book of Proverbs.* JSOTSup 99. Sheffield: JSOT, 1990.

Widengren, G. "The Persian Period." *Israelite and Judean History*, 489-538. Edited by J. Hayes and J. M. Miller. OTL. Philadelphia: Westminster, 1977.

Wiesmann, H. *Das Buch der Sprüche, übersetzt und erklärt.* Bonn: P. Hanstein, 1923.

Wildeboer, D. G. *Die Sprüche.* KHAT 15. Tübingen: Mohr, 1897.

Williams, R. J. "Egypt and Israel." *The Legacy of Egypt*, 257-90. Edited by J. R. Harris. Oxford: Clarendon Press, 1971.

_____. "A People Come Out of Egypt: An Egyptologist Looks at the Old Testament." *Congress Volume: Edinburgh, 1974*, 231-52. VTSup 28. Leiden: E. J. Brill, 1975.

_____. *Hebrew Syntax: An Outline.* 2nd. edition. Toronto: University of Toronto Press, 1976.

Williamson, H. G. M. *Ezra, Nehemiah*. Word Biblical Commentary 16. Waco, Texas: Word, 1985.

Wilson, F. "Sacred and Profane? The Yahwistic Redaction of Proverbs Reconsidered." *The Listening Heart: Essays in Wisdom and the Psalms in Honor of Roland E. Murphy O. Carm.* 313–334. Edited by K. G. Hoglund et al. JSOTSup 58. Sheffield: Sheffield Academic Press, 1987.

Wittenberg, G. H. "The Lexical Context of the Terminology for Poor in the Book of Proverbs." *Scriptura* 2 (1986) 40–85.

Wolters, A. "*Ṣôpîyâ* (Prov 31:27) as Hymnic Participle and Play on *sophia*." *JBL* 104 (1985) 577–87.

Wright, A. "The Riddle of the Sphinx Revisited: Numerical Patterns in the Book of Qoheleth." *CBQ* 30 (1968) 313–34.

_____. "Additional Numerical Patterns in Qoheleth." *CBQ* 45 (1983) 32–43.

Würthwein, E. "Der Sinn des Gesetzes im Alten Testament." *ZThK* 55 (1958) 255–70.

_____. "Egyptian Wisdom and the Old Testament." *SAIW* 113–33.

Zimmerli, W. "Concerning the Structure of Old Testament Wisdom." *SAIW*, 175–207.

_____. "The 'Land' in the Pre-Exilic and Early Post-Exilic Prophets." *Understanding the Word: Essays in Honor of Bernhard W. Anderson*, 247–62. Edited by J. T. Butler, E. W. Conrad, B. C. Ollenburger. JSOTSup 37. Sheffield: JSOT, 1985.

Ethnography and Folklore Studies

Albert, E. "'Rhetoric,' 'Logic,' and 'Poetics,' In Burundi: Culture Patterning of Speech Behavior." *American Anthropologist* 66 (1964) Special Publication, Part 2, Number 6, 50.

Arnott, D. W. "Proverbial Lore and Word-Play of the Fulani." *Africa* 27 (1957) 379–96.

Bascom, W. R. "Four Functions of Folklore." *Journal of American Folklore* 67 (1954) 333–49.

_____. "Folklore Research in Africa." *Journal of American Folklore* 77 (1964) 16–17.

Bauer, R. A. "Day to Day Resistance to Slavery." *Journal of Negro History* 27 (1942) 388–419.

Bohanan, L. "A Genealogical Charter." *Africa* 22 (1952) 301–15.

Champion, S. G. *Racial Proverbs: A Selection of the World's Proverbs arranged Linguistically.* New York: Macmillan, 1938.

Christensen, J. B. "The Role of Proverbs in Fante Culture." *Africa* 28 (1958) 232–43.

Doke, C. M. "Bantu Wisdom-Lore." *African Studies* 6 (1947) 101–120.

_____. *Lamba Folk-Lore.* Memoir of the American Folk-lore Society 20. New York: American Folk-lore Society, 1927.

Dundes, A., ed. *The Study of Folklore.* Englewood Cliffs, N.J.: Prentice-Hall, 1965.

_____. "Who Are the Folk?" *Frontiers of Folklore*, 17–35. American Association for the Advancement of Science, Selected Symposium, no. 5. Edited by W. R. Bascom. Boulder, Co.: Westview Press, 1977.

Dundes, A. and E. O. Arewa. "Proverbs and the Ethnography of Speaking Folklore." *American Anthropologist* 66 (1964) 70–85. Reprinted in *Analytic Essays in Folklore*, 35–49. Studies in Folklore 2. Edited by A. Dundes. The Hague: Mouton, 1975.

Evans-Pritchard, E. E. "Meaning in Zande Proverbs." *Man* 63 (1963) 4–6.

_____. "Sixty-One Zande Proverbs." *Man* 63 (1963) 109–112.

_____. "Zande Proverbs: Final Selection and Comments." *Man* 64 (1964) 1–5.

Finnegan, R. *Oral Literature in Africa.* London: Oxford University Press, 1970.

Fortes, M. "The Structure of Unilineal Descent Groups." *American Anthropologist* 55 (1953) 15–41.

Genovese, E. D. *Roll, Jordan, Roll: The World the Slaves Made.* New York: Pantheon, 1974.

Goody, J., ed. *Literacy in Traditional Societies.* Cambridge: Cambridge University Press, 1968.

Gray, E. "Some Proverbs of the Nyanja People." *African Studies* 3 (1933) 101–28.

Herskovits, H. and S. Tagbwe. "Kru Proverbs of Liberia." *Journal of American Folklore* 43 (1930) 225–93.

Joyner, C. *Down by the Riverside: A South Carolina Slave Community*. Urbana, Illinois: University of Illinois Press, 1984.

Junod, H. P. *Bantu Heritage*. Westport, Connecticut: Negro Universities Press, 1938; reprint ed., 1970.

Knappert, J. *Proverbs from the Lamu Archipelago and the Central Kenya Coast*. Language and Dialect Atlas of Kenya, Supplement 6. Berlin: Reimer, 1986.

Merrick, G. *Hausa Proverbs*. London: Kegan, Paul, 1905; reprint ed., New York: Negro Universities Press, 1969.

Messenger, J. C. "The Role of Proverbs in a Nigerian Judicial System." *Southwestern Journal of Anthropology* 15 (1959) 64–74. Reprinted in A. Dundes, ed., *The Study of Folklore*, 299–307. Englewood Cliffs, N. J.: Prentice-Hall, 1965.

Mieder, W. *International Proverb Scholarship: An Annotated Bibliography*. Garland Folklore Bibliographies 3. New York: Garland, 1982.

Nyembezi, C. L. S. *Zulu Proverbs*. Revised edition. Johannesburg: Witwatersrand University Press, 1963.

Pelling, J. N. *Ndebele Proverbs and Other Sayings*. Guelo, Rhodesia (Zimbabwe): Mambo Press, 1977.

Penfield, J. *Communicating with Quotes: The Igbo Case*. Contributions in Intercultural and Comparative Studies 8. Westport, Connecticut: Greenwood Press, 1983.

Rattray, R. S. *Hausa Folk-lore, Customs, Proverbs, etc.: Collected and Transliterated with English Translation and Notes*. 2 volumes. Oxford: Clarendon, 1913; reprint ed., New York: Negro Universities Press, 1969.

Sahlins, M. *Tribesmen* Englewood Cliffs: Prentice Hall, 1968.

Scheven, A. *Swahili Proverbs*. Washington, D.C.: University Press of America, 1981.

Seitel, P. "Proverbs: A Social Use of Metaphor." *Genre* 2 (1969) 143–61. Reprinted in D. Ben-Amos, ed., *Folklore Genres*, pp. 125–43. Austin: University of Texas Press, 1976.

Simmons, D. C. "Oron Proverbs." *African Studies* 19 (1960) 126–137.

_____. "Protest Humor: Folkloristic Reaction to Prejudice." *American Journal of Psychiatry* 120 (1963) 567–70.

Thomas, N. W. *Anthropological Report on the Ibo-Speaking Peoples of Nigeria.* Part 6, Proverbs, Stories, Tones in Ibo. London: Harrison and Sons, 1914; reprint ed., New York: Negro Universities Press, 1969.

Walser, F. *Luganda Proverbs.* Berlin: Reimer, 1982.

Whitting, C. E. J. *Hausa and Fulani Proverbs.* Lagos: Government Printer, 1940; reprint ed., Farnborough Hants, England: Gregg, 1967.